TERRORISM AND COUNTERTERRORISM

TERRORISM & COUNTER-TERRORISM

A Comprehensive Introduction to Actors and Actions

Henry Prunckun
Troy Whitford

LYNNE
RIENNER
PUBLISHERS

BOULDER
LONDON

Published in the United States of America in 2019 by
Lynne Rienner Publishers, Inc.
1800 30th Street, Boulder, Colorado 80301
www.rienner.com

and in the United Kingdom by
Lynne Rienner Publishers, Inc.
Gray's Inn House, 127 Clerkenwell Road, London EC1 5DB

Library of Congress Cataloging-in-Publication Data
Names: Prunckun, Hank, 1954– author. I Whitford, Troy, 1971– author.
Title: Terrorism and counterterrorism : a comprehensive introduction to
   actors and actions / Henry Prunckun and Troy Whitford.
Description: Boulder, Colorado : Lynne Rienner Publishers, Inc., [2018] I
   Includes bibliographical references and index.
Identifiers: LCCN 2018035340I ISBN 9781626377585 (hardcover : alk. paper) I
   ISBN 9781626377608 (pbk. : alk. paper)
Subjects: LCSH: Terrorism. I Radicalization. I Terrorism—Prevention.
Classification: LCC HV6431 .P778 2018 I DDC 363.325—dc23
LC record available at https://lccn.loc.gov/2018035340

British Cataloguing in Publication Data
A Cataloguing in Publication record for this book
is available from the British Library.

Printed and bound in the United States of America

The paper used in this publication meets the requirements
of the American National Standard for Permanence of
Paper for Printed Library Materials Z39.48-1992.

5 4 3 2 1

Contents

Part 2 Counterterrorism

Tables and Figures

Tables

Figures

Foreword

Although politically motivated murder is an ancient tactic—instances of what would be labeled *terrorist* today can be found throughout written history—terrorism in its contemporary form emerged as an international phenomenon only in the late 1960s. Since then, bombings, assassinations, armed assaults, hijackings, kidnappings, and other forms of hostage taking have become the basic terrorist repertoire.

While weapons and tactics have evolved rather slowly over the past fifty years, terrorist violence intensified in volume and in lethality. The worst terrorist attacks had already escalated from tens of fatalities in the 1970s to hundreds in the 1980s to thousands with the September 11, 2001, attacks against the United States. The scale of the 9/11 attacks not only seemed to obscure the more than three decades of evolution that preceded them but also altered perceptions of plausibility. Attacks that would have been dismissed as far-fetched the day before 9/11 became operative presumptions the day after. These order-of-magnitude increases invited further extrapolation to future terrorist attacks that would involve tens or even hundreds of thousands of casualties. Such a level of violence could be achieved with weapons of mass destruction: nuclear or biological weapons. That terrorists would someday acquire and employ stolen or improvised nuclear weapons was considered by many to be inevitable—to use the popular phrase: not if, but when.

That has not happened. Instead, terrorists have employed the Internet and social media to exhort followers worldwide to carry out low-level attacks—a sort of horizontal rather than vertical escalation. Terrorist campaigns in the twenty-first century are global enterprises. The online exhortations reach huge audiences to inspire distant terrorist attacks. Therefore, terrorism is a global phenomenon, a major feature in current political discourse, often a condenser of society's broader anxieties. Except in failed states or conflict zones, terrorism currently poses little direct threat to human life—personal quarrels, ordinary crime, and organized wars pose far greater dangers—but terrorism has an enormous effect on public perceptions. It merits objective study—based on observing the phenomena and presenting these observations factually, which is not the same as impartial study—simply trying to stay neutral in presenting the argument.

In this regard, Henry Prunckun and Troy Whitford's book takes on the ambitious goal of providing a comprehensive introduction to terrorism's actors and the actions involved in countering terrorism. It provides an explanation of the theory of terrorism, a description of terrorist strategy and tactics, and a broad historical and geographical survey of terrorists. These are necessary starting points for understanding what is essential for effectively combating terrorism while protecting society's essential freedoms.

—Brian Michael Jenkins,
senior adviser to the president
of the RAND Corporation

Acknowledgments

We extend our thanks to the US Department of Defense, the Federal Bureau of Investigation, and other US government agencies, as well as to the various sources cited, for the use of the photographs that appear in this book. In doing so, we point out that their inclusion does not imply, nor constitute, these providers' endorsement.

1

Introducing Terrorism and Counterterrorism

Shoppers had entered the Big C Supercenter looking for bargains, regular groceries, and perhaps that little treat that might be awaiting down an aisle. Nothing distinguished this Tuesday from any other shopping day—customers inspected a stack of brightly colored plastic containers and black plastic chairs displayed at the Supercenter's entrance as they made their way through the glass sliding doors.

Then, at 2:10 P.M. on May 9, 2017, someone set off firecrackers inside the store. Customers were evacuated—this area of Thailand had experienced acts of political violence before. A decades-long Malay Muslim separatist insurgency had been waged in the province, as well as in the provinces that bordered Malaysia—Yala and Narathiwat. Since 2004, it had been reported that the violence resulted in more than 6,500 deaths. There had been indiscriminate bomb and grenade attacks on tourist hotels, discos, bars, shops, marketplaces, and government offices (see Figure 1.1). So, the store evacuation was part of a routine response plan.

But the first set of minor explosions were not the objective of the attack; they were a diversion. The attack came minutes later when a pickup truck loaded with explosives and gasoline detonated while customers gathered outside. There was a fireball; thick black smoke billowed from where the truck was; wreckage was strewn for hundreds of feet. When the debris stopped falling and noise settled, sixty people lay injured, four seriously.

Courtesy of Police Captain Sayoobman Maidtreejon.

Figure 1.1   Thai Explosive Ordinance Disposal (EOD) Squad disarming a bomb on a motorcycle in the south of Thailand.

The subsequent investigation discovered that the bombers killed a canvas vendor and stole his truck, which they used in the attack. Later, six people were arrested: an Islamic teacher and four followers, and a local administrator.

Terrorism has become an almost daily occurrence. Using social media, acts of terrorism can be viewed on smart phones within minutes of their occurring, and mainstream news media provide the world with photographic evidence of terrorists' deeds. We have seen air travelers murdered; ocean cruise liners taken hostage; embassies, department stores, office buildings, and shopping and entertainment spots bombed; people walking along city streets run over; and the list goes on.

As unique as these crimes may appear in the context of what society recognizes as crime, the threat posed by terrorists is by no means new, nor are the ways it is carried out innovative. Terrorists can be traced back to the Roman occupation of Palestine. However, the present-day terrorist phenomenon has attributes that make it different from its historical predecessors. Social and technological changes have influenced the effectiveness of terrorist operations. And the terrorists' philosophies have evolved; their tactics have been perfected, and they have developed new tactics for striking at their targets.

It is obvious that terrorists do not engage their political opponents in combat on a declared piece of turf. To the terrorist, the battlefield can be an urban area, a plane on an international flight, a ship on the high seas; it can be a diplomatic mission in a foreign country, or a crowded shopping center. The terrorist's battlefield can be anywhere and everywhere, wherever a perceived advantage can be gained over a political opponent. They choose the target, the place, and the timing of the attack. But what is terrorism?

Terrorism Defined

The terrorist phenomenon can be described in an almost endless stream of examples, yet a universal definition that can be used as a yardstick to gauge these various acts of violence is less than agreed. The definitions in the literature, which are numerous, show a diversity of political and philosophical views, and these views have given rise to scholars contesting these definitions in a wide-ranging, and sometimes tense, debate.[1]

Reports in the media likewise appear to reflect something beyond what one would expect to be an objective criterion for assessing events involving these types of violence. Many media reports demonstrate varying attitudes to the phenomena and tend to use interpretative ethical and evaluative judgments and observations; for example, "an evil act," "a cowardly deed," "immoral behavior," "senseless destruction."

"The problem of defining terrorism [and hence, a terrorist] is compounded by the fact that terrorism has recently become a fad word often applied to a variety of acts of violence which are not strictly terrorism."[2] For instance, the term "terrorized" has even been misused by the media to refer to those who have witnessed traffic accidents, or communities that have experienced the murder of a local (among many other possible examples). These are upsetting events, for sure, but are these people really *terrorized* by them?[3] Or could it be argued that these media reports are trying to juxtapose an upsetting event with that of a politically motivated attack on innocent people to attract the reader's attention?

The meaning given to terrorist phenomena extends beyond the world of sensationalized journalism and into the realm of geopolitics; even governments cannot agree on what is or what constitutes an act of terrorism. These differences mainly revolve around the issue of what constitutes the political motives that distinguish terrorism from other forms of violence. Take, for instance, the situation in northern Iraq on the Turkish border in 2017. The United States viewed the Kurds as an ally in fighting Islamic State, whereas the Turks labeled them terrorists.

Martha Crenshaw has pointed out that crafting a "'neutral' definition of a method rather than a moral characterization of the enemy [is a dilemma], since the use of the term is not merely descriptive but as currently understood deprives the actor thus named of legitimacy. Since the early use of the term in the latter half of the nineteenth century, it has not been possible to escape a pejorative connotation."[4]

Even the distinction between a political extremist and a terrorist has been debated. Bruce Hoffman argued that many people "harbor all sorts of radical and extreme beliefs and opinions, and many of them belong to radical or even illegal or proscribed political organizations. However, if they do not use violence in the pursuit of their beliefs, they cannot be considered terrorists. The terrorist is fundamentally a *violent intellectual,* prepared to use and indeed committed to using force in the attainment of his goals."[5]

One could view the disagreement about how terrorism is defined by the issues involving the perpetrators and their political use of violence (e.g., people labeled as terrorists may see themselves as freedom fighters), the victims (e.g., victims may be seen by the perpetrator as supporters of their oppressors), and the legitimacy of the methods of attack (e.g., indiscriminate violence may be argued to be part of an asymmetrical conflict).

Returning to the example of the Kurds, one can wonder if they are terrorists, America's allies, or simply a nation in pursuit of state recognition. Therefore, a definition of terrorism should not be dependent on the perpetrator's ethnicity, religion, or cultural background, though these factors may influence perpetrators in thinking in such a radical way (known as radicalization).

Defining terrorism is not just an ideological debate; it is the foundation on which state policy is formulated (e.g., counterterrorism policy). Defining a person or group as a terrorist bestows upon the state the ability to confront the perpetrators in a way that common violent criminals cannot be confronted. A definition that misses its purpose could result in a less than perfect policy. This, in turn, could lead to responses by the state that are ineffectual in dealing with the threat. It could also affect the way a state aids other states in addressing the problem, because there may be a disconnect between the policies of these states.

"All terrorist acts are crimes. . . . All involve violence or the threat of violence, often coupled with specific demands. The violence is directed mainly against civilian targets. The motives are political.

> "The aims of terrorism and guerrilla warfare may well be identical; but they are distinguished from each other by the means used—or more precisely, by the targets of their operations. The guerrilla fighter's targets are military ones, while the terrorist deliberately targets civilians.
>
> By this definition, a terrorist organization can no longer claim to be freedom fighters because they are fighting for national liberation or some other worthy goal. Even if its declared ultimate goals are legitimate, an organization that deliberately targets civilians is a terrorist organization. There is no merit or exoneration in fighting for the freedom of one population if in doing so you destroy the rights of another population."[6]

The actions are generally carried out in a way that will achieve maximum publicity. . . . And finally the act is intended to produce effects beyond the immediate physical damage."[7] As an example of a working definition of terrorism, the US Federal Bureau of Investigation (FBI) defines it according to the Code of Federal Regulations (28 CFR, sec. 0.85), which states: "The unlawful use of force and violence against persons or property to intimidate or coerce a government, the civilian population, or any segment thereof, in furtherance of political or social objectives."[8] The US Department of Defense defines terrorism as: "The unlawful use of violence or threat of violence, often motivated by religious, political, or other ideological beliefs, to instil fear and coerce governments or societies in pursuit of goals that are usually political."[9]

Despite the debate, common ground is found in that terrorism is violence directed against a government (via innocent victims) as opposed to aggression that emanates from a state's military. In this way, the act is political. Although terrorism has individual victims, these are civilians, not military personnel, because terrorists are conducting an assault on society itself. This is an important distinction in identifying terrorist acts. It is accepted that in conventional warfare—state versus state—terror is a natural by-product of the battlefield. However, the generation of terror on the battlefield is not the prime intention of the military engagement. Combat operations are intended to bring one's forces within range of the other's in such a rapid escalation and concentration that they overwhelm the opposing force, thereby destroying or severely disrupting the opposition's command, control, communication, and intelligence (C^3I) structure. The fear of terror experienced by the combatants is not the determining factor as to whether the conflict will result in victory. Warring military forces represent nation-states; terrorists lack the legitimation to use violence that is provided by constitutional and international legal authority.

Although the acts of warring states and terrorists may both be politically inspired, it is important to highlight this political focus to distinguish between not terrorism and war but terrorism and other forms of violence. The crimes of murder and assault are among the most feared acts of violence but are not related to terrorism per se because of the characteristics just discussed (take, for instance, the mass murder in Las Vegas on October 1, 2017).

In sum, the factors of violence (or threat of violence), political motivation, and civilian victims are what differentiate terrorism from other forms of violence and define it as such.[10] "Any action . . . that is intended to cause death or serious bodily harm to civilians or noncombatants, when the purpose of such act, by nature or context, is to intimidate a population, or to compel a Government or an international organization to do or to abstain from doing an act."[11]

Purpose

The purpose of terrorism is to achieve a political goal. Unlike other forms of *political action*—say, lobbying politicians by email and letter writing, organizing petitions, or participating in election campaigns—terrorism is a type of *direct action*. Unlike forms of direct action that society accepts—labor strikes and peaceful demonstrations—terrorism goes beyond these forms of protest by employing violence, or the threat of violence in what is termed violent political action. Violence is used to instill fear that can be manipulated to the terrorists' political ends. Rather than kill a lot of people, as in a conventional conflict, terrorists want a lot of people watching.[12] "Terrorists [use] what has become known as [Sun Tzu's ancient Chinese] doctrine of 'kill one, frighten ten thousand' as their lever in this mismatch of strength of force. This could be argued to be the first pillar in the philosophy of terrorism. It allow[s] an undermanned and under-resourced opposition to engage a much larger opponent to catalyze for political change."[13] Still, some scholars have argued that terrorists have access to modern weapons and knowledge to build improvised systems that can kill more people. Attacks using these weapons and methods generate enormous public outrage, so that "many of today's terrorists want a lot of people watching *and* a lot of people dead."[14]

The drive to use violent political action has been attributed to several factors, including (1) situational factors, such as social or economic factors, or certain events, in a person's life that influence them to see authority as the enemy (e.g., seeing a news report of an air strike that killed people in the country of their ethnic origin); (2) strategic aims, such as political autonomy (e.g., separatists) and historical grievances (e.g., the 1915–1923 Armenian genocide); (3) disruption of government processes (e.g., peacekeeping or nation-building missions in foreign countries); (4) provocation of a reaction that legitimizes grievances (e.g., anti-Muslim immigration polices); and (5) erosion of democracy and personal freedoms (e.g., to impose stricter security). The outcome sought is to destabilize governments by creating unrest that will lay the foundations for political conditions that are necessary for terrorists to exercise some level of control over the country's government.

Tactical and Strategic Objectives

The objective of using fear is to reach either a tactical goal or a strategic position, or both simultaneously. Tactical objectives are goals of an immediate nature, requiring only short-term planning. An illustrative example of a tactical terrorist operation is the June 14, 1985, hijacking of TWA Flight 847 from Athens. The hijackers were members of the militant organization Hezbollah. Hezbollah demanded the release of seventeen Shiite terrorists being held in Kuwaiti jails. Kuwait had incarcerated the terrorists for their part in a series of bombings in December 1983. The tactical objective was therefore the release of Hezbollah members.

In contrast, strategic goals are long-term positions that have a broader scope. An example of a strategic goal can also be seen in this 1985 incident: the hijacking of the TWA flight could have been used by Hezbollah as part of a larger campaign to increase its influence on Kuwait or to have its political stature as an organization recognized.

In many cases, the distinction between tactical and strategic objectives is difficult to distinguish. The Kuwaiti hijacking could have fulfilled both objectives concurrently; however, not all operations have this duality. Some may have only a single focus—for instance, the March 1969 bombing of the cafeteria of the Hebrew University by members of the Democratic Popular Front. The incident was "a warning aimed at the Jewish intellectuals to open their eyes to Zionism and to turn them from it."[15]

Taxonomy of Terrorism

The term *terrorism* is used in a range of contexts with little effort to distinguish between the various taxonomical categories. To some extent this can contribute to the definitional confusion—if there is no separating of the various categories of terrorism, trying to understand one act of political violent action may not make sense when applied in another context.

A taxonomical analysis of terrorism shows that there are four classifications: domestic, transnational, international, and state. Understanding these categories can help place a terrorist incident into conceptual framework that will allow better analysis.

Domestic Terrorism

Domestic terrorism is characterized by a country's national or permanent resident carrying out a political violent action within that nation. Of course, it can be carried out by a group, organization, or movement, but these entities need to comprise members of the target nation and the target of their action needs to be located within the nation's borders. The informal term *homegrown terrorist* has been used to describe this category of terror. To demonstrate what this might look like in practice, let us examine two cases, one historical and one contemporary.

The Weather Underground was a militant left-wing group that operated in the United States in the late 1960s and 1970s with the aim to overthrow the government. It comprised radical American college students and its targets were symbols of US political power. Several bombings were attributed to the group, including the June 14, 1975, bombing of Gulf Oil's international headquarters in Pittsburgh, Pennsylvania; the May 31, 1974, bombing of the Los Angeles office of California's attorney general's office; the June September 23, 1974, bombing of the New York office of the Latin American division of International Telephone and Telegraph; and the August 30, 1971, firebombing of two California prison system offices. Weather Underground's political ideology was influenced by Lenin's theory of imperialism.

The other case is the September 17–19, 2016, bombings in New York and New Jersey by Ahmad Khan Rahimi of Elizabeth, New Jersey. It was alleged that Rahimi detonated three homemade bombs. He was alleged to have used a pipe bomb in an attack at Seaside Park, New Jersey, on September 17, and a pressure-cooker bomb in the Chelsea neighborhood of New York City. Other explosive devises were discovered that day in New York. The next day, several devices were found at a train station in Elizabeth, New Jersey—one of which detonated early on the morning of September 19. The bombings resulted in thirty-one people wounded, but no one was killed. Investigations showed that Rahimi's actions were influenced by a politically interpreted Islamic ideology.

Transnational Terrorism

Transnational terrorism is characterized by an incident that takes place in multiple jurisdictions. For instance, an attack might be planned in one country with the group's members being trained in another country, and when the attack is carried out, its political message is intended to meet the group's strategic objective, which is global in nature.

As a way of contextualizing this, let us examine the case involving the Islamic State of Iraq and Levant (ISIL) (which was also known as the Islamic State of Iraq and Syria, or simply the Islamic State), which sought to establish a caliphate that would traverse the political boundaries of Iraq, Syria, and Lebanon. Because its goal was to create an Islamic state—a strategic position to create a supranational world order—and the group's members were recruited from many countries, this case reflects this category of terrorism. In addition, its victims were also global—by way of example, four American citizens were beheaded in 2014, as well as a French citizen, two British citizens, and eighteen Syrian Arab army soldiers. Moreover, some of the people who lived in the countries occupied by ISIL were displaced, killed, or enslaved. Overall, this example demonstrates what is referred to as transnational terrorism.

International Terrorism

Although the terms *transnational* and *international* may be confused and taken as meaning the same, they represent different concepts. International terrorism is direct political violence orchestrated in one country by perpetrators who are not native or inhabitants of that country. The test here is that the perpetrators are not domiciled in the target country. The 1986 bombing of the La Belle discotheque in Germany by Libyan terrorists demonstrates this. The targets were the US service personnel who frequented the venue. From a US point of view, this was a case of international terrorism because the bombing was an attack on the nation (via its military) in a foreign country.

State Terrorism

State terrorism refers to nations whose rule is founded in widespread fear and oppression. It is the use of political violence by a government against its citizens. It is not the use of terror by a state that promotes third-party actors to carry out attacks, as in the case of state-sponsored terrorism. It is the type of terrorism that spawned the other categories of terror—it originated in the French Revolution of 1793, during which, under Robespierre and the Jacobin government, thousands of people were executed.[16] This period has come to be known as the Reign of Terror.[17] At the time, terror was viewed as a necessity for suppressing civil disquiet. Since that time, dictatorial regimes have exhibited, to varying degrees, hallmarks of state terror. For instance, Saddam Hussein used terrorist methods against the Kurdish population in Iraq's north: torture, murder, rape assignation, forced displacement, and poison gas.

Typology of Terrorism

Now that we understand the taxonomical categories that constitute terrorism, let us look at the types of terrorism. We can do this by constructing a typology. It is important to point out that one codification that is not included in this analysis is that of civil disorder, which is sometime termed civil unrest, even though it is a form of collective violence that disrupts society's normal mechanisms.

Civil disorder is characterized by riots, sabotage, destructive public protest, forceful demonstrations, marches, and sit-ins. This can be conducted in opposition to community social, economic, religious, or political problems. Civil disorder replaces peace and security with a breakdown in social order. It is a criminal offense in most jurisdictions. In cases where law enforcement officers are unable to quell the disturbance, martial law can be declared, and soldiers can be deployed to keep the peace. This form of protest is different from civil disobedience, which is predicated on the philosophy of nonviolence. And it is different from terrorism. The scholarly literature identifies six types of terrorism.

Political Terrorism

Political terrorism is violent behavior that is intended to generate fear through asymmetrical confrontation with the state, but not necessarily by engaging its law enforcement or security service apparatus. It is done with the express purpose of making a political statement. This type of terrorism is characterized by indiscriminate attacks on people and iconic targets that are not connected with the perpetrator's grievance, but by using these targets as a way of making the terrorists' message heard. This type of terrorism may comprise left-wing groups, right-wing groups, and issue-orientated groups.

Religious Terrorism

Religious terrorism bears all the characteristics of political terrorism, but it bears a religious message instead. It instills fear and targets noncombatants to leverage coercion over the state. The goal is religious in nature—which is nevertheless a form of political thought—such as establishing an Islamic caliphate.

Limited Political Terrorism

This could be called separatist terrorism because it is characterized by a revolutionary ethos; limited political terrorism refers to acts of terrorism that are committed for ideological or political motives, but that are not part of a concerted campaign to capture control of the state—perhaps to gain, say, regional autonomy. This type of terrorism would fit with the attacks that have been perpetrated by Basque Homeland and Liberty (ETA) in Spain in support of autonomy for the Basque region.

Lone-Actor Terrorism

Lone-actor has been called "lone-wolf" terrorism in the news media but could also be termed "individual" terrorism because it is characterized by individuals who have no formal connectivity to a terrorist entity. They act alone, largely of their own volition about target selection, timing, and tactics. It is a solitary type of terrorism, though these individuals may be connected to political causes or religious beliefs; this is likely to be a one-way transmission of information—from the outsider to the lone actor.

State-Sponsored Terrorism

State-sponsored terrorism fits under an umbrella of what has been referred to as low-intensity conflict. This applies to various forms of warfare that do not draw armies into direct confrontation. It is used by states and subnational entities to assist third parties to use political violence against the state's enemies. It is warfare by proxy, using terrorist tactics internationally.

In an era where warfare with a power such as the United states, or with a coalition country such as a North Atlantic Treaty Organization (NATO) ally, the costs of escalating a direct confrontation can be prohibitive. Nonetheless, supporting a terrorist group to wage a low-intensity conflict with a large, better militarily equipped country permits the supporting nation to avoid the repercussions that would come in a direct confrontation by allowing it to wage an undeclared clandestine war. Support can be in the form of money, logistics, arms and explosives, training, intelligence, false documents, communication equipment, technology, or whatever is needed to carry out an attack.

Whether a terrorist act is state-sponsored terrorism may be difficult to establish. Investigations may not be able to determine whether a state was involved. Or it may take years to gather enough evidence to establish beyond reasonable doubt the state's involvement, as was the case with Libya's involvement in the 1988 bombing of Pan Am Flight 103 over Lockerbie, Scotland. The reasons states have resorted to this form of foreign policy are many, but mainly these states see terrorism as just another means for conducting foreign relations.[18] Generally, they have designs to destroy and undermine the authority of democratic states, in particular the United States.[19] The use of terrorists as agents of their foreign diplomacy entails low risks, and it is an association that the employing state can deny in public.

Criminal Terrorism

Criminal terrorism could be also called quasi-terrorism because the violence perpetrated resembles that of political terrorism. However, the violence (or threat of violence) occurs during the commission of a crime. The modalities and techniques may be like those of political or religious terrorism, but the perpetrator's intent is not to produce reactions in the wider population. An example is where an armed felon enters a bank and takes several hostages during his escape.

This type of terrorism can also include perpetrators who suffer from pathological issues. Take for instance the case of the shootings at Columbine High School in 1999 in Colorado, during which two psychologically disturbed senior students killed twelve fellow students and a teacher, and wounded twenty-three others, for no obvious reason other than a deleterious choice.

Another example of criminal terrorism is what is called narco-terrorism, because it allows political, religious, and other types of terrorists to obtain funds by selling illicit drugs. It also refers to criminal gangs that use violence to intimidate law enforcement and civilian populations in the areas where they operate. Mexican drug cartels have used kidnapping, robbery, extortion, and murder, at times burying victims in mass graves. In Colombia, Pablo Escobar used assassination as a method to intimidate politicians and law enforcers not to interfere in his narcotics-trafficking enterprise.

Impact on Society

International terrorism is a phenomenon that governments around the world have come to dread. Since the end of World War II there have been hundreds of terrorist groups operating worldwide, each pursuing its own political or radical religious agenda. Likewise, the cases involving terrorism are seemingly endless. There have been aircraft hijackings, hostage takings, embassy and department store bombings, and assassinations of political leaders and diplomats.

The dilemma of how to deal with the problem has been grappled with by political leaders of nearly every nation. Combating this continuing stream of terrorist events has proved a troublesome political issue for democratic governments, especially when trying to protect their citizens and commercial interests overseas. Governments can usually enact legislation to guard against terrorism at home, and develop their domestic law enforcement agencies to detect and deter events on their soil. Governments can also exercise a large amount of control when resolving domestic events, such as hostage situations that have already unfolded. However, when faced with an event overseas—especially one that uses novel approaches—far from their geographic sovereignty, governments are vulnerable. By way of example, post-9/11 terrorism[20] has seen the use of women as terrorists and the recruitment of Western foreign fighters in the Middle East.

Women as Terrorists

Looking at the issue of women in terrorism first, this period in history saw Islamic extremist groups use gender as a means of recruitment. Groups like ISIL targeted women with propaganda to entice them to join their ranks. At the center of the campaign was the message of women as victims, which was intended to stir feelings of dissatisfaction with Western gender norms—for example, the message that Western societies do not respect Muslim women.

Social media played a large role in arguing that the West's view of Muslim women was one of a life of oppression in Islamic society. Photographs were circulated on the Internet depicting Muslim women being sexually assaulted in Srebrenica in 1995. Other photographs showed Israeli troops dealing forcefully with Palestinian children—scenes that were emotionally inciting with no promotion of dialogue that discussed the complexity of these situations. The campaign appeared to have had some success, because in mid-2017 reports showed that one in five ISIL members were women. Other reports showed that these women soon became dissatisfied and sought to exfiltrate themselves from these extremists. Some women were more successful than others, but those who did return to the West were disillusioned with their experience in the cause they served. Many then spoke out against the ideological propaganda of such groups.

Western Foreign Fighters

The mass recruitment of women in terrorist campaigns was part of the wider phenomenon of Western foreign fighters. Many of the people fighting in places like Iraq and Syria in the years 2011 to 2018 were from the West. Some joined because they too were influenced by the dynamics of gender, but rather from a male perspective—reports show that some of these recruits were driven by the desire to protect Muslim women and children, not because they wanted to escape poverty or other economic considerations. Thousands of foreign fighters from Europe, North America, Asia, Australia, and elsewhere are known to have become soldiers in jihadist groups such as ISIL and al-Nusra. It is a matter of public record that these recruits fought in conflicts in Afghanistan and Somalia, but in greater numbers in Iraq and Syria. Some died in combat and some, like Western women recruited to these groups, returned to their native countries.

The holding of radical political views by citizens is not necessarily an issue for a state's security services, but a person who holds these views and has been trained as a "soldier," and has fought in combat, is a different matter. As such, Western governments have, on the one hand, passed laws dealing with the return of foreign fighters (revoking their citizenship, and penalizing offenders with prison sentences) and, on the other hand, have implemented deradicalization programs in schools and universities to challenge extremist ideologies, as well as implemented programs to help terrorists who have denounced beliefs that led them to support violence, and to help them reintegrate into Western society.

Roots of Terrorism

"Terrorism is at least partly a reaction to the particular political, economic, and historical context within which potential terrorists exist."[21] For instance, the catalyst for right-wing terrorism is different from that of eco-terrorism. Nevertheless, terrorism is the use of fear to control the behavior of a civilian population by placing pressure on government authorities to make social or political changes. It seeks to make governing difficult or impossible by causing political destabilization. It has been argued that an act of terrorism is a subjective act.[22] The adage "one man's terrorist is another man's freedom fighter" acknowledges this view.

For perpetrators of terrorism, this view seems to condone their violence. Terrorists hold the freedom fighter belief that helps them justify their actions. For terrorists, society cannot be reformed through existing conventions, such as ballots or debate; it requires violence. Terrorists argue that the state itself is the violent party and can only be countered in the same way. Terrorists see their cause has having a higher purpose and moral standing than those of the state.[23]

The philosophy of terrorism does not entertain the possibility of coexistence between the group and society. Rather it seeks to destroy society.[24] This stance makes it difficult, if not impossible, to negotiate with the group. Nonetheless, this absolutist perspective can change over time. In some instances, the terrorist's cause can take on a more moderate political perspective to achieving its objectives.

The Irish Republican Army (IRA) in the conflict in Northern Ireland is a case in point. After decades of terrorism, through its political wing—Sinn Fein—the IRA sought a compromise through a political solution. However, compromise likely developed because the organization transformed into several political groups. Such transformation is possible when the main group gains recognition from the state or the international community; it can then seek to orient itself toward playing a role in the state's political apparatus. Such a shift often indicates that violence is no longer effective or that its resources or community support have been exhausted.

Ideology

Ideology is central to terrorism. But the ideologies are as diverse as the groups that employ terrorism. In many instances ideologies and the actions undertaken may seem at odds with each other. What is common is the belief that violence will achieve a group's objectives. Building upon the notion that the society the terrorists are attempting to transform is corrupt or immoral, they often will not display compassion for the members of that society. This is particularly a problem for alt-left groups that have emerged in the twenty-first century. Propagating platforms of equity for minority and socially disadvantaged groups and promoting the protection from violence against those minorities, alt-left groups commit acts of terrorism against others who simply disagree with their ideology.

Ideology is stronger than organizational structures. People have committed themselves to an ideology, a social outlook, or a cause without having to become a formal member of an organization. The rise of social media and other forms of Internet communication has given rise to so-called armchair activists, people who share opinions and subsequently serve as a conduit for spreading an ideology.

There is nothing inherently problematic about the spread of ideas. However, individuals who move beyond discussing ideology to direct action using violence are troubling. In some ways the lack of organizational structure means oversight of a group is more difficult. From a terrorist perspective, the lack of organizational structure can be effective in encouraging lone-wolf attacks because the ideology is strong and alluring.

Historically, the ideologies underpinning terrorism have been centered on challenging governments or seeking separatism. A few notable examples include Guy Fawkes, who was part of the failed Gunpowder Plot of 1605, during which Fawkes tried to bomb the British Parliament to remove the Protestant monarchy. Incidentally, it is Guy Fawkes's image that is used by the political activist/hacktivist group Anonymous. In 1914, Archduke Franz Ferdinand was assassinated by an organization known as the Black Hand, which was part of a larger effort to create an independent Serbian state.

In the late nineteenth and early twentieth centuries, anarchist ideology proved a dominant antagonist to existing governments and social order. Particularly strong in Europe, the ideology called for the abolishment of governments in favor of cooperation to rebuild society. Anarchists of this period believed that their cause could be best furthered through violent political action. Anarchist attacks include the assassination of Russian tsar Alexander II in 1881, the assassination of French president Marie-François Sadi Carnot in 1894, and the bombing of the Greenwich Observatory in London in 1894. In 1901, US president William McKinley too was assassinated by an anarchist.

As a contemporary analogy, anarchists of the nineteenth and twentieth centuries were viewed as a threat to national security in the same vein as ISIS or al-Qaeda in the early twenty-first century. Renowned author Joseph Conrad even explored the political dimensions of anarchism and terrorism in his 1907 novel *The Secret Agent*.[25]

Social Darwinism has sometimes been adopted by terrorist groups to justify racially based terrorism. Stemming from Charles Darwin's observations of natural life, some racially orientated groups have conveniently interpreted "survival of the fittest" to mean a collective struggle of one group against another.[26] White separatist terrorists such as the Ku Klux Klan (KKK) have historically used Social Darwinism as their ideology to justify terror.

Anarchism and Social Darwinism are still apparent in the ideologies of some contemporary groups, but as society changes new ideologies have emerged. The advent of environmental issues and reactionary movements to globalism, technology, and animal experimentation has spawned new terrorist organizations and lone-wolf terrorists.

Eco-terrorism is based on environmental ideology that uses ecological degradation as the justification for widespread attacks on people and property. Groups such as Earth Liberation Front have been prominent in this regard. Opponents to using animals for medical research, such as the Animal Liberation Front, have targeted individuals and organizations associated with animal experiments, as well as industry sectors that indirectly support medical testing. They have been responsible for causing millions of dollars of damage.

Ted Kaczynski, the so-called Unabomber, conducted a series of terrorist attacks against sections of American society over a twenty-year period on the justification of his own self-developed ideology, which he expressed in his manifesto, *Industrial Society and Its Future:*

> [I] therefore advocate a revolution against the industrial system. This revolution may or may not make use of violence; it may be sudden, or it may be a relatively gradual process spanning a few decades. We can't predict any of that. But we do outline in a very general way the measures that those who hate the industrial system should take in order to prepare the way for a revolution against that form of society. This is not to be a *political* revolution. Its object will be to overthrow not governments but the economic and technological basis of the present society.[27]

Theory

The strategies and tactics used in military combat operations are absent in terrorist engagements. Terrorism relies not on superior position, forces, or weaponry but on the ability to produce a disproportionate amount of fear—terror—in the opposition, thereby overwhelming and incapacitating them. Terrorism's principal purpose is to frighten people, as opposed to killing or injuring them, although terrorists usually inflict grievous bodily harm or kill people indiscriminately to achieve this end. In contrast to conventional warfare—that is, aggression conducted under the auspices of some specific legal doctrine—the victims of terrorism are those people who are frightened (society itself), not necessarily those who are injured.

The purpose of terrorism is to divide the mass of society from the state's elected incumbent authorities. Through fear, terrorists hope to create a process of disorientation that will lead to the undermining of the social structure. Fear, it is hoped, will lead to a situation where society loses confidence in its elected leaders, spreading confusion that is intended to create frightened individuals who are concerned with personal survival rather than solidarity and cooperation. The purpose of terrorism is to substitute society's independence with insecurity and distrust. If the targeted state's law enforcement or military forces are shown to be inept in dealing with the terrorists, the terrorists will have achieved their objective. There is a long-standing Chinese proverb that summarizes the situation: "Kill one, frighten ten thousand."

Justification for Terrorism

The justification for terrorism is subjective. Earlier in the chapter, we highlighted how terrorist actions of some are rationalized as freedom fighting—characteristically by "intellectuals of the democracy-left" for what has been referred to as "'a culture of excuse and apology' for acts of terror that has risen in parts of the academic and organizational left."[28] But it is a problematic phenomenon that makes terrorism difficult to outright condemn, and this issue has attracted much debate.[29] Take as an example former South African president and apartheid activist Nelson Mandela. He is often seen as a savior by the international community, having jointly won the Nobel Peace Prize in 1993. But early on he broke with the African National Congress (ANC), which supported nonviolence,[30] and cofounded an armed branch of the ANC known as Umkhonto we Sizwe (Spear of the Nation). "He later pleaded guilty in court to acts of public violence, and behind bars sanctioned more, including the 1983 Church Street car bomb that killed 19 people."[31] Given the broad consensus that he was fighting for a just cause, few today would view him as a terrorist, considering his later emphasis on reconciliation, humanitarian work, and social justice, but wasn't he a terrorist at the time of the Church Street bombing? It could be argued that the concept of terrorism is made complex because of the philosophical and political influences that are injected into what should be an objective debate.

The United Nations (UN) has grappled with the justification of political violence. It recognizes the rights of people to pursue national liberation or self-determination specifically when under colonial or dictatorial racist regimes. In recognizing the legitimacy of these types of struggles, it may also be interpreted as accepting political violence. Where the United Nations makes political violence justifiable is when there is a clear distinction between civilian and armed combatants. Further, attacks can be directed only toward military objectives.[32] It is inferred by the United Nations that targeting civilians and nonmilitary targets constitutes terrorism. Given this perspective, one may argue that an indiscriminate military bombing of cities or towns may also be an act of state-sanctioned terrorism.

Given the UN's understanding of terrorism within the context of international law and the problem of subjectivity in justifying acts of terror, it is not surprising that it is still based on a public opinion interpretation to decide if a terrorist act is justifiable. What constitutes a legitimate target for a group struggling for self-determination or national liberation is still open to debate.

While the justification for terrorism tends to be subjective, there are instances where terrorists have developed ideology based on weak political arguments or erroneous religious interpretations. Some notable weak political arguments are evident in terrorist thinking based on race. For instance, white supremacists believe that by nature of their skin color they are superior to other groups and therefore should be the dominant group. Religions have created some of the most psychotic foundations for terrorist actions. Poor interpretations of religious texts have caused some groups to launch terrorist attacks to bring forth an apocalypse. Others have applied selected sections of a religious text but failed to understand these passages' full meaning. Take the term *jihad,* which has been used by many self-described Islamic terrorist groups. For the most part, Islamic terrorists argue that Allah has given them a mandate to kill non-Muslims, and even other Muslims, in what they would view as a defense of the faith. However, jihad is more complex. Some theologians refer to it as the struggle within one's self to be a good Muslim.[33]

An Unjustifiable Act

Despite the complexity inherent in justifying terrorism, it remains intuitively unjustifiable. If the political motive is removed, it becomes apparent that its methods are indefensible; it becomes a criminal act. But it is unlikely it will ever be solely examined from a criminal perspective. So, to establish what acts are justifiable from what are unjustifiable, it is necessary to place terrorism into a theoretical framework that allows closer ethical analysis. In this regard, Just War theory can provide such a framework.

Just War theory sets conditions for armed conflict to be morally justified and the conduct for individuals in war. There are conditions that must be met to assess if the choice to go to war is just: "1) the war must have a just cause; 2) it must be fought with the right intentions; 3) the harm caused in war must be proportionate to the good achieved; 4) it must have reasonable prospects of successes; 5) it must be initiated and waged by a legitimate authority; 6) individuals must discriminate between legitimate and illegitimate targets and attack only legitimate targets—this means no harm to non-combatants; and 7) harm caused through war must be proportionate to the military advantage gained."[34]

Applying Just War theory to terrorism shows that terrorism fails to be justifiable. An illustration are the tactics of Boko Haram. The Nigerian-based terrorist group formed during the 1990s with the aim to introduce sharia (Islamic) law to Nigeria and establish an Islamic state in West Africa. In April 2014, Boko Haram terrorists stormed a boarding school in Borno, Nigeria, kidnapping 276 teenage girls and subsequently forcing some to marry the terrorists. Boko Haram began releasing a few of the schoolgirls two years after their capture. In 2018, the terrorist organization committed a similar attack, storming a girls' school and kidnapping a further 110 girls.[35] By choosing to focus its terror attacks on young girls, Boko Haram could be easily criticized for not adhering to Just War principles. While the group may believe it has a just cause and is fighting with the right intentions (both conditions are highly subjective), it lacks legitimacy. It certainly did not distinguish between military and non-military targets. Kidnapping young civilians had no military advantage. It was simply to instill fear into Nigerians by showing deficiencies in the state's security forces.

Another case of a clearly unjustified terrorist attack took place in Nice, France, in 2016. On this occasion a terrorist drove a truck through a crowd on Bastille Day, killing seventy-seven people. ISIS claimed responsibility for the attack. Like with the Boko Haram terrorist attacks, there is no rationale that could be used to justify this attack. There were no military targets, nor was there any military advantage; the only purpose was to create fear and a sense of insecurity among the people of France.

Through the lens of Just War theory, one can appreciate that there is no justification for terrorism. It is almost inconsequential if the terrorist believes they are fighting a just war or fighting with the right intensions.

Counterterrorism

Governments address unacceptable behaviors by enacting legislation that makes them crimes. Usually, a crime is punished by a fine or imprisonment. But just because a law is enacted does not mean that the behavior will cease. Although there are many criminological theories that explain why people commit crimes, in general the theory underpinning the rule of law is that it sets a standard for the communities to abide by and acts as a deterrent for those who are contemplating doing otherwise. It also serves as a way to isolate those who persistently commit crimes and to effect punitive retribution for pain and suffering caused to victims.

The responsibility for preventing and controlling crime is passed to a police force, which can take many forms depending on the scope of the jurisdiction covered by the law—from local parking inspectors to officers of a nationwide policing agency, with a wide range of agencies and law enforcement, regulation, and compliancy laws in between.

Regarding the crime of terrorism, the policies, laws, strategies, and tactics are not usually called crime prevention or crime control; they are referred to as counterterrorism. This is a term that encompasses all measures to prevent and control terrorism by law enforcement and intelligence agencies, as well as the military. These measures include both defensive measures[36] and offensive measures. As a guide, defensives measures aim to prevent and deter events, whereas offensive measure preempt and respondent events (see further discussion in Part 2 of this volume).

Study Questions

1. Explain the difference between terrorism and war.
2. Describe the four types of terrorism and explain the difference.
3. Explain what is meant by *guerrilla warfare* and give an example.
4. Explain what is meant by "kill one, frighten ten thousand."
5. Explain the theory behind terrorism. As a tactic, describe what it is trying to achieve.
6. Reflecting on the debate in the literature, explain if there is ever a justification for terrorism.
7. Discuss the significance of ideology for a terrorist organization.
8. Explain why the United Nations and other international bodies have difficulty in defining terrorism.
9. Political violence is not necessarily the domain of extremist groups, but why do they choose it over other avenues for political change? Discuss.

Learning Activities

1. In some political circles, the terms *terrorism* and *terrorist* are still debated. Given the lack of scholarly agreement, argue either for or against the continued use of these terms.
2. Undertake a SWOT analysis (strengths, weaknesses, opportunities, threats) that assesses terrorism in terms of its ability to meet the strategic objective of political/social change. Using a case study of a terrorist attack (one of your choice), identify the strengths, weaknesses, opportunities, and threats of the group that committed the attack. Drawing on the findings of your analysis, discuss why the group's strategic goals were or were not achieved. What are the impactions of your conclusion for policy?

Notes

1. Lukasz Kamienski, "Defining Terrorism: Issues and Problems," in Frank Shanty (ed.), *Counterterrorism: From the Cold War to the War on Terror,* vol. 1 (Santa Barbara: Praeger Security International, 2012), 7–12.

2. Brian Michael Jenkins, *The Study of Terrorism: Definitional Problems* (Santa Monica: RAND, 1980), 1.

3. Compare more appropriate synonyms, such as frightened, shocked, alarmed, appalled, scared, startled, and dismayed.

4. Martha Crenshaw, *Explaining Terrorism: Causes, Processes, and Consequences* (New York: Routledge, 2011), 2.

5. Bruce Hoffman, *Inside Terrorism*, rev. and expanded ed. (New York: Columbia University Press, 2006), 38, original emphasis.

6. Boaz Ganor, "Terrorism: No Prohibition Without Definition," October 7, 2001, https://www.ict.org.il/Article.aspx?ID=1588#gsc.tab=0.

7. Jenkins, *The Study of Terrorism*, 3.

8. US Department of Justice, Federal Bureau of Investigation, *Terrorism 2002–2005* (Washington, DC, 2017).

9. US Department of Defense, *Dictionary of Military and Associated Terms* (Washington, DC, 2017), 234.

10. These elements of terrorism are captured in 22 U.S. Code § 2656f(d)(2): "premeditated, politically motivated violence perpetrated against noncombatant targets by subnational groups or clandestine agents."

11. United Nations, *Report of the Secretary-General's High-Level Panel on Threats, Challenges, and Change: A More Secure World—Our Shared Responsibility* (New York, 2004), 52.

12. Brian Jenkins, "International Terrorism: A Balance Sheet," *Survival* 17, no. 4 (July–August 1975), 18.

13. Henry Prunckun, "The First Pillar of Terror—Kill One, Frighten Ten Thousand: A Critical Discussion of the Doctrinal Shift Associated with the 'New Terrorism,'" *Police Journal: Theory, Practice, and Principles* 87, no. 3 (2014).

14. Brian Michael Jenkins, "The New Age of Terrorism," in David G. Kamien, *The McGraw-Hill Homeland Security Handbook* (New York: McGraw-Hill, 2006), 119, emphasis added.

15. From a transcript of an unpublished taped interview by Bill Hillier of *Peace News* (London) with a ranking member of the Democratic Popular Front in London on May 16, 1969: "Democratic Popular Front: We Are Marxist-Leninists," in John Gerassi (ed.), *Towards Revolution,* vol. 1 (London: Weidenfeld and Nicolson, 1971), 235.

16. Bernard Lewis, "The Isma'ilites and the Assassins," in Marshall W. Baldwin (ed.), *The First Hundred Years: A History of the Crusades,* 2nd ed., vol. 1 (Madison: University of Wisconsin Press, 1969).

17. *Dictionnaire de l'Académie Française,* 5th ed. (Paris: Académie Française, 1798), 3,187.

18. Ariel Merari says: "Terrorism is useful for its sponsors as long as it does not become counter-productive in strategic and political terms. As a rule of thumb, the state sponsors of terrorism wish to remain below the threshold of punishment that is set by the states against which terrorism is directed. In this sense, it is the target countries of state-sponsored terrorism that determine the scope and form of this kind of warfare by their responses or lack of responses to it." Quoted in Brian L. Davis, *Qaddafi, Terrorism, and the Origins of the U.S. Attack on Libya* (New York: Praeger, 1990), 171.

19. For instance, Qaddafi had for some time promoted the downfall of all democracies, not only that of the United States. He wanted to replace democratic structures with what he called the "Third Universal Theory." Qaddafi's theory rejected capitalism and communism, constitutions and man-made laws, political parties, and representative democracy. To this end, Qaddafi made it clear that he wanted to see the ultimate demise of the United States. Qaddafi said: "Parliaments are the backbone of traditional democracy prevailing in the world today. Parliament is a misrepresentation of the people and parliamentary systems are a false solution to the problem of democracy." He went on to say: "This is an obsolete structure. Authority must be in the hands of all of the people." Muammar Qaddafi, *The Green Book* (Tripoli: Green Book World Center for Research and Study, 1980), 9–12.

20. Scholars such as Willard M. Oliver have argued that the events of September 11, 2001, resulted in governments adapting enhanced domestic security measures. This policy shift has manifested itself in a new age of policing, the era of homeland security. Oliver argued that over the centuries, policing has proceeded through three eras: the political (1840–1930), the reform (1930–1980), and the community (1980–2001). These developments in policing, Oliver posited, are based on four policing models: traditional, community, problem-oriented, and zero-tolerance. Willard M. Oliver, "The Fourth Ear of Policing: Homeland Security," in *International Review of Law, Computers, and Technology* 20, nos. 1–2 (2006). Other scholars include a fourth model: intelligence-led policing; see for example Jerry H. Ratcliffe, *Intelligence-Led Policing*, 2nd ed. (New York: Routledge, 2016).

21. Audrey Kurth Cronin, "Sources of Contemporary Terrorism," in Audrey Kurth Cronin and James M. Ludes (eds.), *Attacking Terrorism: Elements of a Grand Strategy* (Washington, DC: Georgetown University Press, 2004), 20–21.

22. Arthur Garrison, "Defining Terrorism: Philosophy of the Bomb, Propaganda by Deed, and Change Through Fear and Violence," *Criminal Justice Studies* 17, no. 1 (September 2004), 259.

23. A. Parry, "Terrorism: From Robespierre to Arafat," cited in Garrison, "Defining Terrorism."

24. Muhammad Kamal, *The Meaning of Terrorism: A Philosophical Inquiry*, NCEIS Research Paper 1, no. 1 (Melbourne: University of Melbourne, 2008).

25. Born Józef Teodor Konrad Korzeniowski on December 3, 1857, Conrad was a Polish British writer who has been regarded as one of the greatest English-language novelists. "Conrad" was his third Polish given name, but he anglicized it as well as his first name to form his writer's identity of "Joseph Conrad." See Jeffrey Meyers, *Joseph Conrad: A Biography* (New York: Scribner's, 1991).

26. Richard Weikart, "The Origins of Social Darwinism in Germany, 1859–1895," *Journal of the History of Ideas* 54, no. 3 (July 1993), 469.

27. Theodore Kaczynski, *Industrial Society and Its Future*, unpublished manuscript (1995), 1, emphasis added.

28. Michael Walzer, "Five Questions About Terrorism," *Dissent* 49, no. 1 (2002), 9.

29. See for example Walzer, "Five Questions About Terrorism," 5–11.

30. Elleke Boehmer, "Postcolonial Terrorist: The Example of Nelson Mandela," *Parallax* 11, no. 4 (2006).

31. Andrew Bolt, "The Dark Side of Nelson Mandela," *Herald Sun,* December 8, 2013.

32. United Nations High Commission for Human Rights, Human Rights Terrorism, and Counter-Terrorism, *Fact Sheet* no. 32 (2008).

33. *The Quran,* translated by Abdullah Yusuf Ali (1934), 4:74–76, 202 and 17:33, 703.

34. Jonathan Parry, "Just War Theory, Legitimate Authority, and Irregular Belligerency," *Philosophia* 43 (2015), 177.

35. Tara John, "Boko Haram Has Kidnapped Dozens of Schoolgirls, Again: Here's What to Know," *Time,* February 26, 2018, http://time.com /5175464/boko-haram-kidnap-dapchi-schoolgirls.

36. The purely defensive side of dealing with terrorism is sometimes referred to as anti-terrorism. See Hank Prunckun, *Scientific Methods of Inquiry for Intelligence Analysis,* 2nd ed. (Lanham: Rowman and Littlefield, 2015), 283.

Part 1
Terrorism

Terrorism

2

Contemporary Forms of Terrorism

Contemporary terrorism has distinct characteristics that differentiate it from the strategies and tactics used in the past. The factors that have caused the modern form have stemmed from the use of social media and Internet communications. It could be argued that contemporary forms of terrorism are notable for having less reliance on organizational structures and a greater focus on spreading ideology. These features make for a greater challenge for law enforcement and security agencies—how do authorities "arrest" an ideology? Yet within a terrorist apparatus, there are fundamental aspects that remain central. Specifically, terrorism is the rejection of the prevailing views of society with little concern for those that hold those values.

Before examining contemporary forms of terrorism, let us first review terrorism's long history. An understanding of the history of these events is important so we can set modern-day terrorism in context. This is more than an academic exercise of gazing back through history; context is important when formulating policies that address terrorism.

Historical Perspectives

Political events in Europe, the British Isles, Africa, the Middle East, Southeast Asia, and South America have brought the phenomenon of terrorism to world prominence. This in turn has generated extensive literature on the subject. David Rapoport developed a theory that he called the four waves of modern terrorism.[1] The current, and fourth, wave began with the 1979 Islamic Revolution in Iran. It was preceded by the anarchist movement of the late nineteenth century (first wave), the anticolonial movement that began in the 1920s (second wave), and the political and social radicals of the 1960s (third wave). However, it should not be assumed that terrorism was restricted to these periods in history. Examples of terrorism can be traced as far back as the Zealot struggle in Palestine in 48 C.E.

Antiquity

It could be argued that the first event involving the makings of terrorism is that of the Zealots, a group of Jewish nationalists dedicated to resisting Roman rule. Between 6 C.E. and the fall of Masada in 70 C.E., the Zealots carried out unconventional war against their Roman occupiers. The type of operations could be construed as guerrilla warfare—small groups of irregular fighters engaging larger numbers of regular troops. For example, they operated from the mountains of Galilee, striking at Roman targets and the villages of Jews who collaborated with the Romans.

Nevertheless, beginning about 48 C.E. the Zealots divided their activities between military guerrilla operations and terrorist-type activities. That is, the Zealots began employing assassins, known as *sicarii* (dagger-men), who would infiltrate the Roman-controlled cities and assassinate prominent Jewish collaborators. The Zealot *sicarii* continued their campaign of targeted murder for the next twenty years, until the guerrilla group grew strong enough to seize Jerusalem and incite general rebellion.

Another tactic employed by the Zealots was that of hostage taking. Throughout the fifth decade of that century, the Zealots would kidnap members of the Staff of the Temple of Guard and hold them for ransom. Their release would be conditional upon the Romans safely returning captured guerrilla fighters. These examples highlight the emergence of two important tactics of political violence that have since manifested themselves in the repertoire of the contemporary terrorists—assassination and kidnapping.

Middle Ages

Beginning in the eleventh century, the Order of Assassins held Persia and Asia Minor in terror for approximately 150 years using the tactic of murder. The Order was an underground Shiite splinter sect of Nizari-Ismaili based in Alamut, Persia. In the main, the Order's purposes and procedures were those of the Ismailites, with the additional practice of secretly murdering religious and political opponents using daggers. The killings planned by the leaders of the sect were carried out by a group of followers known as the *fidawi* (devotees).

> The name Assassin, by which the sectaries are known in both Moslem and western sources, is now known to be a corruption of hashish, taker of hashish, or Indian hemp, which the sectaries were believed to use in order to induce visions of paradise and thereby fortify themselves to face martyrdom. The stories told by Marco Polo and other eastern and western sources of the "garden of paradise" into which the drugged devotees were introduced to receive a foretaste of the eternal bliss that awaited them after the successful completion of their missions are not confirmed by any know Isma'ilite source.[2]

The Order's influence began to wane in the decades leading up to the Mongol invasion around 1270. History suggests that in remaining centuries of the Middle Ages, and throughout the sixteenth and seventeenth centuries, no new terrorist movements came to notice.

Eighteenth Century

Although we can identify individual terrorist events as far back as the ancient world, the terms *terrorism* and *terrorist* are relatively recent, dating only from the French Revolution. The fifth edition of the 1798 *Dictionnaire de l'Académie Française* referred to *terrorisme* as "système, régime de la terreur."[3] During the period, Robespierre led the Committee of Public Safety; unsurprisingly the term *terrorisme* was used in a positive sense—the Jacobins[4] were using desperate measures, collectively known in history as the Reign of Terror, to crush any possibility of counter-revolution.[5] However, after Robespierre and twenty of his lieutenants were beheaded on July 27, 1794, *terrorist* lost its positive connotation and "became a term of abuse with criminal implications."[6] This change in rhetoric can be seen as a contributing factor in the current debate about the definition of terrorism: Is it an objective description of the phenomena or is it a pejorative term?

Nineteenth Century

A hundred years later, another terrorist movement began, this time operating in Russia. Between January 1878 and March 1881, the

Narodnaya Volya (People's Will) was responsible for a concerted campaign of terror aimed at tsarist authorities.

Existing at the same time as the People's Will was anarchist terror. Elsewhere in Europe, the activities of anarchists were characterized by an individual approach, whereas the activities of the Narodnaya Volya took the form of a unified movement. The leading theoreticians of the Narodnaya Volya saw terrorism as an ethical alternative to the choice of allowing the carnage that would have resulted from a mass insurrection. They saw the death of innocent people from their terrorist operations as an acceptable consequence of their struggle: preferable to the deaths that would have followed conventional warfare.

The anarchists' philosophy viewed individual terror as a means of arousing revolt among the masses. Anarchists advocated the concept of what has become known as propaganda by deed. They argued that intellectual propaganda was meaningless. They maintained that their message, disseminated in newspapers, public meetings, pamphlets, and elsewhere, was being distorted by the bourgeois press and orators. Nevertheless, anarchist ideologists argued that practical demonstrations—including assassinations and bombings—could not be ignored. Such activities were considered to be a "bell" that could wake the "sleeping consciousness" of the masses.

Twentieth Century

Terrorism in the twentieth century is themed with a decline in anarchist movements and a rise in terrorist events attempting to further separatist or independence causes. It then returns to more ideological grounds as terrorist groups adopt left- or right-wing political outlooks. Fascism and socialism formed the two opposing ideological views after World War I. In the postcolonial era, after World War II, terrorist groups were intertwined in pro-communist or anti-communist struggles, but within those ideological camps they also sought independence from colonial rule.

During the Cold War (1945–1989), terrorist activities were often part of the broader struggle between Russia and the United States. Terrorist groups were often state-funded by either Russia or the United States as part of their proxy wars. On a domestic front in the West, terrorism is informed by the counterculture of the 1960s, with the creation of groups such as the militant Black Panthers, and a resurgence of extreme reactionary groups such as the Ku Klux Klan.

The rise of the New Left terrorist groups in the 1960s and 1970s marked the beginning of modern terrorism. At the end of the Cold War in 1989, new forms of terrorism emerged, or at least new ideologies. Environmental issues, animal rights, abortion, technology, and globalization all proved causes that used terrorism to further a political or social agenda. However, at the end of the twentieth century, Islamic extremism became the dominant terrorist activity, with 9/11 ushering in what is perceived as the period of global terrorist threats.

Post–World War I

Post–World War I, there appears to have been a shift in the ideology driving the perpetrators of terror, from a predominantly left-wing stance exhibited by the anarchists to one taken up by those on the right of politics. Although it is wise not to overstep the conclusions made in political analysis, especially regarding terrorism, it is reasonable to say that during the post–World War I period in Europe, terrorism was dominated by an aggressive patriotic ideology. As an example, take the Russian group known as the Black Hundreds, an ultranationalist political movement that supported the House of Romanoff. The group was reported to have promoted pogroms against the Jews and endorsed other extremist strategies that ensured the reign of the monarch. Of course, there were other groups that were on this side of the political spectrum: Irish nationals, German nationals, Armenians, Macedonians, and the Croatian Ustasha.

Pro-nationalist/self-determination objectives reflected wider changes taking place in Europe at the end of World War I. The fall of the Austro-Hungarian Empire had shepherded in several new autonomous states on the European continent. The rise of nationalism, groups seeking self-determination, and terrorism during this period are exemplified in the formation of the Irish Republican Army.

Like many terrorist organizations, the Irish Republican Army was a product of splintered political groups. The initial IRA formed in 1917 and was part of the Anglo-Irish War of Independence. During that time, it used guerrilla tactics, conducting raids, ambushes, and sabotage to force the British government into negotiating an independent Irish state. The Anglo-Irish Treaty of 1921 allowed the establishment of the Republic of Ireland in the south but left Northern Ireland under British control. Some in the IRA were unsatisfied with the Anglo-Irish Treaty and the IRA divided into two factions, one in support of the treaty and the other against. Those who were pro-treaty were then considered the regular Irish Army, while those against were deemed an illegal terrorist group.

Post–World War II

History shows that after World War II, there was a fear that there might be a resurgence in fascist or neo-Nazi ideology; but that did not prove to be the case. Instead, Europe settled into reconstruction. What did occur was a shift in the extremist political landscape in Africa, the Middle East, and Asia. In the main this was due to the authoritarian regimes that took power after the war in places such as Eastern Europe, the Balkans, and Spain. The power of national armies and the efficacy of their secret police forces helped limit the rise of underground groups.

In contrast, Africa saw the start of a postcolonial period of violence associated with liberation. In Algeria in 1954 a war for independence began that lasted seven years. The campaign was augmented by a terrorist component against the French colonists. There was also the Mau Mau Uprising in Kenya. Between 1951 and 1959 the colony's population was subject to acts of murder, assassination, and arson by Mau Mau revolutionaries.

In the Middle East, Palestine was the focus of political violence. Historical records show that the mandated power—Britain—was the subject of terrorist attacks by two Zionist paramilitary groups—Irgun and Lehi (known also as the Stern Gang)—opposed to what was considered illegal occupation.[7] Although an armistice was signed by the right-wing Irgun and the British government during the war years, elements of Lehi continued to operate against Arab targets until 1948–1949.

Asia was the site of the Chinese Revolution and the Vietnamese war against French colonial rule. After 1954, when the French were defeated at Dien Bien Phu, the United States entered the dispute and in the early days of the conflict experienced numerous acts of terrorism. The US response is well documented, as is how that conflict ended.

Modern Terrorism

The 1960s, 1970s, and 1980s were a time during which separatist political movements took hold. It was a global phenomenon, with direct political action being used against states in South and Central America, the Caribbean, Africa, and Europe. It was during this period that urban guerrillas came into being. Inspired, no doubt, by Carlos Marighella's book *Minimanual of the Urban Guerrilla*,[8] this period is characterized by a revolutionary theme.

Calls to overthrow governments by groups ranged from the Tupamaros in Uruguay to the Red Army in Japan, the National Liberation Army in Brazil, the Montoneros in Argentina, the Red Army in Germany, the Red Brigades in Italy, and the Black Panthers, Weather Underground, and the Symbionese Liberation Army in the United States, as well as a host of others. These groups were sometimes called the New Left. They were distinguished by their moving away from a Marxist outlook of class struggle to one that embraced an intellectual focus on issues that examined rights, such as civil rights, gay rights, women's rights (e.g., the right to choose abortion), gender equality, sexual rights, and the legalization of drugs. They still sought to overthrow governments, but their agenda had widened.

During the late 1970s and the 1980s there was a decline in New Left terrorism but a rise in extreme-right groups. In Europe, the United States, and Australia there was a significant increase in right-wing-inspired domestic terrorist events. In 1980, neofascist groups carried out bombing attacks in Italy, Germany, and France, killing and injuring hundreds.[9] In the United States, a range of right-wing extremist groups emerged, forming militias to further causes such as white supremacy, antigovernment sentiments, and Christian fundamentalism. Groups such as American Front Skinheads were active in planting explosive devices in the United States, as was the anti-Castro group Omega 7. The Justice Knights of the Ku Klux Klan were also involved in several shootings.

In Australia, National Action rose to prominence and was placed under surveillance by the Australian Security Intelligence Organization (ASIO) after allegations it had firebombed a trade union official's car and stormed government buildings. Also, a white supremacist group known as the Australian Nationalist Movement, led by Jack van Tongeren, committed several arson attacks on Chinese restaurants and businesses.

Instructing these modern terrorists were underground publications[10] like the now notorious *Anarchist Cookbook*.[11] Written in 1969 by William Powell, who was nineteen years of age at the time, it was originally published in 1971. It was a manual providing instructions on how to make improvised explosives, weapons, and even illicit drugs. The influence of the book has been alleged to be behind a pressure-cooker bomb explosion in 1976 at Grand Central Station in New York and linked to the Boston Marathon bombing in 2013. The author has for some time distanced himself from the publication and has openly regretted its distribution. *The Anarchist Cookbook* is over forty years old and has been reprinted several times, but only in recent times have governments made moves to restrict or ban copies.

New Terrorism

The term *new terrorism* came into vogue in the 1990s to describe a tactical shift in terrorist attacks, or at least terrorist planning.[12] Although scholars are not in complete agreement as to whether new terrorism should occupy its own place in history, the argument is that what distinguishes it from old terrorism is the use of weapons that will result in mass casualties. These weapons include nuclear, biological, chemical, and radiological devices.

An example of one such attack is the 1995 chemical attack on a Japanese subway by the doomsday cult Aum Shinrikyo. Using sarin gas, the cult's attackers triggered five devices on three lines of a Tokyo subway during rush hour. The poison gas killed twelve people. In addition, the chemical attacks left fifty commuters with severe injuries and caused temporary vision problems for another 5,000.

To date in the United States, there has not been a mass-casualty chemical terrorist attack. However, one of the 1993 World Trade Center bombers, Nidal Ayyad, had worked at a chemical company in New Jersey and used that position to obtain chemicals to make the bomb used in the 1993 attack. He had also stolen cyanide and planned to release it into office-building ventilation systems.[13]

The most infamous mass attack to date is 9/11. There is a voluminous body of literature, public debate, and discussion over the 9/11 attack, so further examination is not required here. However, the attack forms part of new terrorism because of its level of destruction and degree of sophistication in its planning. It is cited as one of the most expensive terrorist attacks in history and its impacts were felt worldwide. At the time, it was thought that 9/11 was the beginning of a new, larger, and more expansive series of terrorist attacks. However, post-9/11 terrorism has become more makeshift.

Post-9/11 Terrorism

Terrorist attacks since 9/11, such as the Boston Marathon bombing in 2013, the London bombings in 2005, the London Bridge attack of 2017, and the attack in Nice, France, in 2016, have all been conducted on a smaller, less costly scale, but still with significant impacts. Post-9/11 terrorism is less organized, with most attacks orchestrated by small terrorist cells or lone actors. The use of homemade explosives, knives, and even motor vehicles has become a common feature in terrorist attacks. "This increase was seen in many OECD [Organization of Economic Cooperation and Development] countries resulting in a 650 per cent increase in deaths to 577 from 77 in [for example] 2014."[14]

Despite the potential threats of chemical or mass-scale attacks, it is the smaller, more frequent attacks that are proving the most difficult to address. In the post-9/11 period it is mostly (but not always) the spread of radical Islamic ideology that has driven terrorism. Individuals and small collectives can in many ways, through social media and other communication technologies, selfradicalize or be radicalized by propaganda groups. They can also be inspired by the actions of others. Smaller, more dispersed groups and individuals can create terror events that instill fear and divide a community.

The spontaneity of these smaller attacks has led to higher security in public places, such as at sporting and entertainment events and in shopping districts. They have also contributed to the increase in surveillance throughout many parts of the world. The smaller terrorist attacks have been effective in creating a hypersensitivity to terrorism that is changing how many societies traditionally function. The terrorist threat is now everywhere and anywhere.

Although examples of early terrorism have been examined, it needs to be reiterated that these were isolated acts and terrorism's systematic manifestations did not emerge until the French Revolution, with widespread application coming only after World War II. Also, it is important to understand that although these examples from antiquity through to the French Revolution and beyond were the genesis of modern-day terrorism, they also differ greatly from today's acts of terror primarily due to their evolution.

Terrorism grew out of the need to combat overwhelming conventional forces, the same as guerrilla warfare. Whereas guerrilla operations are conducted in unconventional conditions of engagement and directed at military targets, terrorism branched off, striking at non-combatants through murder and kidnapping. From there, Robespierre developed the phenomenon's systematic characteristic. This manifestation was further advanced by nineteenth-century Russian terrorists and European anarchists who, from different perspectives of course, attempted to justify their violent political activities through complex philosophical arguments. From this genesis, then, evolved the ideology that has fueled terrorist movements since World War II.

Although we can see that terrorism is certainly not a new phenomenon, terrorist operations have undergone important changes. Social and technological changes, for instance, have had a profound effect on the purpose and objectives of contemporary terrorism. As such, democratic states now face a different threat to their stability than what would have been posed by terrorist movements in centuries past.

Whereas terrorist groups of the past can be classified by the politics of the period, today's terrorism is, arguably, influenced by globalization. Anticolonial movements emerged at the end of World War II, communist movements thrived during the Cold War, and transnational Islamic extremists proliferated post-9/11. This makes terrorism in the post-9/11 world a transnational phenomenon in several ways—the causes being pursued, how terrorists operate, and the outcomes of their attacks.

Left-Wing Terrorism

During the twentieth century, left-wing terrorism was attributed to communist rebels and Marxist-Leninist groups fighting against capitalism, or what was perceived as imperialism. Set within the context of the Cold War, groups such as Action Directe carried out attacks in the name of repelling what they perceived as the Americanization of Europe. During the 1980s, the Basque Armed Revolutionary Workers' Organization, with a membership of only twenty people, bombed US companies in France and Spain.

The international terrorist organization the Japanese Red Army was formed in 1970. It took part in airline hijackings and attempted bombings in the United States. Other left-wing groups active during the late twentieth century were more focused on domestic issues. Groups like the Black Liberation Army in the late 1960s and 1970s were formed as anticapitalist groups with a socialist and pro–African American political stance. The group carried out bombings, murders, and robberies. The ideology driving much of the left-wing terrorist activities during the 1960s and 1970s helped give rise of the counterculture and the New Left throughout Western democracies.

After the collapse of the Soviet Union and the end of the Cold War, there was a decline in left-wing terrorism, specifically by groups that openly advocated Marxist-Leninist doctrine. In the twenty-first century, left-wing terrorism has reemerged under the ideological banner of the antifascist movements such as Antifa. In 2017, New Jersey listed Antifa as a domestic terror group. While it has yet to use the violent tactics seen internationally, it does use political violence.

Antifa targets conservative governments. Antifa ideology features a pro-multicultural agenda, the protection of social and ethnic minorities, and the socialization of government. Much of its platform is mainstream liberal politics, but it has adopted violence and intimidation as its method to promote its agenda—instilling fear in society. Unlike the left-wing terrorist groups of the late twentieth century, Antifa has no leadership structure; it is an ideology with methods that individuals subscribe to and act upon independently and without central coordination. This is done via social media and various forms of Internet communication.

Right-Wing Terrorism

There is a spectrum of right-wing ideology encompassing race, nationalism, and a perceived need for protection against government control. In the contemporary sense, right-wing terrorist groups, or alt-right groups, are associated with neo-Nazi or fascist movements. They are typically anti-immigration and have a preoccupation with purity of race.

Within right-wing terrorist ideology is at times a strong sense of Christian fundamentalism. In the United States, groups like the National Alliance, the World Church of the Creator, and the Aryan Nations are recognized as being in the forefront of right-wing political extremism. Commonly, these groups believe their nation has been overtaken by nonwhites as part of an attempt to eradicate the white race. They exhibit a hatred for what they might describe as big government or government control. On issues like gun control, these groups interpret attempts to curb gun violence as an attempt to disarm people as part of a greater scheme to subjugate the entire population.

Right-wing ideology tends to be influenced by ideas of Adolf Hitler's *Mein Kampf* and the *Turner Diaries*. The *Turner Diaries* remains a seminal and inspirational work for the alt right. Written by William Pierce in 1978 under the pseudonym Andrew McDonald, the book is a fictional tale of a race-based revolution. The book traces the activities of a group opposed to Jews, homosexuals, and nonwhites as they undertake a series of bank robberies, murders, and guerrilla warfare that leads to the novel's protagonist and his group overthrowing the US federal government. Many right-wing terrorist groups view the work as a prophecy and often look at politics through the ideological lens of this fiction.

Notably, within the United States, right-wing terrorism justifies itself as a prelude to a larger race war. The Ku Klux Klan, for example, was active in the mid-twentieth century, but has a history dating back to the post–Civil War period. During the middle to late twentieth century, the KKK was reacting to the desegregation of schools and universities and the advances being made by the civil rights movement. Throughout that period, the KKK murdered, shot, and lynched people. As the organization grew in prominence, the FBI infiltrated and disrupted many of the KKK's activities as part of its counterintelligence program (COINTELPRO). Because of law enforcement efforts, today the KKK is fragmented and less organized than it was once.

In the 2000s, Stormfront was at the forefront of developing right-wing ideology. It was bringing together white nationalist groups across the world using its websites and social media platforms. At the heart of its ideology was a pro-white oratory. There were also suggestions of anti-Jewish rhetoric. Within the ideology was a religious aspect that focused on Christianity. Its introductory literature made use of selected biblical quotes as a justification for its cause. The essence of their problem was that multiculturalism does not work and causes society to fragment, thus creating conflict. The group's gullible argument was that it is only through a nationally inspired homogeneous culture that peace can be achieved.

Right-wing terrorism is also characterized by reference to fascist-sponsored terrorism, or militant nationalism. Death squads or progovernment groups may take unofficial action against the domestic population to ensure that the ruling government maintains power, helping quash dissent. Some examples include the Bonnet Gang and Davo Death Squad, both of which are alleged to have conducted extrajudicial killings of drug traffickers in the Philippines.[15] Often death squads and militant nationalists are trained by government military or police (albeit covertly) or comprise former police and military personnel.

Single-Issue Terrorism

Single-issue terrorism is also known as special interest terrorism and seeks to use fear to bring about a specific outcome. Its absence of ideology makes it different from right- and left-wing terrorism. Members of a special interest group may hold a wide variety of political and social views but are brought together on one common issue.

Notably, single-issue terrorism has been represented on animal liberation, the environment, and anti-abortion fronts. Single-issue terrorism, especially when focused on the environment or animal rights, has not received the same resourcing or attention from law enforcement as has international terrorism. This lack of attention has generated criticism for those targeted by these factions, and targets often struggle to highlight the impact these groups have on their business or way of life.

Animal Rights Terrorism

Animal rights terrorists are specifically motivated by a zeal to protect the health and well-being of animals, specifically those used in medical experiments. Universities have been a target for animal rights terror attacks, but other targets have emerged—those who provide animal transportation services, or banks and investors that have a financial interest in animal medical experiments.[16]

Notable animal rights terrorist groups include the Animal Liberation Front (ALF) and the Earth Liberation Front (ELF). The ALF was founded in the United Kingdom (UK) in the mid-1970s with the objective of stopping what the group claimed to be the exploitation of and cruelty toward animals. By the late 1970s, the ALF had set up branches in the United States. The ALF did not have a formal membership in the sense of registration and fees. It chose direct action over an organized structure. Direct action is individual-centered and is best described as a lone-wolf operation inspired by a group's ideology. Direct action is the commission of a form of criminal activity that will cause economic loss of property damage. These activities may include vandalism, arson, animal releases, harassing telephone calls, and threats to individuals involved in conducting animal-based experiments or testing using animals. Such groups also target companies that do business with companies that are conducting testing on animals.

Since 2002, as reported by the Federal Bureau of Investigation, there has been an increase in violent rhetoric of animal rights groups as well as the use of improvised explosives. In 2003, two pipe bombs were detonated at a research center in northern California. Both claims of responsibility called for the cessation of what the perpetrators believed were acts of animal cruelty. One statement of responsibility suggested that while buildings could be protected, it would be impossible to protect individual employees. The homes and cars of customers and suppliers of the research centers were considered legitimate targets. In 2004, the FBI estimated that since 1976, the ALF and ELF committed more than 1,100 criminal acts and caused damages estimated at approximately US$110 million.[17]

Anti-Abortion Terrorism

Since the legalization of abortion in the United States, clinics and their staff have been the subject of political violence. The National Abortion Federation has been compiling records of violence and campaigns since 1977, and its figures present what could be described as a relentless campaign against abortion clinics. From 1977 to 2016, a total of 7,731 acts of violence were committed. This includes eleven murders, forty-two bombings, and four cases of kidnapping.[18]

The Anti-Defamation League refers to anti-abortion violence as a forgotten terrorism.[19] At the fore of anti-abortion violence have been groups such as Operation Rescue, Promise Keepers, and the Army of God. Despite allegations, Operation Rescue denies any involvement in violence and publicly denounces violence. Promise Keepers is a Christian organization that does not openly advocate violence. The Army of God is perhaps more sympathetic to those who commit anti-abortion acts of terror. Its website makes martyrs out of terrorists like Paul Jennings, who murdered medical doctor John Britton in 1994.

Within the realm of anti-abortion terrorism, groups appear not to take ownership of specific acts of terror but rather suggest that those who commit them have done so on behalf of these groups.

Eco-Terrorism

Eco-terrorism has two very diametrical interpretations. It can refer to the violence used to support environmental causes and it can refer to acts of political violence that deliberately cause environmental damage. In the context of contemporary forms of terrorism, it is the first definition that is of interest.

Eco-terrorism rose to prominence between 1998 and 2005, with a notable example being the 1998 arson attack on a ski lodge in Vail, Colorado, which gave the phenomenon prominence and initiated public hearings in the United States. In response to eco-terrorism, a multiagency investigation was launched called Operation Backfire. The operation successfully brought about several prosecutions and is credited with disbanding several eco-terror groups.[20]

Earth First! is an example of an eco-terrorist group that was formed in the United States in the 1980s and spread to many countries, including Britain, Australia, and Canada. Few of Earth First!'s goals were ever realized, with several members being convicted of conspiracy to damage the Rocky Flats nuclear weapons plant, the Diablo Canyon nuclear power–generation facility, and the Palo Verde nuclear power–generation station.[21] Such acts demonstrate that eco-terror tends to focus more on sabotage and less on actual violence. However, there has been a tendency to persecute offenders in the United States under the Patriot Act.[22] This has caused some to question the necessity of distinguishing between eco-terrorism and eco-sabotage.

Religious Terrorism

Religious terrorism is commonly motivated by one or more of three goals: bringing about the apocalypse, creating a religious government, and religious cleansing of a state.[23] Apocalyptic terrorism aims at bringing about the prophecy of the end of the world. Most major

religions, and even some cults, share an end-of-world vision characterized by a day of judgment, followed by the inception of a new
world. However, religious terrorist groups see themselves as key
players in the prophecy.

Within the Christian faith, some notable groups include the Concerned Christians and Army of God. The Concerned Christians were
a Denver, Colorado–based sect campaigning against new age spiri-
tualism. In 1999, its leader had prophesied the end of the world; so in
preparation for the millennium, he moved members of the sect to
Jerusalem. According to Israeli police, they were planning many violent acts and possibly the planting of an explosive in a mosque. The
sect aimed to cause a holy war between Jews and Muslims and thus
bring about the second coming of Jesus.[24]

A more notorious example of apocalyptic religious terrorism is the
Japanese Aum Shinrikyo religious cult's 1995 attack on a Tokyo subway. The attack killed thirteen and injured hundreds. The leader was
Shoko Asahara, who had planned several more attacks. Authorities
said the attacks were in part designed to bring forth the apocalypse.[25]

Creating a religious government is easier to comprehend than
efforts to bring about the apocalypse[26] because it has familiar political connotations. Much of the efforts of Islamic State of Iraq and
Syria were focused on establishing a religious government built on
sharia (Islamic) law within a certain geographic area. History now
shows how this fanatical plan failed, causing innumerable people to
be killed, injured, and left homeless. Some additional examples of
this credulous obsession are the efforts of Hezbollah to create a Shiite religious government in Lebanon, and Hamas's efforts to establish
a Sunni Palestinian state.[27]

Religious cleansing is essentially a euphemism for genocide
along sectarian lines. It is predominantly undertaken against religious
minorities by the dominant religion of a state. Where the dominant
religion attempts to kill or remove people of another religion, terror
cells that are unofficially state sponsored or state trained (e.g., death
squads) may be used. Alternatively, religious minorities can use terrorism to protect their interests within the state. Like the objective
of creating a religious government, religious cleansing has strong
political motivations as well. Often underlying religious terrorism is
a political agenda that may include sovereignty or separatism.

Terrorists seeking to expand their influence can use religious
cleansing as an opportunity to recruit and gain support for their

agenda. Groups can harness support from victims of religious cleansing if the group can frame it within the context of their own struggle and share the same religious faith. For example, the outbreaks of violence in Myanmar in 2017 exhibited a religious tension that existed with the Muslim Rohingya and the dominant Buddhist authorities in the region. Certainly the dispute was multifaceted, but it provided an opportunity for Islamic terrorists to exploit it in terms of recruiting supporters—people who would not previously have been supporters if it were not for the religious maltreatment. Essentially, if a terrorist group can show a religious connection with their cause, they are able to galvanize support.

Criminal Terrorism

There are three important facets to criminal terrorism. The first is that terrorist groups will sometimes resort to criminal activities, like bank robberies, to fund their terrorist activities. Second, terrorist and criminal organizations will cooperate with each other when there is a financial or political advantage. Third, criminal organizations will embark on terrorist activities to protect their interests by inciting community fear.

To be effective, terrorist groups require funding. It is likely there will be ideological restraints on the kind of criminal activities a terrorist group may undertake. Typically, terrorist groups have little issue targeting financial institutions or state-run enterprises for their criminal activity. Bank robbery is often a lucrative means of obtaining funds fast. Regardless of a terrorist group's political ideological leanings (left or right), banks are often associated with assisting a corrupt or immoral society. Other crimes include immigration fraud, counterfeiting, and drug and weapons trafficking.

Part of the contemporary terrorist paradigm is the partnership between organized crime and terrorist groups. Traditionally, the two entities were separate law enforcement issues. The old view was that organized crime was motivated by illicit business profits, while terrorists were motivated by politics and ideology. There appeared little in common between them. However, in 2001 the United Nations noted that there were closer links than initially thought.[28] It was suggested that through cooperation, crime organizations and terrorist groups had the opportunity to gain several benefits. For example, within the context of the drug trade, it is suggested that terrorist groups can benefit through controlling territory where drugs are cultivated and transported while organized crime groups control the trafficking of drugs.[29] Both then enjoy the profits of the drug trade, which can fund further activities of each group.

Criminal organizations may also resort to terrorist activities to protect their own interests. In 1993, five car bombs were detonated in Rome, Florence, and Milan, Italy, killing at least ten. The Sicilian mafia had also used a car bomb to murder anti-mafia judge Paolo Borsellino. The rationale for the bombings was to instill fear and cause destabilization of the Italian government and protest anti-mafia legislation being enacted.[30]

Anti-Government Extremists

Where once anti-government extremism was the domain of anarchists, in modern times it has increasingly become a rejection of what it commonly known as the New World Order and globalism. The phrase "New World Order" was first made prominent by George H. W. Bush at the end of the Gulf War (August 2, 1990—February 28, 1991). Energized by a successful United States–led UN coalition against the Saddam Hussein regime in Iraq, Bush had suggested that the way the world responded to Iraqi aggression was a model for dealing with future aggression and ushered in a new global order under the guidance of the United Nations and US leadership.

Later, Bill Clinton, after he was elected president, undertook substantial economic reform that emphasized the need for globalization and freer trade. This reform had some negative impacts on US manufacturing and blue-collar jobs. Many around the world viewed the New World Order and globalization as a move toward one world government and the removal of individual and national freedoms. Beginning in the 1990s there was a resurgence of groups and individuals rejecting big government. According to the Southern Poverty Law Center in the United States, in 2015 there were 998 various anti-government groups including militias in operation.[31]

Not all these groups are terrorists but there are some that have been placed on the US list of domestic terrorists. Anti-government terrorists will target government buildings and institutions perceived as sponsoring the ruling government. Sovereign Citizens is one example of a listed domestic terrorist group that is anti-government. The Sovereign Citizens movement is active in the United States, Australia, and Canada. Those who identify themselves as Sovereign Citizens do not believe they are subject to taxation, laws, or institutions within their country.

In Australia, law enforcement intelligence has uncovered plans to disrupt court proceedings with paint bombs and kidnap judges and judicial officers as well as a police officer.[32] Like other movements, Sovereign Citizens has no formal organizational structure but has a refined ideology. Often it is individuals or small groups who plan terrorist activities. A common factor in anti-government terrorism is its propensity to foster lone-actor attacks or attacks orchestrated by a handful of people. The Oklahoma Bomber, Timothy McVeigh, is likely the most well-known anti-government terrorist. Another example would be Theodore John Kaczynski, the Unabomber (see discussion of terrorism types in Chapter 1).

Radical Separatist Groups

Separatist groups are characterized by a drive to identify with a specific political individuality. They see their community as unique and separate from the greater society in which they live. Often a separatist group will identify with a specific religious or ethnic disposition, but there can also be social differences. Separatist groups often seek full or partial autonomy from the country wherein they reside. This may involve establishing a small, separate self-governing municipality or a completely new state within the existing state.

There are many separatist groups across the world. In Iraq, Syria, and Turkey there are the Kurdish peoples. Separatist movements are also active in the south of Thailand, the Philippines, and Spain. The motivations of separatist groups are relatively easy to identify and, unlike other contemporary terrorist groups, separatist groups have a clear organizational structure and leadership. Separatist groups are quite politically focused, which provides an ideology and a direct-action approach.

Separatist groups have used terrorism as means to pressure governments into negotiations to grant them their demands. The Palestine Liberation Organization, the Liberation Tigers of Tamil Eelam, the Chechen Republic, and the Irish Republican Army are well-known examples of groups that have been engaged in this form of terrorism. While most ruling governments state that they do not negotiate with terrorists, a lack of success in countering terrorism through law enforcement or military means suggests there may be a role for negotiation specifically when there is a clear political objective of the separatist group that can be addressed.

In some instances, there may be more than one separatist terror group operating within a jurisdiction, and these groups may even be competing for sovereign territory. For example, in Thailand's south, there have been up to six active separatist groups. While some of these groups have sought peace talks, the dominant group—Barisan Revolusi Nasional—was not interested in negotiations and would not discuss political issues with other separatist groups. The chaotic nature of multiple separatist groups makes the phenomenon difficult to combat, and even more problematic to negotiate.

Study Questions

1. Discuss the distinction between acts of terrorism and acts of sabotage. Place this discussion in the context of animal rights and environmental groups.
2. Discuss the effectiveness of direct action as opposed to organizational leadership.
3. Explain the central purpose of contemporary terrorism.
4. Explain how contemporary terrorism might be different from its historical roots. Then discuss if there is an evolution and what might drive that evolution.

Learning Activity

Write a tactical law enforcement briefing paper that profiles a terrorist group. The report should comprise several sections: the group's historical background (if it is a long-standing organization), key individuals, the group's ideology, current media reports of its activities, and its tactics.

Notes

1. David C. Rapoport, "The Four Waves of Modern Terrorism," in Audrey Kurth Cronin and James M. Ludes (eds.), *Attacking Terrorism: Elements of a Grand Strategy* (Washington, DC: Georgetown University Press, 2004).

2. Bernard Lewis, *The Assassins: A Radical Sect in Islam* (London: Weidenfeld and Nicolson, 1969), 108–109.

3. *Dictionnaire de l'Académie Française*, 5th ed. (Paris: Académie Française, 1798), 3,187.

4. "Jacobin" was the name given to the members of a radical French political club that played a controlling part in the French Revolution (1789–1799). The name of the club was derived from the club's original meeting place—a Jacobin monastery.

5. George Rude, *The Crowd in the French Revolution* (Oxford: Oxford University Press, 1967).

6. Walter Laqueur, *The Terrorism Reader* (Boston: Little, Brown, 1977), 6.

7. J. Bower Bell, *Terror Out of Zion: Irgun Zvai Leumi, LEHI, and the Palestine Underground, 1929–1949* (New York: St. Martin's, 1977); Paul Wilkinson, *Terrorism and the Liberal State* (London: Macmillan, 1977), 50–51.

8. Carlos Marighella, *Minimanual of the Urban Guerrilla* (Boulder: Paladin, 1985).

9. Nick Grothaus, "Right-Wing Terrorism," 2011, http://handofreason .com/2011/featured/right-wing-terrorism.

10. And publications such as Abbie Hoffman's *Steal This Book* (Cambridge, MA: Da Capo, 1996).

11. William Powell, *The Anarchist Cookbook* (El Dorado, AR: Ozark, 2002).

12. Walter Laqueur, *The New Terrorism: Fanaticism and the Arms of Mass Destruction* (New York: Oxford University Press, 1999).

13. Eben Kaplan, "Targets for Terrorists: Chemical Facilities," December 11, 2006, https://www.cfr.org/backgrounder/targets-terrorists-chemical-facilities.

14. Institute for Economics and Peace, *Global Terrorism Index 2016* (New York, 2016), 2–3.

15. Clare Baldwin and Andrew Marshall, "Between Duterte and a Death Squad: A Philippine Mayor Fights Drug-War Violence," March 17, 2017, https://www.reuters.com/article/us-philippines-drugs-mayor/between -duterte-and-a-death-squad-a-philippine-mayor-fights-drug-war-violence -idUSKBN16N33I.

16. Federation of American Societies for Experimental Biology, "Report on Animal Rights Extremism," March 24, 2014, http://www.animalright sextremism.info/news/media-conferences-and-press/faseb-report-on-animal -rights-extremism.

17. John E. Lewis, "Testimony Before the Senate Judiciary Committee," Washington, DC, May 18, 2004, https://archives.fbi.gov/archives/news /testimony/animal-rights-extremism-and-ecoterrorism.

18. National Abortion Federation, "Violence Statistics and History, 2017," https://prochoice.org/education-and-advocacy/violence/violence-statistics -and-history.

19. Anti-Defamation League, "Anti-Abortion Violence: America's Forgotten Terrorism," September 4, 2012, https://www.adl.org/news/article/anti -abortion-violence-americas-forgotten-terrorism.

20. Lauren Kirchner, "Whatever Happened to 'Eco-Terrorism'?" January 27, 2015, https://psmag.com/environment/whatever-happened-to-eco-terrorism.

21. "Man Gets 6 Years in Plot to Damage A-Plants," *New York Times,* September 8, 1991.

22. David Thomas Sumner and Lisa M. Weidman, "Eco-Sabotage Should Not Be Mistaken for Eco-Terrorism: Guest Opinion," 2013, http://www .oregonlive.com/opinion/index.ssf/2013/10/eco-sabotage_should_not_be _mis.html.

23. Heather S. Gregg, "Defining and Distinguishing Secular and Religious Terrorism," *Perspectives on Terrorism* 8, no. 2 (2014).

24. B. A. Robinson, "The 'Concerned Christians' Cult—Originally of Denver CO," 2002, http://www.religioustolerance.org/dc_conc.htm.

25. Charlotte Alfred, "20 Years Ago, A Shadowy Cult Poisoned the Tokyo Subway," *World Post,* March 20, 2015, https://www.huffingtonpost .com/2015/03/20/tokyo-subway-sarin-attack_n_6896754.html.

26. Gregg, "Defining and Distinguishing Secular and Religious Terrorism," 2014.

27. Gregg, "Defining and Distinguishing Secular and Religious Terrorism," 2014.

28. Rob McCusker, "Organised Crime and Terrorism: Convergence or Separation?" *Standing Group Organised Crime eNewsletter* (European Consortium for Political Research) 5, no. 2 (May 12, 2006), 3–5.

29. Rachel Ehrenfeld, *Narco-Terrorism* (New York: Basic, 1990).

30. John Tagliabue, "Bombings Laid to Mafia War on Italy and Church," *New York Times,* July 15, 1994, http://www.nytimes.com/1994/07/15/world /bombings-laid-to-mafia-war-on-italy-and-church.html.

31. Southern Poverty Law Center, "Active Antigovernment Groups in the United States, 2015," https://www.splcenter.org/active-antigovernment -groups-united-states.

32. Australian Broadcasting Corporation, "Sovereign Citizens: Terrorism Assessment Warns of Rising Threat from Anti-Government Extremists," *7.30 Report,* December 1, 2015, http://www.abc.net.au/news/2015-11-30 /australias-sovereign-citizen-terrorism-threat/6981114.

3

Radicalization

Leaders and disaffected members of political or issue-motivated groups make a conscious decision to use terrorism to further their cause. Not all members or supporters of a group will subscribe to the use of extreme violence without some justification. The process used to enlist participation in terrorist activities is known as radicalization.

Definitions of radicalization have two central tenets. First, there is an agreed understanding of existing and accepted social, political, or religious ideas. Second, attempts to undermine or reject those existing accepted norms are an expression of radicalization. Radical views within themselves are not a danger to the safety of individuals and communities. Radical views can challenge long-held biases or social disadvantage. However, radical political, social, or religious views become a threat to security when those views are manifested as violent extremism. Consequently, it is possible to have radical political, social, or religious groups that are nonviolent. Nevertheless, violence is adopted by groups and aggrieved individuals who seek to change the way the society is organized or functions.

Violence is an old and well-used medium for expressing a political position. This chapter examines some of the causes and mechanisms of radicalization, with emphasis on violent extremist radicalization.

Motivations

According to the US Department of the Army[1] there are four motivational categories for terrorist groups: separatist, ethnocentric, nationalistic, and revolutionary. However, there tends to be crossover among the categories.

Separatists will seek to create a new independent state within an existing state. Often they are seeking religious freedom or political autonomy. The Bangsamoro Islamic Freedom Movement in southern Philippines and the United Front for the Independence of Patani in southern Thailand are just two examples of separatist movements in Asia. But perhaps the most well-known separatist struggle is that between Israel and Palestine in the Middle East.

An ethnocentric motivation is based on the perception that it is race that defines a society and that it is only through having a society with one race that there can be peace and cooperation within that society. Ethnocentric groups, as the definition suggests, believe that some races are superior to others. As an example, white supremacy groups such as Aryan Nations or the Ku Klux Klan advocate that the white race is superior to other races.

Nationalistic motivations may share similar outlooks to those of the separatist and ethnocentric views. Nationalists are motivated by the preservation of and devotion to the state, believing their nation's interests and qualities are better than those of other nations. Often a nationalist movement will use race to define the nation and display ethnocentric views. A nationalist group is likely motivated by a desire to create a new nation based on its understanding of nationalism or retaliate against what it perceives as a change for the worse in its society. The Irish Republican Army and Basque Homeland and Liberty movement in northern Spain are some examples of nationalistic groups with separatist leanings.

Revolutionary motivations are aimed at removing the established government and replacing it with a new political or social structure. Traditionally, the motivation for revolutionary terrorism has been associated with communist ideology. However, groups like Boko Haram in Nigeria show revolutionary motivations in their attempt to overthrow the Nigerian government in favor of an Islamic state.

Historical and Group Grievances

Many of these motivations are embedded in historical or group grievances. A historical grievance means there has been some past conflict between peoples or states. Past conflicts or old injustices may continue to resonate with a section of society and may be viewed as the cause of some contemporary disadvantage. For instance, some argue that the partition of the Ottoman Empire after World War I was the origin of Islamist opposition to the West.[2]

Perhaps a more pronounced example of a historical grievance that has led to terrorist action and divided the West and Arab world is the Israel-Palestine conflict. Like the Ottoman Empire example, the state of Israel was established in 1948 by a United Nations resolution that divided British Palestine into Jewish and Arab states. The move created a significant historical grievance that remains central to any attempt to bring peace to the Middle East.

Historical grievances can provide a focus for terrorist motivations. Perceptions of injustice—real or imagined—can be a motivation for groups to act and make political change. Historical grievance can be reasoned as a just cause for contemporary action. History can be used as part of the radicalization process when it is used to highlight a past grievance and how it has shaped contemporary problems experienced by the individual or social group.

A group grievance is often a response by a collective who believe they are suffering an injustice or inequality within their state or community. The grievance may not have a historical basis and can be a response to a change in government policy or economic or social structure. A distinctive trait of a group grievance is that individuals collectively identify and respond to a given political, social, or economic change. The group can be collectively radicalized through their grievances and its rejection of the social or political change they may be experiencing. The solution they seek to their grievance can be outside acceptable protest or political action because they reject the so-called new structures by adopting extreme violent measures given that they do not view the new structure as legitimate. According to the aggrieved group, the social contract between the group's members and wider society is perceived as null and void.

Personal Grievances

Personal grievances naturally follow similar patterns of those with historical or group grievances, but are based on an individual's perception. A personal grievance can manifest into radicalization through a personal interpretation of events either historical or contemporary. Timothy McVeigh, the Oklahoma Bomber, and Ted Kaczynski, the

Unabomber, are two examples of terrorists who had personal grievances and radicalized themselves through their own unique perception of changes taking place in American society.

McVeigh was a returned veteran from the first war in Iraq who
had difficulty adjusting to civilian life. Without employment or a
wide circle of friends, he had begun to reject contemporary American society and questioned the federal government's response to
the Ruby Ridge siege in Idaho as well as the Waco, Texas, siege.
His selfradicalization was supplemented with his reading of *The
Turner Diaries,* a pro-white revolutionary novel that has served as
the inspiration for others who believe that a race war is coming to
the United States.[3]

Kaczynski was a selfradicalized anarchist with a distaste for
technology. A former mathematics lecturer, he wrote his own manifesto, *Industrial Society and Its Future.* Reclusive and working as a
lone wolf, he remained elusive, driven by a personal grievance
against the changing nature of American society.

Personal grievance, as an act of terror, requires a political or
sociopolitical context. Without either such agenda, it is simply an
act of criminal violence. Both McVeigh and Kaczynski are illustrative of the necessary context required to differentiate lone-actor terrorism from acts of violence that might be described as mass or
serial murder.

Terrorist Idols, Martyrs, and Leaders

Radicalization of groups or individuals to conduct acts of terror
involves a promise that the act will not only assist the cause and effect
change but also ensure the perpetrator is revered and idolized. Importantly, individuals radicalized to commit terrorist acts want to be
remembered. Former chief Crown prosecutor Nazir Afzal described
British teenagers as being radicalized by ISIS because those teenagers
saw Islamic State fighters as "pop idols" and described a form of
"jihadimania" taking root among young British Muslims.[4]

Efforts to curb terrorism in Britain have unintentionally created
a mystique around this phenomenon. Being a terrorist can also be
perceived by disadvantaged people as an opportunity to have purpose and meaning. In Gaza, Hamas members are often seen as war-
riors, nationalist heroes, and pop idols.[5] In conditions of poverty,
disadvantage, or perceived grievance, joining a terrorist group or

undertaking an act of terror gives the individual or group status, purpose, and meaning.

Radicalization also involves the acknowledgment of martyrs as symbolic leaders to a cause. A martyr is someone who has given their life for a cause. History is filled with people who have sacrificed for a political or social cause. Martyrdom is viewed as the ultimate sacrifice a person can make. From Joan of Arc to Martin Luther King Jr., martyrs represent unparalleled commitment and are often role models for those who share the same ideology.

While the notion of martyrdom is discussed in more detail later in this chapter, an important distinction needs to be made here between martyrs and suicide terrorists. A martyr in the traditional sense will be persecuted and executed for their beliefs. This is distinct from a suicide terrorist in that their actions tend to be aimed at publicizing a cause. The difference in interpretation may be subtle for some but is nonetheless important to acknowledge.

Martyrdom

A narrow definition of a martyr is someone who suffers or is killed because of a religious or political belief. Within Christianity, Islam, and Judaism, martyrdom is symbolic of faith and commitment. The question of Islam-inspired terrorist martyrdom is often discussed when trying to assess terrorist motivations. Some scholars refer to quotes within the Quran that appear to indicate that it is permissible and even desired that a person die in the protection or pursuit of Islamic ideals. Terrorists may suggest that verses in the Quran make it permissible to commit suicide attacks to further a perceived religious cause. The passage often cited is "And do not kill anyone which Allah has forbidden, except for a just cause."[6] Further, there is a suggestion that martyrdom has rewards. "Let those (believers) who sell the life of this world for the Hereafter fight in the Cause of Allah, and who so fights in the Cause of Allah, and is killed or gets victory, we shall bestow on him a great reward."[7]

While it is important to understand the religious reasons used by people, it is equally important to acknowledge that these reasons are not universally recognized by the Muslim faith as a justification for terrorist attacks. Further, the use of the Quran to justify such actions is commonly refuted.

Rational Choice Theory

Rational choice theory has its foundations in the economic and social sciences. It means that people will carefully think through the benefits of some action and weigh them against the costs before making a choice.[8] Further, it emphasizes the role of individual action as being central to social exchanges. The theory suggests that the individual is driven to make choices based on rewards versus penalties. Even the threat of a penalty or promise of a reward can have an impact on individual choice.[9]

A shortcoming of the individual in rational choice theory is the place of collective action. If, as the theory suggests, social exchange is based on individual action built on benefits and costs, then how is collective action explained? The subject literature on rational choice theory suggests that people take part in collective action when there is an individual benefit that will be extended only to the members of that group. However, rational choice theory can be a lens to view radicalization. The theory provides an opportunity to structure thinking around choices made by individuals to join a terrorist group or commit an act of terror.

But a decision to join a terrorist group, seen through the lens of rational choice, may involve an individual evaluating the benefits and costs of such involvement. The benefits may include the kind of prestige some associate with being a member of a terrorist organization. Or the decision to join may be the promise of escape from poverty or simply the belief that through their association with a terrorist group the person will gain benefits that nonmembers would not receive. Alternatively, it may be a decision made upon a threat—that failure to support the group or undertake terrorist action will result in their individual circumstances being made worse.

Rational choice theory can assist in identifying motivations for joining terrorist organizations. It may also apply some incitation to the terrorist actions of lone individuals. Regardless, like many theories, it is only a lens to view a problem, so it should be a complementary approach to other possible motivations.

Mass Radicalization

Mass radicalization involves the conversion of a large part of a population. It occurs when there is a distinct conflict with a group outside the major group. An example of mass radicalization was the sentiment of many Americans after the September 11 attacks.[10] One notable change in American outlook after the attack was the rise in patriotism and support for the establishment—the president, the military, and government agencies. Moreover, there was a renewal of "American values" and a rebirth of the idea that the United States was disliked because of its freedoms and democratic ideals.

Mass radicalization is evident in the impact of any act of terrorism against the in-group or wider society. Mass radicalization serves to forge the social fabric of the in-group and can be a cohesive instrument for leaders of this group. Mass radicalization has also occurred within the out-groups when they are targeted by in-groups. Using the 9/11 example again, while it galvanized non-Muslim Americans, it also alienated American Muslims. Subsequently, some of these people were galvanized as a community of outsiders.

On occasion, mass radicalization can be deliberately brought about through a concept known as jujitsu politics. The concept was first introduced by Richard Gregg in his work *The Power of Non-Violence*.[11] As the title suggests, his ideas were focused on nonviolent protest. Jujitsu politics uses the force of a larger group against itself. It forces or places the dominant group into a position of using violence against a nonviolent group. Within the arena of world public opinion, a dominant group that perpetrates violence against a nonviolent group will often attract criticism and the nonviolent group may even recruit supporters or even activists.

There are numerous examples of jujitsu politics at work. Perhaps a visually significant example is the 1989 pro-democracy movement in Tiananmen Square in China. The image of a lone man standing in front of a line of military tanks and the violent action allegedly taken against protestors brought international criticism to China. From a view of terrorist radicalization, the notion of nonviolent political jujitsu is absent, but the method is still the same. A terrorist group using violence to incite a larger power to commit violence against a smaller power can radicalize supporters into activists and activists into terrorists, because the violent act of the larger power becomes a justification for the smaller group to undertake violence.

Hatred

Hatred is often the product of a personal, group, or historical grievance. It is the emotion that stems from the experiences felt by people.

Group hatred makes the use of violence easier, and it can lead a group to act irrationally.

Inciting hatred is a form of radicalization for both in-groups and out-groups. An act of violence upon one group will likely create hatred in another group. Also feeding hatred are the notions of racism, xenophobia, social stratification, religious intolerance, and fanaticism. These negative feelings may lead an individual or group to conflict or extremist behavior.

Another aspect of hatred and the justification for violence and terrorism is dehumanization, which involves taking away the human qualities of an individual or group. It can also involve the spread of propaganda suggesting an individual or group possess either beast- or demonlike qualities. Dehumanizing an enemy has a long history in many civilizations. The early Roman Empire viewed outsiders as barbarians. In the 1930s and 1940s, Jewish people were portrayed as rodents by the Nazis. In the 1970s, the Iranian Ayatollah Khomeini called America the "Great Satan." Such descriptions were designed to dehumanize individuals and groups. During the twentieth century, both world wars saw a range of visual imagery that portrayed the enemy as nonhuman. The images of the beastlike German soldier or the monkey-featured Japanese solider were designed to divorce fighting and killing the enemy from the act of killing humans.

As part of radicalization, dehumanization allows violent activity to have some form of legitimacy, particularly where civilian casualties are concerned. In the current conflict between Islamic extremists and more moderate or secular states, dehumanization occurs along the lines of infidels versus fanatics. From the perspective of the Islamic extremist, killing or committing acts of terror against non-Muslims is permissible. The implicit message is that because they are not Muslim, they are therefore less human—much like the early Roman's view of the Germanic barbarians.

At the other end of the spectrum is the perspective that those Muslims who behave as fanatics lack the intellectual capacity to reason effectively and consequently lack some essential human traits. While not as stark as the beastlike images of World War II propaganda posters, the dehumanization tactics are similar in that each side believes the other is not possessing fully developed human behaviors and therefore violent acts may be justified.

Essentially, hatred and dehumanization are methods for radicalization. They are used as justification for violent acts. But they can also unify groups against other groups. Neither hatred nor dehumanization is necessarily rational, but they are commonplace within conflicts.

Recruitment

Recruiting terrorists is a complex task. There are probably as many mechanisms to recruit people as there are reasons why individuals are open to radicalization. There are many mechanisms and reasons why people become radicalized, so it is worth investigating some of these to understand how radicalization may occur in the recruitment process.

The decision to form or join a radical group must come from an individual, who may have made a rational choice. An individual with knowledge of a group's cause may decide to join the group. As rational choice theory suggests, it could be based on benefits that nonmembership cannot provide. The benefits may be a sense of belonging, prestige, security, or financial reward. Recruitment is also enhanced if the group can create a sense of mystique about its influence or show it has the resources to supply the individual with their needs.

Using influence or coercion, recruiters may target individuals who identify or are sympathetic to the cause. Recruiters exploit personal grievances or grievances experienced by the individual's family or the social community they are part of. The recruit may have seen discrimination because of their beliefs and have a sense of not belonging to the more dominant societal group. A recruiter may use that experience as a mechanism to attract people to the group by providing a historical or contemporary explanation for why the recruit is feeling alienated. The recruiter may then explain that their group is also subject to the same discrimination and motivations, thus making a connection. The recruit may then feel a sense of belonging and be more open to radicalization.

Irrespective of the individual's motivations to join the group, the recruiter needs to be aware of what motivates people and use those motivations to groom the individual. While there is a great deal of psychology behind the recruitment, it is apparent that joining a radical group seems to be particularly attractive to young people. The rebellious or questioning nature of youth allows for a greater opportunity to recruit this demographic. In many cases youths are at a developmental stage when they often feel uncomfortable with political authority in all its guises. It is advantageous for recruiters to capture and use that sense of rebellion for their own ends.

An essential part of the recruitment process is isolating individuals from ideas and groups that may be in opposition to the recruiter's. Isolating a recruit from different views and interpretations can happen either by the actions of the radical group or through the individual withdrawing themselves. Prisons, places of worship, and the Internet with its social media websites can create insular environments where one idea is perpetuated and dominates as the "right" idea.

Prisons

There are two dominant perspectives regarding radicalization in prisons. One view is that there is seldom enough information about an individual's experience in prison to establish if he or she was radicalized once incarcerated.[12] In addition, in some instances the radicalization may occur after the individual leaves prison and finds association with a religious group. Leaving prison communities can also be an isolating experience and it is at this time an individual can be susceptible to radicalization.

The other view about prison radicalization is that prisons, by their physical and social environments, are incubators for radical thinking. Another perspective is that it is not necessarily the prison that causes radicalization but the reentry into society. In understanding this problem, it is worth examining it from both perspectives to assess the prison experience as a factor.

The nature and conditions of imprisonment can provide the necessary environment for radicalization. The prison population is often already marginalized from the dominant ideology of society and its inmates may already have anti-establishment tendencies. As prisoners are socially marginalized from mainstream society, they often seek social, political, or economic explanations for their own experiences and reasons for their marginalization. In some instances, while in prison, they may be led to new religious ideas that provide them with a sense of exclusivity, giving meaning to their social alienation. Unfortunately, these new religious ideas may take the form of a psychotic theology.

When an inmate undertakes a religious conversion in prison, it has a distinct impact on their worldview and their sense of individual identity. In some cases, there is a feeling that their exclusion from wider society has a religious meaning and they begin keeping within groups that share that same religious worldview. Through religious conversion, a prisoner is also able to develop a new self-identity. Converting to a religion can provide them with an identity that is not necessarily associated with their crime. Further, as prisons are organized along group lines, it is natural that a convert or someone of the same religion will associate within their own group.[13]

The prison environment is somewhat tribal and subsequently it is argued that these unique circumstances can create an incubator for extremists. In the case of Denmark, there have been concerns raised by authorities that without proper religious instruction, prisoners, particularly new converts, will be influenced by other prisoners who may not have a complete understanding of the faith, or their understanding may be characterized by distorted extremist views, particularly regarding Islam. Consequently, there has been a call for more regular visits of imams into prisons.[14]

Places of Worship

Places of worship have a role in the radicalization as well as the deradicalization process. They are the focal point of a religious community and are influential on their followers. Consequently, it is not surprising that places of worship are subject to scrutiny by law enforcement and intelligence agencies. Places of worship provide forums for religious individuals to share their faith and receive religious instruction. Places of worship can on occasion be insular and removed from the broader society in which they are located—or they can be active participants in the wider community. The role of places of worship in radicalization depends on the role they have in the community and the tone set by the prevailing religious instructor.

The Red Mosque in Pakistan is an example of how places of worship can be places of radicalization. Initially established and funded by the United States, the Red Mosque was both a place of worship and a recruitment facility for those fighting Russians in Afghanistan. After hostilities between Russia and Afghanistan, the leadership of the Red Mosque pledged allegiance to Osama bin Laden and brought sharia law to Pakistan.

Throughout the early part of the twenty-first century, the Red Mosque provided free education to Pakistani children. Offering free food and accommodation, the Red Mosque taught students to recite the Quran, instilling an extremist interpretation of Islam into the curriculum. The attraction of sending students to the Red Mosque was that it offered free education and boarding facilities. It was an offer that resonated with the poor of Pakistan.

Places of worship that can provide social services, such as education or outreach programs, and that meet the needs of the community will often capture the interest of people regardless of the message that accompanies the services. The blend of meeting a community's need is not unusual across all faiths and has been a staple of most evangelical religions.

Places of worship can also function to prevent radicalization. In 2015, the French simplification minister reportedly argued that more mosques would provide better conditions for Muslim worship because they would reduce radicalization by addressing the perception of disadvantage.[15] In Morocco, there have been many programs designed to avert extremism within places of worship. Morocco has established an official list of imams and created a directorate of religious education. It has also established a religious council in Europe for expatriate Moroccans. Most of the regulations on places of worship in Morocco are easier to implement than those in many other states. The Moroccan king is the central religious leader and has an authority that keeps radical Islamists out of mainstream religion.[16]

Social Media

Social media have provided an effective forum to disseminate information and therefore galvanize support for political issues. A range of factors make the Internet an effective platform in radicalization. The online environment allows widespread engagement with people that would be very difficult if not impossible without such technology. It also allows individuals to find ideas and communities that share the values they are interested in. Social media is also a stylized environment. Terrorist groups have understood that the medium allows direct, unfiltered communication with their followers. Able to bypass traditional mainstream media, radical groups can style their message unhindered and create whatever image they are seeking. Take for instance the widely distributed ISIS magazine *Dabiq*. It was an online magazine published by the Islamic State of Iraq as a means of recruiting converts to extremist jihadism. It began publication in July 2014 and appeared in several languages, including English. It was later replaced by *Rumiyah,* also an online magazine by Islamic State. This magazine started in September 2016 and, like its predecessor, was released in several languages, including English, French, German, Indonesian, Russian, and Uyghur.

Some terror groups were skilled at disseminating their propaganda through social media. There has been much analysis of the techniques used by groups like ISIS that suggests that social media communication, while seeming spontaneous, is artificial and controlled.[17] Studies also suggest that social media are less about circulating operational information such as weapons manuals and tactics and more focused on spreading ideology.[18]

Social-networking websites are reported to include the more popular social media platforms because of their wide area of coverage and great audience reach. These platforms can potentially be used by terrorist organizations to make initial contact. Often it is the high-profile social media sites where individuals with an interest in radical ideology first contact groups or in some instances radical individuals. Terrorist groups may seek out individuals who they believe are likely to be persuaded to commit an act of terror. And because of this role played by social media forums, they are scrutinized by law enforcement and intelligence agencies for illegal activity.

When a person contacts a radical group, the group may attempt to isolate the person from others online, or from family and friends. Isolating an individual takes place through the group's members constantly communicating with the individual and even suggesting that the individual begin to break off contact with others—specifically, people who do not share the same radical views. At this point in the radicalization process, the targeted individual will be directed to use a more secretive form of communication.

Such services are designed to be harder to intercept and track because these are encrypted for privacy. Some of these types of services have little, if any, monitoring of the content being transmitted. Using these types of privacy platforms, the recruiter can continue the radicalization process by assessing the level of contribution the individual might be able to make. A recruiter will later assess the individual's level of radicalization and willingness to participate in terrorism. In some instances, it may be that the individual is suited to finding others who could be radicalized, or to travel to locations to take part in conflict, or even to commit acts of lone terrorism.[19]

In other instances, social media are also used by provocateurs. It is common for an opposition to use social media and pose as a member of a group or follower of an ideology and incite violence. The purpose of this is to bring the target group into disrepute or cause the wider society to condemn the group's activities. A provocateur would aim to incite an event that would damage the reputation of the targeted group and in doing so gain support for their own group.

Study Questions

1. List three of the main causes of radicalization and describe each.
2. Explain two measures you think could be used to address radicalization, one in places of worship and the other in prisons.
3. Discuss the pros and cons for using rational choice theory to understand radicalization.
4. Explain what might be some of the signs that an individual could be becoming radicalized.

Learning Activity

Search for possible extremist posts on social media sites and evaluate the content of these messages. Are these posts predominantly ideological or tactical? Present your evaluation as a short briefing.

Notes

1. US Department of the Army, *A Military Guide to Terrorism in the Twenty-First Century* (Washington, DC: US Department of Defense, 2007), 5.
2. Ussama Makdisi, "'Anti-Americanism' in the Arab World: An Interpretation of a Brief History," *Journal of American History* (September 2002), 546.
3. William Luther Pierce writing as Andrew Macdonald, *The Turner Diaries* (Charlottesville, VA: National Vanguard, 1978).
4. Nigel Bunyan, "Senior Muslim Lawyer Says British Teenagers See ISIS As 'Pop Idols,'" *The Guardian,* April 5, 2015, https://www.theguardian

.com/world/2015/apr/05/senior-muslim-lawyer-says-british-teenagers-see
-isis-as-pop-idols.

5. John West, "Hamas Fighters Are Gaza's Idols," *Reuters,* December
26, 2000, https://www.paldf.net/forum/showthread.php?t=5586.

6. *The Quran,* translated by Abdullah Yusuf Ali (1934), 17:33, 703.

7. *The Quran,* 4:74–76, 202.

8. John Scott, "Rational Choice Theory," in Gary Browning, Abigail
Halcli, and Frank Webster (eds.), *Understanding Contemporary Society:
Theories of the Present* (London: Sage, 2000), 126.

9. Scott, "Rational Choice Theory," 131.

10. Clark McCauley and Sophia Moskalenko, "Mechanisms of Political
Radicalization: Pathways Toward Terrorism," *Terrorism and Political Violence* 20, no. 3 (2008), 427.

11. Richard B. Gregg, *The Power of Non-Violence* (Philadelphia: Lippincott, 1934).

12. Gaetano Joe Ilardi, "Prison Radicalization: The Devil Is in the
Detail," conference paper presented at the Global Terrorism Research Centre,
Melbourne, Monash University, December 31, 2010, 1.

13. Jon Marts, "Radicalization in Danish Prisons," in *Danish Institute for
International Studies Brief* (2008), 2.

14. Marts, "Radicalization in Danish Prisons," 4.

15. Henry Samuel, "French Minister Agrees That Lack of Mosques Encourages Radicalisation," *The Telegraph,* April 7, 2015, http://www.telegraph
.co.uk/news/worldnews/europe/france/11519452/French-minister-agrees
-that-lack-of-mosques-encourages-radicalization.html.

16. Mohamed Tamek, "Morocco's Approach to Countering Violent
Extremism," presentation at the Washington Institute for Near East Policy,
Washington, DC, May 16, 2014.

17. Jytte Klausen, "Tweeting the Jihad: Social Media Networks of Western Foreign Fighters in Syria and Iraq," *Studies in Conflict and Terrorism* 38
(2015), 2.

18. Klausen, "Tweeting the Jihad," 2.

19. Geoff Dean, Peter Bell, and Jack Newman, "Dark Side of Social
Media: Review of Online Terrorism," *Pakistan Journal of Criminology* 3,
no. 3 (January 2012).

4

Targets

In Chapter 1 we discussed what terrorism is. We defined it as involving violence (or threat of violence), political motivation, and civilian victims—the three elements that differentiate terrorism from other forms of violence. Because the targets are civilians—noncombatants—we need to analyze their approach to attacking civilians, which varies depending on finances, material resources, knowledge, and capability. The strategy of a terrorist, or a terrorist group, also influences the countermeasures a state may take.

Target Selection

History shows that there are two categories of targets—human and physical—but a third is worth discussing because it is becoming a target in its own right—cyber. These categories can be classified as one of four types: officials, military, business, and private parties.[1] Officials can include government officials (e.g., diplomats) and their official personnel, as well as official buildings, such as embassies or high commissions. Military targets include uniformed defense personnel and civilian support staff, as well as military bases and buildings. Business targets include the range of personnel and buildings used by and for commercial services, as well as industrial manufacturing, storage, transportation, and the like. Private parties include all other targets that do not fit into the first three types.

There are many logical and mathematical models for explaining target selection. But arguably the easiest to understand and use is also the best in analyzing how terrorists select their targets. This approach follows the scientific law of parsimony, or Occam's Razor. This straightforward model is called vulnerability analysis. There are three elements to this analytical model: target attractiveness, ease of attack, and target impact. It can be stated as an equation or depicted diagrammatically (see Figure 4.1). As an equation, it is expressed:

*target attractiveness + ease of attack +
impact on the target = vulnerability*

Attractiveness

Of the three elements of vulnerability, attractiveness is probably the key consideration. Recall that the purpose of terrorism is to install fear in a population. To this end, committing violence, or threatening its use, is what terrorists do to manipulate public opinion to their political end. Target attractiveness is therefore at the center of a terrorist's thinking. Yes, terrorists want to kill civilians, but more important they want to have a lot of people watching—"kill one, frighten ten thousand."[2] It is not the killing that is important; it is the fact that

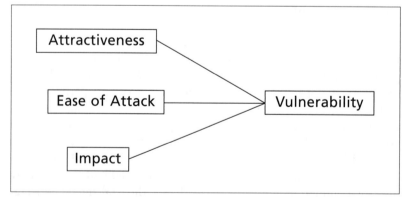

Figure 4.1 Vulnerability Analysis

people will notice the killing. It is hoped that people will internalize this trauma, and that this emotion will manifest itself in fear.

Following this reasoning, the attractiveness of the target is paramount. Silently killing a person at night in a back alley will not be as attractive as driving a delivery-type van through a crowned pedestrian area, as was the case in Barcelona, Spain, in August 2017. On August 17, at the height of Spain's tourist season, a man drove a van along the famous Las Ramblas Boulevard. For hundreds of meters, he drove at high speed, running down people and cyclists on the footpath. In the aftermath, over a dozen people lay dead and over a hundred injured. Islamic State claimed responsibility for the attack.

Comparing the two examples—a dark backstreet killing and murdering people in a crowded area in broad daylight—it might seem obvious that selecting a prominent target is what terrorists would choose in planning an attack. However, there are levels of attractiveness in selecting prominent targets. As an example, take the Barcelona case. It received immediate worldwide media coverage. The city is world renowned and draws tourists—in the millions—from across the globe. Many people have either been there, know someone who has, or might be planning to visit one day. Instead, if the target had been a less prominent place, say Dubois, Idaho—a town of about 700 people—there would not be many people outside the community who would know of it. As such, people hearing a news report—perhaps days after the event—though they would naturally feel sympathy for the victims in a small town, would unlikely experience the same level of anxiety as resulted from the terrorist event in Barcelona.

In this regard, selecting a target is a matter of recognizability. If we look at how this might be categorized by a terrorist, four groupings immediately present themselves—local, regional, national, and international. Clearly, a target that is internationally recognized would be the most attractive. Least would be a hay terminal in a remote, rural, farming community.

The concept of international recognition is tied to the notion of symbolism. It is about the imagery or representation of the target. The more the target is known, the more attractive it is. The more it is valued, the more attractive it is. This rationale goes a long way in explaining why terrorists target commercial aircraft. Passenger flights are universally understood by people the world over. However, in the current era of homeland security that has manifested since the 9/11 attacks, airline security is at such a high level of vigilance that terrorists have shifted their targets to those that are still attractive but easier to attack.

Ease of Attack

What might *easy* look like to a terrorist? There are two aspects to thinking about this issue. The first is gaining enough information about the target to be able to carry out the attack, and the second is the security surrounding the target. Regarding information gathering, the task is known as reconnaissance, which involves collecting vital pieces of information to infiltrate, execute the attack, and exfiltrate if getting away is part of the plan. History shows that exfiltration is not always conducted—autogenic massacres are common.

It follows that if there is little information about the target, conducting an attack will be more difficult, especially in the first two stages of the attack—infiltration and execution. It also follows that if there are security measures in place, an attack will be problematic. Getting to the target and carrying out the attack could be thwarted because of security.

By way of example, take aircraft security. Pre-9/11, it was easy to gain access to a plane's cockpit. Post-9/11 it is near impossible. As a demonstration of this, on March 24, 2015, the pilot of Germanwings Flight 9525 was locked out of the cockpit by his copilot. The pilot was unable to gain entry and the copilot crashed the aircraft in the French Alps. Moreover, carrying a weapon aboard has been made manifestly more difficult. The statistics are astronomical when it comes to the numbers of weapons, and devices that could be used as weapons, being carried by passengers who have passed through airport checkpoints. Granted, the majority of these are associated with innocent errors of judgment; nonetheless, it shows how rigorous passenger security has become. Managing the vulnerabilities of these attractive targets has resulted in terrorists shifting their gaze to softer targets, including

> night clubs, movie theaters, busy shopping malls and large stores, popular restaurants, concert halls, university campuses, public swimming pools, indoor ice skating rinks, and generally any busy enclosed area, as such an environment allows for one to take control of the situation by rounding up the kuffar[3] present inside and allows one to massacre them while using the building as a natural defense against any responding force attempting to enter and bring

the operation to a quick halt. Similarly, characteristics of a good target location include low light conditions, as it grants one the ability to maneuver between the people, taking advantage of the confusion and killing as many of the kuffar as physically possible.[4]

Impact

Even if attacking a target is determined to be easy, the impact factors need to be considered. Impact is associated with attractiveness, but it more about the metrics of the attack, rather than symbolism. To this end, a terrorist is likely to try to estimate the numbers of people who could be killed and injured by the attack. If we look at past events, we see that a suicide bomber who walks into a crowed marketplace and detonates an explosive vest is not going to kill as many people as they would if they impregnated the vest with nails or ball bearings. In addition, when calculating the impact, it would not escape the terrorist that wounds from scrap-metal shrapnel are far more graphic, even in the dead, which in turn contributes to the emotional impact of the viewers.

This type of impact is known as an effect-based attack. There are also event-based attacks that use the calculus of, say, monetary impact, or physical disruption. Examples of event-based attacks that come to mind are those that target critical infrastructure—electric power and water supply; the gas, dieseline, and gasoline supply chain; major rail and roadways; and so on.

How a terrorist brings these three factors together is the same process that an intelligence analyst uses to determine what will be protected and how best to do that, but in reverse. The terrorist will weigh the three factors—attractiveness, ease, and impact— to determine which target to select.

Reconnaissance

Reconnaissance is the act of assessing a location for important features.[5] It is a military term and in that context is often used to gather information about what is ahead of, say, advancing troops. Reconnaissance should not be confused with intelligence gathering, though the two are related.

Reconnaissance is characterized by immediate or short-term objectives associated with a larger force. For instance, a scout might be sent ahead of a larger contingent of soldiers to reconnoiter the safest path through a river valley or around a village. A scout may also be tasked to take up a position to make observations for advancing troops, especially if the battlefield is likely to change before troops arrive. Other examples can be cited, but the point is that intelligence gathering is about reducing uncertainty through some form of analysis. Some scholars have described this as prediction. Reconnaissance lacks this analytic step.

In an operational context, a terrorist who is in the process of selecting a target will need to conduct some form of reconnaissance. This reconnoitering can be a physical act of scouting or conducted via open-source information research, or both. Returning to the 2017 terrorist attack in Barcelona, the terrorists involved in that event needed to collect information relating to the three elements of vulnerability. They needed to know how attractive the La Rambla venue would be, and how easy it would be to gain access to the pedestrian mall, and to gather information that would help them assess the attack's impact.

Compared to a military installation, reconnoitering a public place is not difficult if the scout blends in with the environment. Failing to do so will call attention to the scout and jeopardize the attack. In a busy shopping district, then, the aim is to look like a typical shopper—travel alone; dress neat, yet casual; carry a shopping bag; look in windows; and take photographs using a smart phone, like a tourist would do. Photographs in this context are referred to as target accusation photos.

The adage "a picture is worth a thousand words" also applies to terrorist reconnaissance. The purpose of a target accusation photograph is to provide information to plan the infiltration route and what equipment will be needed. These visual data also assist in determining when and where the attack will take place. Of course, photographs are not necessary; terrorists can sketch the venue's details from memory, as well as make a mental list of issues that require consideration.

If the plan includes exfiltration, then a separate reconnaissance mission is needed. Things a terrorist might consider are placement of a getaway vehicle, caching a change of clothes/disguises; food and water; cash (relying on any digital money facility will leave a paper trail); and false identification papers and passport. There will be a need to locate a safehouse and the escape routes that will be traversed. A test run of this exfiltration plan may also be part of the reconnaissance mission.

Human Targets

Historical events show that humans are by far the most selected type of target for terrorists. In this regard, targeting strategy falls into one of two categories: indiscriminate and discriminate.

Indiscriminate

The indiscriminate targeting of people provides a large physiological leverage to causing anxiety. This is because of the nature of random variation—"Will I be the next victim?" There are numerous examples of people having been murdered at random. In some of these situations, security agencies may have had intelligence that indicated an attack was in the planning, but it was not precise enough to disrupt the operation. Other attacks came as a surprise. And it is surprise that establishes the phenomena of terror—shock and unpredictability, especially in the face of government safeguards.

We have seen the everyday effects of these in the weeks and months after an attack. People will cancel travel plans, change travel plans, avoid certain venues, or implement personal security measures. Although we have suggested that indiscriminate killing of civilian targets is random, it is not random in the sense that the people who are killed and injured have not been selected for some reason. Often terrorist groups will choose what Bruce Hoffman[6] termed a target set. A target set may be an ethnic population, a religious sect, members of a political party, people in a certain social or economic class, and so on. A target set represents a subgroup of society, so it is not indiscriminate in that way. But the potential victims who comprise a target set will be random—they will not be selected for who they are, but rather for what they represent by being at the target site.

On June 3, 2017, three terrorists associated with ISIS conducted an attack on London Bridge. The incident involved driving a van along the footpath so that it would run down pedestrians on the bridge. After crashing the van, the three ran to nearby Borough Market, where they stabbed people in the Southwark restaurant district. The result was eight people dead and forty-eight injured. The deaths included four unarmed police officers. The attack ended when the three terrorists were shot dead by police.

In this example the attackers selected their target set, but not the individual victims—these people happened to be on London Bridge and in the Borough Market when the terrorists attacked. The bridge and market were symbolically important for reasons already discussed with regard to vulnerability. The people were important only because they were part of the overall symbolism. It mattered not who they were, where they were from, or what their personal belief systems were. In contrast, discriminate killing targets the person.

Discriminate

Take the case of the discriminate kidnapping and hostage incident that involved US general James Dozier in Italy in 1981. At the time, he was NATO's deputy chief of staff for land forces in southern Europe. NATO was planning to deploy a nuclear missile in Sicily as a response to the Soviet Union's SS-20 nuclear missiles, which were targeting Europe.

The Red Brigade[7] was a left-wing group dedicated to removing Italy from the North Atlantic Treaty Organization. With the potential NATO missile deployment as a backdrop, Dozier was kidnapped from his apartment in Verona on December 17 and held hostage. But, unlike the kidnapping, and later murder, of Italian prime minister Aldo Moro in 1978, General Dozier was freed by Italian police after forty-two days.

As noted, indiscriminate targeting is based on randomness, but it does feature a distinct target set. With discriminate targeting, we see that some degree of randomness still exists—the Red Brigade could have selected any number of people involved in NATO, but they specifically targeted General Dozier. We also see that rather than having a general (indiscriminate) target set, here there is an identified target. The purpose of discriminating in target selection is to aim the political message at a particular audience; in the case of Dozier, it was NATO.

Physical Targets

In order to understand how terrorists approach the issue of targeting—whether these are physical objects, buildings, or facilities (known as assets)—we need to examine the theory by which such decisions are made. This theory is found in military doctrine.

In military terms, targeting is about selecting assets that assist the enemy to conduct war. These targets can be military related or civilian if they facilitate the military. Examples of the former are military bases, naval shipyards, barracks, arms caches, and so forth. Examples of the latter include highways and rail facilities that allow, say, the transportation of troops and arms; telecommunication facilities; and utilities, such as gas, water, and electrical power. The logic behind targeting is to destroy objects that the enemy can least afford to lose, and that provide the attacker with the greatest advantage. Ultimately, targeting is intended to reduce or eliminate the enemy's ability to carry out offensive operations and then degrade their defensive ability to the point that the area under conflict can be physically occupied (temporarily or permanently) by the attacker. The same analytic process of vulnerability analysis is used to make these determinations. Nonetheless, military targeting follows the laws for armed conflict by limiting collateral damage and civilian casualties.

Deliberate

Militaries approach targeting from two points of view—deliberate and dynamic. Deliberate targeting is characterized by a planning process. This starts with articulating the end-state of the conflict—that is, the mission's goal, aim, or objective. This ties in with the political aim for the mission as dictated by the nation's leadership. Targets are usually developed by intelligence analysts, whose job it is to examine information about the enemy and their area of operation and assess how best to inflict damage.

Dynamic

Because the objective of deliberate targeting is to pave the way for occupation, the time frames for removing the targets can be between twenty-four and seventy-two hours of lead time. This provides time to assess the damage and follow up with further attacks if needed. However, sometimes analysts do not have all the information they need to identify all the targets, or the enemy has moved them, switched to alternative resources, and so on. So in these circumstances dynamic targeting is used. Dynamic targeting is characterized by immediacy. For instance, advancing troops encounter opposition and call for the impediments to be eliminated. Or it could include, say, pilots returning from a mission observing a target and taking the opportunity to attack (known as a target of opportunity).

* * *

So how does military targeting theory apply to terrorist targeting? Although militaries operate within the legal framework of just war (*jus bellum iustum*), and they do not target civilians—applying great control to limit collateral damage—the facts used, and the logic employed in selecting targets, have parallels to terrorist targeting. The objective of terrorists is to instill fear in the wider population, so they too use vulnerability analysis to reverse engineer the process. Table 4.1 summarizes the aspects of these processes that are alike and those that are different.

Cyber Targets

Cyber-crime is not cyber-terrorism, but cyber-terrorism is a form of cyber-crime, just as terrorism is a form of crime. What denotes a cyber-terrorism event is also what defines terrorism's physical manifestations—it is politically motivated, targets nonmilitary assets, and is aimed at intimidation through fear.

So how can a network of electronic equipment, electrical cables, and data storage devices be a target for terrorists? Recall that for an event to be classified as terrorism, it needs to cause harm to life, or threaten harm. Reflecting on this presents the answer. The Internet provides *the* vital means for accessing data that, in a long list of examples, are critical to the safety and well-being of individuals and whole communities. It also provides *the* vital means for communicating with industrial systems. This is known as SCADA: supervi-

Table 4.1   Terrorist and Military Targeting Characteristics: Physical Targets

Terrorist	Military
Planning is involved	24–72 hours lead time
Great symbolic importance	High-value asset
No military targets	Exclusively military targets
Civilian casualties	No or very limited civilian casualties
Long-term political campaign	Military mission–oriented
Deliberate targets	Deliberate and dynamic targets

sory control and data acquisition. The Internet is used to monitor and control manufacturing and industrial processes that include electrical power generation; utilities such as water, gas, and waste treatment; oil and gas pipelines; power transmission lines; wind farms; parts of airports and seaports; rail transport facilities; and so on.

The Internet is also used by public health facilities such as hospital and medical clinics. In May 2017, the WannaCry malware spread across the Internet and infected hospitals in the United Kingdom, causing the National Health Service's computers to become encrypted. In effect, this made all infected computers useless. However, this was not a terrorist event. It was a crime event because the perpetrators demanded a ransom to be paid before they would unencrypt the affected computers. Had there been a political motivation behind the attack, as well as the objective to cause harm, it would then have the hallmarks of terrorism.

The point is, rather than using physical means of inflicting human casualties, a terrorist can target devices or systems controlled via the Internet to instill fear. In addition to the health system, cyber targets can include any device or system connected to the Internet—dam floodgates, power grids, traffic controls for road and rail, and the like.

The targets can have direct impact on people's lives, or indirect or consequential impact. Targeting a hospital system would have direct consequences, but the same effect could be accomplished by switching of the power grid—emergency generators can operate only a short period of time.

Kill Chain

The term *kill chain* finds home in military circles. It is used to describe the series of events that are performed when executing an attack. Nonetheless, the concept has applicability to how terrorists target because they use the same logical process. By understanding the kill chain process, law enforcement and security agencies can use vulnerability analysis to protect assets.

There are several versions of the kill chain described in the subject literature, but one of the simplest is this: (1) determine the political end-state for the attack; (2) identify the target (using vulnerability analysis); (3) undertake reconnaissance of the target; (4) surveil the target to ensure that conditions have not changed; (5) select the most effective type of force and its delivery; and (6) conduct the attack. If the mission is military, this would also include postattack evaluation and exploitation of intelligence data, if any. However, a terrorist's kill chain may end with the attack, or attack and exfiltration. Evidence that suggests that some objective evaluation of the political outcome is ever done by terrorist groups is lacking. Otherwise, they would conclude that terrorism is ineffective in bringing about their political end-state. A case in point is the so-called caliphate that Islamic State attempted to create. On November 21, 2017, the Iraqi prime minister, Haider al-Abadi, announced that Iraq had militarily defeated Islamic State. The president of Russia, Vladimir Putin, also declared victory over the terror group in Syria.

Counterterrorism

Understanding the logic that underpins the kill chain thought process can assist counterterrorist analysts in planning defensive strategies. This planning is analogous to the strategies used in artillery counter-battery fire. When an enemy launches an artillery barrage, the procedure is to determine the location of the enemy fire and return the bombardment to end the attack. Knowing that this will happen, the enemy will have tactics in place that allow them to fire and move (or shoot-and-scoot). Anticipating this tactic, the counter-battery commanders will also locate places where enemy relocation is most logical and fire on those positions too. And so goes the strategy of counter-strategy thinking.

Applied to a terrorist's kill chain logic, an analyst can examine this thinking process and look for opportunities to disrupt or eliminate target weaknesses that might be exploited.

Study Questions

1. List the elements involved in vulnerability analysis.
2. Discuss the concept of target attractiveness at play in the mind of a terrorist.
3. Explain the role of reconnaissance in terrorist targeting.
4. List the three major target categories, and give an example of each.

Learning Activity

Although there has been much discussion and policy surrounding the protection of potential human and physical targets, the discussion about cyber targets is still rather obscure. It could be argued that the discussion has centered on criminal events, such as the WannaCry ransomeware worm, but what if terrorists shift from attacking physical and human targets to a strategy that focuses on the Internet. Discuss the likelihood of this happening by providing evidence that this is or is not a possibility.

Notes

1. Patrick T. Brandt and Todd Sandler, "What Do Transnational Terrorists Target? Has It Changed? Are We Safer?" *Journal of Conflict Resolution* 54, no. 2 (2010).

2. Henry Prunckun, "The First Pillar of Terror—Kill One, Frighten Ten Thousand: A Critical Discussion of the Doctrinal Shift Associated with the 'New Terrorism,'" *The Police Journal: Theory, Practice, and Principles* 87, no. 3 (2014).

3. According to scholars, the English spelling is *kifir*, meaning those who do not believe. See Cyrill Glasse, *The New Encyclopedia of Islam* (New York: Altamira, 2003), 247.

4. Anonymous, "Just Terror Tactics," *Ramiyah,* May 4, 2017. *Ramiyah* was the underground magazine published by ISIL as an instrument of propaganda and to inspire people to join the movement. Thirteen issues were published between September 2016 and September 2017.

5. For a detailed discussion, see Henry Prunckun, *How to Undertake Surveillance and Reconnaissance: From a Civilian and Military Perspective* (South Yorkshire, UK: Pen and Sword Military, 2015).

6. Bruce Hoffman, *Inside Terrorism*, rev. and expanded ed. (New York: Columbia University Press, 2006) 230, 268.

7. *Brigate Rosse* in Italian.

5

Methods and Weapons

The theory underpinning terrorism is to instill fear—"kill one, frighten ten thousand." The objective behind this philosophy is to undermine the authority of the state, causing the population to lose confidence in the government to carry out its mandate. How does this translate into action? The transition from wanting to do something to doing it requires some form of methodology—a way of turning ideas into action.

How terrorists approach this problem depends on whether they are part of a group or acting as individuals. This is because of capability, which is a function of knowledge and resources. The capability of a group is usually greater than that of an individual. The greater the capability, the greater are the methods available. There could also be a great intent to carry out an attack because the group dynamics may play into generating and sustaining desire and expectation to follow through with a plan. This is not to discount that the same intent may be held by an individual, but it is a more compelling case that greater desire will be held by groups of like-minded people. We see this dynamic played out in society in general—it is why people establish clubs, teams, support groups, associations, institutes, organizations, and so on.

This is not to say that an individual is not able to do this on their own but that the likelihood is reduced. So, what about the lone actor? Although the term has been applied to individuals, when their capability is analyzed we realize that they do not act in a vacuum. They gather ideas by reading terrorist propaganda, listening to podcasts, and watching sermons, all of which provide not only psychological persuasion to produce desire but also knowledge about how to carry out an attack and information about where to acquire resources. So, can these lone wolves be considered independent actors, or are they part of a group who simply have no physical contact? Either way, the method of attack requires operational strategies, tactics, and weapons.

Operational Strategies

Operational strategies represent the thinking that underpins why terrorists select one method of attack over others. Operational strategies act as the basis for combining people and resources that will yield an effective output. It is important to note the difference between an output and an outcome. The output of a terror attack is an event that will cause fear. To be effective, it needs to have the factors discussed in Chapter 1—violence (or threat of violence), political motivation, and civilian victims. Output can be thought of as the production of cogs on an assembly line. Outcome is why one produces outputs. In manufacturing, the outcome of producing cogs is to make money. In terrorist terms, the attack output is to undermine the state (the latter being the outcome).

The first step terrorists take in deciding what methodology they will use is to examine their capability: What knowledge and resources do they have?

Knowledge and Resources

Che Guevara once wrote, "strategy means the analysis of the objectives we wish to attain."[1] He advised his revolutionary readers to assess the enemy's operational ability—"manpower, mobility, popular support, weapons, and leadership."[2] Although not expressed in the terms that a terrorism scholar might examine regarding capability, his words achieve the same insight—look at capability.

Capability is a function of knowledge and resources. It forms half of the equation that describes threat. A threat is not a declaration made in an argument between two parties but an analytical expression of two factors—capability (knowledge and resources) and intent (expectation and desire). By the time people embrace terrorism as a way of dealing with their grievances, it is not unreasonable to say that their mind-set has become inflexible, and their behavior too rigid for calm discussion and compromise. So, the intent half of the threat equation (i.e., their expectation of success and their desire to carry out an attack) is assumed.

It is not on the opposition's capability that terrorists focus, it is on their own capability. Do they have the necessary knowledge to construct, say, an explosive device? Do they have the material? If the answer is no, are they able to acquire these? A terrorist who has great intent to set off a nuclear device, but no understanding of what it would take to develop one, or the resources to construct it, is of little threat if that is all he or she wants to do.

However, if they apply Che Guevara's advice[3] and work through their capability, they will eventually come to a determination about what they can realistically use as a weapon. If they do this, they then become a threat—intent and capability come together. They then start their planning process.

Planning

Although we have covered the topic of target selection in Chapter 4, we will recap to lead into our discussion of the planning stage of a terrorist operation. Recall that the kill chain is the process followed in attacks. It comprises several steps, one of which is target identification. Target selection is done by assessing its vulnerability, and tied to this is determining the best method of attack—weapons acquisition and deployment.

If a group of terrorists have determined that they have only a modest knowledge of explosives and little chance to obtain materials to fashion a bomb, their choice of weapon system will change. So rather than setting off a bomb in, say, a crowded concert hall, they may use guns—weapons that they have access to and knowledge of how to use.

Planning also includes how the group will fund the operation. Because purchasing weapons on the black market is usually more expensive than buying them legally, funding is an issue to be resolved as part of the resources issue. Take, for instance, the case of the Symbionese Liberation Army. In 1974, this left-wing revolutionary group robbed a bank in San Francisco, California, to obtain cash to help fund its underground operations.[4] It is axiomatic that the more money a person has, the more resources he or she can potentially acquire. It also stands that money can purchase knowledge—for example, advisers, mentors, and expert instructors, as well as technicians to perform functions that take years of experience to develop. Robbing a bank is a logical way to obtain large amounts of money, and in 1974 it was perhaps the only way. At present, the same can be done via other methods that we will discuss in Chapter 6, on financing.

Tactics

With most competitive endeavors, there are different approaches to "winning." Take chess as an example. Tactics are a sequence of moves intended to limit your opponent's options to attack, and at the same time enable you to strike a decisive blow. Tactics are immediate or short-term projections of power, whereas strategy relates to a longer-term or overarching thinking about winning.

History shows that there are several recurring approaches that terrorists use in trying to gain advantage, including hostage taking, kidnapping, hijacking, bombing, armed assault, and assassination. The group's desired outcomes, based on its organizational capabilities, will influence the tactics used. Hostage taking, kidnapping, and hijacking tactics are used to force a target either to negotiate a set of demands or to extort money. Bombing, armed assault, and assassination have been aimed at generating fear, and these incidents usually form part of a larger campaign of violence.

High-Risk Tactics

One way to look at the tactics used by terrorists is to categorize them as high-risk or lower-risk. This is not to say that this is the only way of looking at tactics, but this is a convenient method to distinguish what makes up the moves terrorists take. By understanding tactics, law enforcement and security agencies can devise countermeasures, which we discuss at the end of this chapter.

Hostage taking, kidnapping, and hijacking are all high-risk tactics that require a sophisticated level of planning, which includes the ability to collect targeting information as well as the ability to convert these data into focused intelligence. It also requires the ability to coordinate logistics.

Hostage Taking

A hostage is a person who has been taken and held as security until a demand has been fulfilled. The fear is that if the demand is not met, the hostage will be injured or killed. The length of time the hostage is held can range from hours to months.

Hostage taking for ransom is a much used means for funding terrorist activities. There are an abundant number of potential targets to seize as victims, because there is never the ability to provide an absolute level of personal protection—even presidents and the Pope have been attacked.

The attraction of hostage taking as a tactic is that the event creates a form of drama—a show, or stage production in a way. People's lives are placed in the most precarious of situations. A hostage situation has all the makings of theater—a sinister plot, victims, murder weapons, and powerful emotions all wrapped up in an evil message.

The longer it takes to resolve, the better the image, because, after all, it is fear that terrorists want to incite in society. These situations attract the attention of the media because the risks are high.[5] It is for these reasons that hostage situations must be considered a separate and distinct form of terrorism requiring independent examination. The preceding characteristics of hostage taking serve to establish an external picture of the situation—why it is appealing and how it affects those outside the immediate situation (anyone who is not a hostage, hostage taker, or negotiator).

On the morning of December 15, 2014, Man Haron Monis walked into the Lindt Café at Martin Place in Sydney, Australia. He was bearded, wearing a black cap and a headband that bore an Arabic inscription. He ordered a coffee and cake, and then calmly waited for the moment to act. He unzipped his blue sports bag and withdrew a sawed-off 12-gauge pump-action shotgun. He forced the shop's manager to lock the doors and telephone the emergency number. Monis forced some of the hostages to appear in front of a black-and-white Shahada flag and video his demands. Monis required them to refer to him as "brother" in recording the following message:

> This is a message to Tony Abbott [who was at the time the Australian prime minister]. We're held here hostage and the Brother has three requests. One is to get an [Islamic State] flag and he will release one hostage. The second is for the media to inform the other brothers not to explode the other two bombs, which are also in the city. There are four bombs altogether here. The third is for Tony Abbott to contact the Brother via live web, somehow, and he will release five hostages.[6]

The terrorist's demands were not met; he was killed. His actions lacked sophisticated planning, intelligence, and logistical support. The operation was a failure. But not all high-risk tactics end in failure. Take, for instance, the tactic of kidnapping.

Kidnapping

Kidnapping is like hostage taking, but with hostage situations the usual feature is a terrorist holed up behind a barricade with the victims. Kidnapping, by contrast, is characterized by the abduction of a person: taking them to a secret location and holding them there.

Kidnapping not only involves taking an individual by force but can also involve threatening them, or deceiving/luring them into a situation where they can be abducted. Kidnapping is carried out for political purposes as well as for ransom (to fund terrorist activities).

Historical events show that the reason kidnapping has a higher success rate than hostage taking weighs on three factors: lack of trust between the parties; the power to bargain resides with the kidnapper; and there is a risk that the victims will be killed. These factors are supported by either fear of or collusion with the local population—the former because the terrorists share some of the ransom with them, and the latter because of cultural or religious respect, knowing the geographic area better than the authorities, and persistence—the ability to wait months or years for the outcome they want.

Governments have used kidnapping to bring terrorists to trial—in effect using the terrorists' tactic on themselves. This is sometimes called extraordinary rendition or forced rendition. The term *rendition* is used in the sense of *delivery*. Take, for example, the 1987 case involving the Lebanese terrorist Fawaz Younis, who in September 1987 was kidnapped when he was lured onto a yacht in Italy. Authorities took him to the United States, where he stood trial, was convicted, and served a prison sentence.

Hijacking

Passengers know that flying is statistically an exceptionally safe mode of transport. Nonetheless, when it comes to the helplessness experienced when someone other than the pilot is in command of the flight, not much else compares.

Airline hijackings occurred sporadically in the 1920s through 1950s. However, in the politically charged 1960s, the number of incidents escalated worldwide. The 1970s recorded the most hijackings. In the 1980s the numbers dropped and have continued to decrease since (see Table 5.1).

Although a high-risk tactic, hijacking appeals to terrorists because of the vulnerability presented by an aircraft in flight, and the defenselessness of the passengers and crew. In the main, the prevention methods that have proved fruitful are defensive in nature. Examples of these include passenger screening, luggage screening, physical isolation of aircraft to security-cleared personnel, cockpit security, and enhanced security procedures for crew. Offensive security has been in the forms of better training for aircrews and the insertion of covert operatives aboard certain flights. In the United States, these airborne officers are deployed by the US Federal Air Marshal Service, and in other countries by equivalent agencies.

Although an aircraft in flight is not an ideal place to go on the offensive against armed terrorists, the alternative not to engage them may have catastrophic consequences. Take, for instance, the three ill-fated flights of September 11, 2001: American Airlines Flight 11, American Airlines Flight 77, and United Airlines Flight 175. All three led to horrific consequences as they were crashed into the World Trade Center in New York and the Pentagon in Washington, D.C. Evidence shows that the passengers aboard United Airlines Flight 93 that day went on the offensive. Though they were not successful, they saved many lives, and the devastation they prevented was immense.

Table 5.1   Numbers of Airline Hijackings Worldwide

1920s	1930s	1940s	1950s	1960s	1970s	1980s	1990s	2000s	2010s
1	1	4	3	13	50	30	14	16	8

Note: The 2010s covers 2010 to 2017.

Yet studies conducted since that event—the world's most notorious series of hijackings—show that the public has not been deterred from flying, and that air travel remains a very safe means of transport.

Despite facing what might appear as an impossible hijacking situation, counterterrorist operations have been conducted with great success. Take the 1976 rescue of 248 passengers who were aboard an Air France flight from Tel Aviv to Paris. The flight was hijacked by members of the Popular Front for the Liberation of Palestine–External Operations (PFLP-EO) and the German Revolutionary Cells. It was diverted to Entebbe airport in Uganda. Idi Amin, then dictator of Uganda, allowed the terrorists to stay while negotiations were conducted. In exchange for the hostages, the terrorists demanded the release of forty militants who were in Israeli jails and thirteen others imprisoned by other countries.

The Israeli government authorized a raid to rescue the hostages, conducted by the Israeli Defense Forces. The planning and logistics needed to carry out a raid some 2,000 kilometers away, in an openly hostile country, were enormous. Regardless, the raid succeeded despite several casualties. All terrorists were killed, their demands were not met, and Idi Amin suffered international humiliation for his political and military ineptitude.

Low-Risk Tactics

High-risk tactics require not only a high degree of planning but also a large amount of resources to be able to achieve some level of effectiveness. Many terrorists who are unable to attain this turn to low-risk tactics. These do not require the same capabilities, yet allow them to create anxiety, avenge perceived wrongs, negate the opposition's political process, or carry out political murders.[7] These tactics include bombing, armed assault, and assassination.

Bombing

The use of a bomb as a means of instilling fear is likely to be the prime tactic on the list. The image of militant political movements has been symbolized by a bomb. It represents sudden, uncontrollable destruction. The anarchist movements in the United States and Europe in the late 1800s and early 1990s used bombs. Perhaps one of the most extensive uses of bombs in a single terror campaign was conducted by followers of Luigi Galleani, an Italian anarchist. In 1919 an estimated thirty-six dynamite bombs were mailed to prominent politicians, newspaper editors, businesspeople, and justice officials. The number of bombing incidents that took place before this, and the number since, are almost uncountable.

On any given day, news accounts from around the world report the death and destruction caused by bombings. The capability to manufacture a bomb is based on the relatively simple principle that producing a rapidly expanding gas that is somehow confined will produce a bomb. The rate at which the material burns (i.e., the production of the gas) and, if necessary, the method of containment determine the size of the blast.

The destructive effects of the blast are due to three factors: shock wave, heat, and fragmentation. Shock is caused by the sudden expansion, heat by the burning, and fragmentation by both, with the shock wave causing destruction of the surrounding environment and sometimes including shrapnel that may be designed into the device. It follows that the bigger the bomb, the more explosive the charge it will carry.

At one point in time, commercially manufactured, high-grade explosives could be readily purchased. Because of safety issues and criminal use of these explosives (e.g., safecracking), they were limited by law to those with a genuine need, for instance, miners. Like many things that have been restricted, the economic law of supply and demand comes into play. Explosives being illegal did not prevent criminals from obtaining them. Theft and bribing those with access are two methods that immediately come to mind. For others, there was improvisation—that is, the use of other combustible materials that could achieve a similar result. Phosphorous and chlorate mixtures (e.g., match heads) and gunpowder are among the most widely known.

Moving up the scale are nitrate-based fertilizers, reported to be the most used explosives because of their low cost and high explosive yield. These comprise a mixture of ammonium nitrate and fuel oil. This type of device was used by the American terrorist Timothy McVeigh. On April 19, 1995, McVeigh detonated such a truck bomb in front of the Alfred P. Murrah Federal Building in Oklahoma City.

Far more sophisticated improvised explosive devices (IEDs) can be created using military-grade weaponry or parts.[8] These have been seen in conflict zones such as Iraq, Syria, and Afghanistan in the form of roadside bombs and antipersonnel booby traps. Suicide bombers are a type of booby trap, and although their use may appear novel, the concept is not. Suicide has long been used as a means of delivering explosive charges. Take for instance the kamikaze dive-bombers of World War II. These were pilot-guided bombs comprising modified aircraft to hold explosives. Perhaps this was the source for the idea of the 9/11 terrorists to fly commercial aircraft into what they saw as symbols of Western civilization.

In the 2010s, suicide bombers have been typified by individuals wearing explosive vests (belt bombs), or driving vehicles loaded with explosives (car bombs).[9] Whereas kamikaze attacks had a military goal—to cripple key US naval power—a suicide terrorist is using psychology to instill fear. Paralyzing an aircraft carrier cannot be compared to killing people in, say, a shopping market. The scale of the impact is not the same. The former is strategic; the latter tactical. The University of Chicago reported that in 2016 there were 392 suicide attacks worldwide.[10] This resulted in 4,611 people killed and 9,085 wounded. Vehicle-borne bombs outnumbered belt-bombing incidents. This is likely because the quantity of explosives a car or truck bomber can carry is far greater than what an individual can wrap around the body.

Armed Assault

Arguably, bomb attacks can deliver more destruction, with less effort, than other forms of attack. Bomb making is relatively uncomplicated and there are numerous publications that provide advice on how to make bombs. Bomb-making materials can be purchased or improvised—for example, the simplest bomb of all, the Molotov cocktail. It was once used in regular warfare but has been adapted by urban guerrillas and terrorists alike.

Law enforcement and national security practitioners have learned many lessons about vulnerability and risk, and have implemented protective measures. As these fortifications and new operating procedures begin to reduce terrorists' ability to deliver bombs, naturally they look for other venues of attack (called attack vectors). This problem leads terrorists to opt for armed attacks using small arms, knives, and blunt force trauma.

In November 2008, a group of radical Islamic terrorists launched simultaneous raids across the city of Mumbai, India. The attack lasted four days and although the terrorists used explosives and fire, they also used AK-47 assault rifles. In the end, they killed over 160 people and wounded about 300. One venue they attacked was the Leopold Café. It was a popular meeting place for meals and drinks in South Mumbai. Two terrorists, using their Kalashnikovs, fired on the restaurant patrons. At least ten were killed and many others wounded.

The efficiency of high-caliber weapons, using high-velocity projectiles, is that they deliver devastating wounds. This, combined with the ability to fire in either semiautomatic or fully automatic mode, makes military assault rifles far more effective than, say, single-shot weapons. Assault rifles can fire many hundreds of rounds per second. With muzzle velocities greater than hunting-type rifles, these weapons can reach targets at range, and their projectiles are able to penetrate armor.[11]

Assassination

Ilyich Ramirez Sanchez, known as Carlos the Jackal, is reported to have said, "To get anywhere, you have to step over corpses."[12] What the Venezuelan-born terrorist meant was that to achieve a political goal, those who stand in the way must be eliminated. Assassination is an effective means of targeting such people.

The tactic goes back centuries. Shakespeare's *Macbeth,* and some 2,000 years before that Aeschylus's *Agamemnon,* portrayed the use of assassination in a dynastic setting. History is beset with other examples in many other political settings. In some ways, it is the most personal form of violence—a one-on-one relationship between the assassin and the victim. Most times, it is carried out at close range, as was the attempt on President Ronald Reagan by John Hinckley Jr. in March 1981. However, it can of course be done with a sniper rifle, remote-controlled explosive charge, or letter bomb.

Often, assassinations are nothing like the scenes depicted in cinema, where an assassin draws a high-powered rifle out of a black tactical bag, coolly assembles its parts, checks the telescopic sight, fixes the silencer to the muzzle, and loads a round into the chamber. Then, in his secluded perch, he waits for his target. Regardless of the context, assassination is a low-risk tactic because it requires little in the way of planning aside from just knowing where the target will be and thinking of a way to get close enough to deliver the fatal blow.

Terrorist Weapons

On September 15, 2017, two men detonated a bomb on a train that had stopped at the London suburban station of Parsons Green. The bomb went off, injuring almost thirty people, many of whom suffered severe burns. However, the bomb did not explode as planned, most likely because the terrorists lacked the knowledge needed to construct it properly.

The subsequent criminal investigation discovered that the bomb was a relatively simple device comprising triacetone triperoxide as the main charge, which is an inefficient explosive. Its instability was unlikely known to the terrorist who constructed the bomb because the device only partly exploded.

Such bombs can be made from instructions available on the Internet. In fact, this type of technical information is not new to the online age. Take for example William R. Powell's 1971 book *The Anarchist Cookbook*.[13] It was originally published by Lyle Stuart, a left-leaning publisher that published other controversial titles and hence drew the attention of the FBI. Nonetheless, the book went to press, sold thousands of copies, and has been reprinted several times in the ensuing decades. Declassified FBI documents show that although Powell wrote his book based on information that was publicly available, he lacked the scholastic skills to understand the nuances of what he was translating and so made errors in the text: "The formulas and procedures presented concerning the production of high and low explosives cannot be called incorrect, but they are not always complete and therefore could present a hazard to anyone using the information."[14]

One could look at the partially failed attempt to blow up the Parsons Green commuter train as an indicator that, although such weapons information is available and the process of constructing some of these is simple, it required a high degree of knowledge to do so. Reflecting on the factors that compose a threat—intent and capability—we note that capability requires both knowledge and resources. So, regarding the Parsons Green bombing, the terrorists may have had resources and knowledge, but their knowledge was likely to have been flawed and thus they lacked the skill to craft the device.

History presents us with other examples of failing to understand weapons. There was the March 6, 1970, accidental detonation of an explosive device in the Greenwich Village safe house of Weather Underground. Although the group had exploded bombs before, its success may have been due more to luck rather than to a high degree of skill and knowledge, gauging from this catastrophic error. Two of the terrorists were killed in the blast, three other Weathermen were injured (and escaped the scene), and the four-story townhouse collapsed and burned.

Small Arms

Small arms are defined as lightweight weapons that individuals can carry and use on their own. They can be divided into different categories, but a helpful way to view the many types of small arms available to terrorists is to view them according to type. They can be categorized into rifles (including semiautomatics), shotguns, submachine guns, and handheld weapons.

Rifles are weapons that are fired from a shoulder-held position. Although the barrel lengths of rifles vary, the barrel is designed to be of sufficient length to ensure a bullet will hit its mark with some degree of accuracy. Longer barrels mean greater distance and greater accuracy. Shorter barrels are used in close-quarter situations.

Rifles are therefore designed to kill at a distance. A long barrel offers the operator greater accuracy because the projectile has more time to develop a spin, which will keep it stable in flight. Accuracy of the bullet is provided by a helical pattern of raised channels known as lands within the barrel that cause the bullet to spin. The spinning of the bullet provides gyroscopic stability while the bullet is in flight. This contrasts with a shotgun, which has a smooth bore.

Rifles, other than hunting varieties, are usually semiautomatic, though some can be switched to a fully automatic mode. These types of weapons are technically classed as submachine guns. Like semiautomatic handguns, the weapon can fire a round as fast as the operator can pull the trigger. In this regard, many targets can be engaged within a short amount of time. It is effective in that each round can be delivered to the target without using excess additional ammunition that a fully automatic weapon would use.

Rifles used by terrorists can be of any variety—from sporting guns to hunting rifles—but bearing in mind that the terrorist's objective is to kill people, common wisdom would dictate that a weapon that can fire many rounds and fire them quickly would be more attractive than, say, a single-shot, bolt-action weapon.

Looking at what is available on both the legal and black markets, we note that there are a range of weapons that are distinguished by their caliber, action, size, and magazine capacity. These characteristics also determine the popularity of the weapon and, following the economic law of supply and demand, determine the weapon's price. At the low end are sporting and hunting rifles and at the high end are military assault rifles. This also applies to shotguns and handguns.

Shotguns used for tasks like pheasant hunting or in sporting competitions are usually configured as single-shot, single-barrel, or single-shot, double-barrel (e.g., used by skeet shooters). Some weapons are found as over-under arrangements with a shotgun barrel under a small-caliber rifle, such as a .22 or .22 magnum. But these are intended for shooting at a single target. Although they can be used in terrorist attacks, more effective weapons are of high caliber and rapid fire. That is why a lever-action, pump-action, or semi-automatic shotgun would be more appealing. Shotguns tend to be used for close-range attacks.

The historical record shows that shotguns are not necessarily a weapon of first choice by terrorists, but the advantage a shotgun has is its psychological impact. Wounds caused by a shotgun blast are not the same as a bullet in that a shotgun blast tends to rip apart human flesh and body organs, making those wounds nearly impossible to surgically repair. The blast of a shotgun is much louder than a rifle's "crack," which adds to the psychological impact on the victims.[15] Shotgun barrels can be sawed off, which makes the gun more concealable, as was the case in the 2014 terrorist incident at the Sydney Lindt Café. Man Haron Monis used a sawed-off 12-gauge shotgun that he carried in a sports bag.

Shotgun cartridges are available in several specifications with various sizes of shots or slugs. Using shot as a projectile in some ways overcomes the disadvantage of a single firing. Because shotguns have smooth bores (i.e., no riflings that cause a single projectile to spin) and relatively short barrel lengths, the shot spreads, forming a wide pattern. As distance from the muzzle increases, so does the spread of the shot. One of the reasons riot police have used shotguns is for this characteristic—a crowd can be dispersed with only a few shots being fired. Also, if a small-sized shot is used, it is less likely to result in fatal wounds (unless fired at close range). Slugs are a different proposition. These are single projectiles, weighing more than a rifle slug. Combined with the massive throwing power of the charge, slugs can deliver on the order of two tons of knockdown power. But, unlike with a rifle, their range is much shorter.

This does not mean, however, that single-shot, bolt-action rifles are not in demand by terrorists. Take, for instance, the likes of the Ruger model 6903 in .308 caliber. Fitted with a telescopic sight, such a rifle can be used by snipers. This is because the .308 cartridge—considered suitable for large game—has technical specifications similar to those of the NATO 7.62×51-millimeter round. So there is no hard-and-fast rule as to what will appeal to a terrorist, though submachine guns are very attractive.

Submachine guns differ from machine guns in that they are portable, operating as shoulder-fire weapons. They are lighter and able to be carried by an individual. Some are smaller, with no shoulder stock, allowing them to be concealed and fired like a handgun. Like rifles, their barrels are rifled for accuracy. They are fed by a detachable clip that holds the ammunition. Their main advantage is speed. Automatic weapons are capable of firing hundreds of rounds per minute, but the advantage is also a drawback because it requires the operator to carry a large amount of ammunition. And this is not an easy task, because of weight and bulk. This factor makes maneuverability difficult.

Handguns are manufactured in two types—revolvers and pistols—and are designed for concealment. The former is configured with a revolving cylinder that holds the cartridges; hence its name. The latter is a semiautomatic that is fed via a magazine clip. Handguns are designed to kill at close range. Revolvers feature a cylinder that rotates as each shot is fired. Depending on the caliber and size, these usually hold between five and seven rounds (most hold six rounds; hence the name *six-shooter*). Revolvers fire one round each time the trigger is pulled, making them single-shot weapons. For terrorists, these are less attractive because of the slow rate of fire.

Pistols offer a faster rate of fire because they are semiautomatic. This means that loading of the next round is done automatically, thus requiring the operator to merely pull the trigger in rapid succession. The capacity of a pistol varies by manufacturer and model, but a pistol holds twice or more the number of rounds as a revolver.

Generally, pistols are more appealing to terrorists because they hold more rounds and have a higher rate of fire. However, revolvers are less prone to jamming and malfunction, because their actions require fewer parts and the mechanism for advancing the next round is not susceptible to breakdown.

Arms of War

Legislation defines what is classified as a small arm or a weapon of warfare, the distinction usually being made by the weapon's caliber. As a guide, .50 caliber and larger would be considered a weapon of war. That is not to say that weapons of smaller caliber are not used by militaries—they are; this distinction places emphasis on the fact that these types of weapons have only one purpose—to wage war.

Because the projectiles used in these weapons are, by definition, large, the size of the weapons is also large. Sometimes they require two people to carry and set up. Their firepower makes them attractive to terrorists, but paradoxically their size makes them less attractive.

There are many practical considerations about their size and weight that prevent their deployment. The other consideration is availability—they are manufactured in smaller numbers, are not widely distributed, and are easier to detect by customs and border protection services. Ammunition for these weapons presents a similar problem—it is large and heavy, and its sources of supply are scarce. The cost of these weapons and their ammunition is exponentially more than, say, a semiautomatic pistol for which cartridges can be purchased at a sporting goods store. For the same price, a terrorist group can buy a lot of small arms.

Some arms of war that fall into this category include machine guns like the Browning M2, recoilless rifles (see Figure 5.1), and grenade launchers.

Explosives

Explosives are substances that when ignited release energy, and while doing so create an explosion; hence their name. It is the sudden release of energy that causes the destruction. This energy is in the form of intense pressure and heat, as well as light and sound. The size of the explosive charge is measured by the quantity of explosive material the device contains—for instance, five kilograms of high-explosive.

Explosives are categorized as either high- or low-explosive by the speed at which the material they contain burns, and therefore the rapidity at which the gas that is generated expands. Military-grade explosives are designed for consistent performance and safe han-

Photograph by Staff Sgt. Daniel Love. Courtesy of the US Army.

Figure 5.1 Soldiers firing an M3 Carl Gustaf 84-millimeter recoilless rifle.

dling.[16] Compared to field-expedient (e.g., homemade) explosives, the yield is greater. This also applies to commercial-grade explosives, like those used in the mining industry. And, like weapons of war, such high-quality explosives are under tight control. Many carry serial numbers or have forensic details of their batch and other such information recorded. This helps criminal investigators trace the device to its origin (a technique known as walking back the cat).

It is not always possible, nor is it wise, for terrorists to use military- or commercial-grade explosives because of the forensic fingerprint they leave. Trying to obtain these superior-grade devices also attracts the attention of undercover operatives; and history shows that many would-be terrorists have been stopped at this stage of their operations. It is no wonder that many terrorists turn to building improvised munitions.

Decades of unconventional war have perfected this art into a science. For instance, special forces are regularly trained in field-expedient explosives devices.[17] The information from such training courses has now filtered out of military circles and into the public domain. This means knowledge of these techniques lowers the profile of terrorists setting out to build these devices, thus attracting less attention than if they tried to purchase higher-grade devices on the black market.

Until the 9/11 attacks, large quantities of nitrate-based fertilizer could be purchased without drawing undue attention. Legislation, policy, and procedures have changed this. Still, many improvised bombs can still be fashioned without much difficulty—take for instance the pressure-cooker bombs used by the Boston Marathon bombers in 2013.

Firebombs

Firebombs are a type of incendiary device that is made using improvised materials and techniques. These are different from incendiary bombs that are dropped by aircraft. These types of weapons are used to start fires, and it is the heat and flames of the fire that cause the damage. Military-grade incendiary bombs use materials such as napalm, thermite, magnesium powder, chlorine trifluoride, and white phosphorus, but homemade fire bombs typically use a flammable liquid such as gasoline, kerosene, or dieseline. The most recognizable fire bomb is the Molotov cocktail.

The Molotov cocktail is easy to make using a corked glass bottle as a container of the flammable liquid and a wick (in place of a fuse), usually made from a rag soaked in the liquid. For this reason, these devices are also called bottle bombs. Anyone can make these and history shows that they have been employed by urban gangs and protestors as well as guerrillas and terrorists, with great effect. The Finns used the bombs against Soviet tanks during World War II. The Finns coined the name for this type of bomb as an insult to mock the Soviet foreign minister at the time, Vyacheslav Molotov.

To use the bomb, the thrower lights the wick and tosses it at the target. The glass container smashes on impact, releasing the flammable liquid. The fuel is immediately ignited by the flaming wick. The amount of fuel in the container is the usual determinant for the splash radius, but distances of up to about 1.2 meters in diameter are feasible. The resulting fireball is intended to set the target alight.

Variations of this device have been developed that include adding thickening agents to the liquid. This helps the burning liquid adhere to the target's surface, and depending on the thickening agent used, the ingredient causes the smoke to become black, adding to the bomb's psychological impact.

Booby Traps

The name of these devices says it all—traps set to kill or maim. The term *booby* refers to the unsuspecting victim who inadvertently triggers the bomb himself. Although pranksters have for centuries set traps in good humor—like an exploding cigar—the booby trap is deadly.

It is associated with improvised devices that are akin to the military land mine or antipersonnel mine. Triggering these devices is done by the victim—walking along a path, opening a door, switching on an electric light, turning on the ignition of a vehicle. The settings and methods of triggering these devices vary depending on the materials used and the ingenuity of the bomb maker. There are also manufactured devices for military use. These devices usually resemble objects that the target regards as valuable or as, perhaps, souvenirs. Although these devices are produced for combat troops, they can find their way into the hands of terrorists.

These types of devices are effective because they exploit human curiosity, habit, or the need for self-preservation. For instance, take a situation where law enforcement or security personnel raid an apartment used by terrorists. In the main, they are looking for evidence and intelligence to help their inquiries. If they find a pile of papers—the top pages containing diagrams and maps—their curiosity is piqued as to what this might mean, as well as by the sheets underneath. However, lifting the pile (i.e., the bait) may be the trigger that sets off a boobytrap.

Habit is another human behavior that lends itself to setting a booby trap—a victim-activated ambush. If a terrorist knows his target takes the same route to work each day, at the same time, it is easy to set a trap for the victim to trigger—say a trip wire across a walking path. Self-preservation might involve the setting of a booby trap in, say, a fire escape and telephoning in a bomb threat. When the occupants of the building try to leave, they detonate the bomb.

Booby traps comprise three parts: the firing mechanism, the detonator, and the main charge. The three components work in series, creating a firing chain. That is, the firing device sets off the detonator, which in turn sets off the main charge.

Booby traps are developed and deployed using cunning, so law enforcement and security personnel need to be mindful of their use when searching terrorist-incident scenes, as well as the places occupied by terrorists. The procedures for disarming these devices include neutralization, destruction in place, removal of the main charge, and disarming by hand. These procedures need to be conducted by trained specialists who are members of an explosive ordnance disposal unit.

Vehicle Ramming

The use of vehicles as a weapon is not new, though its use by terrorists has developed since about 2010. Vehicles have been weaponized before by criminals, gangs, and people suffering from psychotic episodes. As an example of the latter, in 1973 Olga Hepnarová drove a truck into a crowd of some twenty-five people waiting for a tram in Prague, killing eight and injuring another twelve. In a letter she sent to two newspapers, she explained that the attack was revenge for the hate she felt from society.[18]

Criminals have long recognized the potential of vehicles as weapons; they have used them in a variety of applications, such as to ram commercial and retail outlets to steal goods, and to breach automated teller machines to steal cash. Because vehicles require little effort to weaponize, it is not surprising that terrorists have adopted and adapted them for killing.

Unlike other weapons, vehicles are legal and in plentiful supply (i.e., will not alert authorities to their acquisition, unlike explosives and arms). Anyone who can drive can use them (i.e., no special training) and there is virtually no planning involved (i.e., can be carried out by a lone assailant with no financial backing); any publicly trafficked area becomes a potential killing zone. Moreover, it is not possible to erect defensive barriers everywhere a vehicle could possibly be used to kill pedestrians or other motorists. The popularity of vehicle ramming is evidenced by the prevalence of such attacks and the large number of people killed since 2010 in France, Stockholm, London, Israel, the United States, and Canada.

Cyber Weapons

A cyber weapon can take the form of either a piece of computer hardware or a program—that is, a software application. The latter is sometimes known as a cyber bomb.

Cyber weapons have been popular in cinema and fiction. Although the portrayal of weaponized computers and software programs has been somewhat simplistic, they can be complex.[19] Nevertheless, their design, creation, and use are usually associated with security and intelligence agencies. This is because such agencies have the means to oversee their development, and the know-how to effectively deploy them against an adversary.

But history shows that this is not always the case. Individuals and criminal groups routinely use cyber weapons to target corporations and to extort money from individuals. In the main, these attacks take the form of tricking the operator of a computer device (e.g., the owner of a smart phone, tablet, laptop, or desktop) into installing a malware[20] agent. Once installed, the program executes its payload— the instructions to steal information, corrupt data, perform a destructive operation, or observe and report.

Given the potential for destruction, one would assume that using a cyber weapon would be an attractive option for terrorists. However, experience demonstrates that this is not so. To date, there have been no incidents where a cyber weapon has been used by terrorists to cause damage to a target population. There have been numerous cases where malware has been used to steal money, and, as we know, theft is one means terrorist organizations use to finance their operations. This is not to say that terrorists use malware in this way; it is nonetheless an acknowledgment that the use of cyber weapons cannot be discounted as a fundraising avenue.

Scholars are not in complete agreement as to why terrorists have not employed cyber weapons, but the consensus centers on the argument that it is too expensive to develop an effective cyber weapon to attack, for example, a SCADA system. Supervisory control and data acquisition systems are combinations of computer hardware, data communication networks, and software programs that allow the management of industrial processes, such as pumps, sensors, motors, electrical transmission and switching devices, and many more. SCADA systems are at the core of managing the operations of critical infrastructure— electricity, gas, water, effluent, transport networks, sea ports, airline traffic, and the like. Although most examples of critical infrastructure would fall into the category of having high symbolic value, it appears that instances of penetration or attempted penetration have been linked to intelligence agencies of foreign countries. Various estimates have been made about how much a SCADA cyber weapon might cost a terror group. These vary because the underlying assumption differs, yet they are consistent in that the sum would be more than US$1 million. By comparison, a vehicle-delivered bomb would be far less expensive.

The other argument for terrorists not developing a cyber weapons capability is that perpetrating a cyber attack lacks the media propaganda that comes with seeing the fire and flames, the bodies and carnage, that are associated with kinetic destruction. Regarding suicide bombers, there is no martyrdom in cyber-space.

Does all this mean that there is no place for cyber weapons in a future terrorist strategy? Certainly not, but it does suggest to intelligence analysts that if such a weapon were used, it would indicate that the group has access to large financial resources and highly skilled technical help, both perhaps supplied by a third party.

Chemical, Biological, Radiological, and Nuclear Weapons

Chemical, biological, radiological, and nuclear weapons are probably the most feared terrorist weapons. The images of people slowly suffocating on a subway platform because of sarin gas, or of a building full of people exposed to anthrax spores, make for thrilling plots for fiction writers, but these incidents are not fictitious.

In March 1995 the Japanese terrorist organization Aum Shinrikyo released sarin gas into five Tokyo subway train carriages. The attack killed twelve commuters and seriously injured many dozens more. Estimates are that some 6,000 people sought medical treatment for the effects of the deadly nerve agent.

Beginning on September 18, 2001, and extending over several weeks, letters were mailed to several media offices and two US senators—these letters contained anthrax spores. The attacks resulted in five deaths as well as infecting seventeen others with the potentially lethal bacteria.

During the 1950s the military acronym *ABC* was coined to describe atomic, biological, and chemical weapons. Some years later, it was replaced by *NBC* for nuclear, biological, and chemical weapons—a change in terminology that reflected the technological advancements being made. The acronym has now been modified to express the threats currently posed by radiological devices or, as they are also known, dirty bombs. In the 2000s, the term *CBRNE* began to make its appearance in military, law enforcement, and emergency management circles, denoting chemical, biological, radiological, nuclear, and explosive weapons. The acronym's added *E* denotes the threat presented specifically by improvised explosive devices, such as the IEDs used in the 2013 Boston Marathon terrorist bombing.

Although one might be drawn to the conclusion that CBRN weapons are a phenomenon of the post-9/11 era, history demonstrates that people with political motivations have used these weapons for a long time. By way of example, take the US government's authorization of plots to assassinate Cuban dictator Fidel Castro during the 1960s. According to the 1975 report by the US Senate's Church Committee,[21] the Central Intelligence Agency (CIA) attempted to use chemical and biological agents to kill him—plots involving poisoned cigars, impregnating his diving wetsuit with toxic bacteria, as well as other schemes using lethal chemical agents were devised.

More recently, there was the case of the poisoning of Alexander Litvinenko with polonium-210. Litvinenko was a former intelligence officer with the Russian Federal Security Service (FSB), and its predecessor, the KGB. He escaped Russia and was granted political asylum in the United Kingdom. It was there that in November 2006 he was given a lethal dose of the radiological material, most likely in a cup of tea. Scotland Yard concluded that the attack was probably carried out by Russian agents because the manufacture of polonium is only available from state-regulated nuclear reactors.[22]

Arguably, the most feared threat from a terrorist group is detonating a nuclear device. The death and suffering that would result are terrifying. The sight of the mushroom cloud from the 1945 Japanese atomic bomb raids can still send a cold shiver up the spine of even the most robust individual.

Study Questions

1. List six types of small arms and describe their characteristics.
2. Discuss the difference between small arms and weapons of war.
3. Explain how field-expedient bombs are constructed, for example, the Molotov cocktail.

continues

Study Questions (continued)

4. List a chemical, biological, radiological, or nuclear weapon that might be of interest to a terrorist group and explain why.
5. Describe the difference between acts of terrorism committed by groups and by so-called lone wolves.
6. Explain what considerations are involved in the operational planning of a terrorist event.
7. Explain the difference between strategies and tactics.
8. List the various tactics that are commonly used by terrorists.

Learning Activities

1. Small arms are manufactured by companies that specialize in their design and are mass-produced for legitimate civilian, law enforcement, and military markets. These markets are regulated; because of this, the more desirable terrorist weapons are difficult, if not impossible, to obtain. Evidence suggests that those wanting to acquire weapons are now turning to field-expedient manufacturing processes, such as 3D printing. Research this issue and then discuss the arguments for and against the viability of a terrorist group employing 3D printing to produce weapons.
2. Select a one-year period and a geographic location—Australia, Canada, France, Germany, Italy, Spain, the United Kingdom, or the United States—and search Internet news reports for terrorist events in the chosen country. Although it is not essential to collect a report for every event, it is important to gather as many as is practical. Categorize the tactics used in these events, as we have done in this chapter, into the various low-risk and high-risk tactics. Now, describe the results—are there more low-risk or high-risk events? What external factors many have influenced this (consider factors such as the time frame and country selected, and the groups carrying out these criminal acts). Think critically, like an intelligence analyst, being mindful that the data collected using this method can be considered exploratory only, meaning that no firm conclusions can be drawn.

Notes

1. Ernesto "Che" Guevara, as quoted in J. Boone Bartholomees Jr., "A Survey of Strategic Thought," in J. Boone Bartholomees Jr. (ed.), *Guide to National Security Policy and Strategy* (Carlisle, PA: US Army War College, 2004), 94.

2. Bartholomees, "A Survey of Strategic Thought," 94.

3. Che Guevara, *Che Guevara on Guerrilla Warfare,* with an introduction by Major Harris-Clichy Peterson (New York: Praeger, 1961).

4. See David Bolton, *The Making of Tania Hearst* (London: New English Library, 1975).

5. David Jacobsen with Gerald Astor, *Hostage: My Nightmare in Beirut* (New York: Donald I. Fine, 1991).

6. As reported by Patrick Begley, "Sydney Siege Over: Lindt Café Gunman Forces Hostages to Appear in Videos," *Sydney Morning Herald,* December 16, 2014, http://www.smh.com.au/nsw/sydney-siege-over-lindt -cafe-gunman-forces-hostages-to-appear-in-videos-20141215-127wgy.html.

7. Jeffrey D. Simon, *The Terrorist Trap: America's Experience with Terrorism* (Bloomington: Indiana University Press, 1994).

8. US Department of the Army, *Field Manual* no. FM-5-31: *Boobytraps* (Washington, DC: US Department of Defense, 1965).

9. Christopher Reuter, *My Life Is a Weapon: A Modern History of Suicide Bombing* (Princeton: Princeton University Press, 2004).

10. University of Chicago, "Attacks by Year," http://cpostdata.uchicago .edu/search_results_new.php.

11. Rick Sarre, "Gun Control in Australia," *Salus Journal* 3, no. 3 (2015), 6.

12. Paul Elliott, *Assassin: The Bloody History of Political Murder* (London: Blandford, 1999).

13. William R. Powell, *The Anarchist Cookbook* (New York: Lyle Stuart, 1971).

14. Federal Bureau of Investigation, from undated declassified internal memorandum regarding Powell's *The Anarchist Cookbook.*

15. Tony Lesce, *The Shotgun in Combat* (Cornville, AR: Desert, 1979).

16. There are two types of explosives: primary and secondary. Primary explosives are characterized by their sensitivity to vibration, impact, friction, and heat. These types of materials will detonate if their sensitive threshold is exceeded. In comparison, secondary explosives (also called base explosives) are more tolerant of these influences.

17. For example, US Department of the Army, *Improved Munitions Handbook* no. TM 31-210 (Washington, DC, 1969).

18. Roman Cilek, *Ja Olga Hepnarova* (Prague: Afera, 2016).

19. For a detailed discussion, see Henry Prunckun (ed.), *Cyber Weaponry: Issues and Implications of Digital Arms* (New York: Springer, 2018).

20. The term *malware* is a shorthand expression for malicious software. The term is used to categorize several types of programs that are designed for hostile intent. Such programs include adware, ransomware, scareware, spyware, Trojan horses, viruses, and worms.

21. US Senate, Select Committee to Study Governmental Operations with Respect to Intelligence Activities, *Alleged Assassination Plots Involving Foreign Leaders* (Washington, DC: US Government Printing Office, 1975).

22. Jamie Grierson, "Litvinenko Inquiry: Russia Involved in Spy's Death, Scotland Yard Says," *The Guardian,* July 31, 2015, https://www.theguardian.com/world/2015/jul/30/litvinenko-inquiry-russia-involved-spy-death-scotland-yard.

6

Financing

No act of terrorism can be performed without resources. Therefore, disrupting terrorist finances by blocking the funds or confiscating them is essential to controlling terrorism. Understanding how and where terrorists come by their funding is pivotal to the effectiveness of law enforcement operations.

If the personification of terrorism has ideology as its heart, then funding is certainly its central nervous system. It should not be surprising that without adequate funds, terrorist organizations are limited in the size, scope, and impact of their activities. According to the US Council on Foreign Relations, the 9/11 attacks were estimated to have cost US$500,000, the 2002 bombing of a Bali nightclub about US$50,000, the 2004 Madrid train bombing between US$10,000 and US$15,000, and the 2005 attacks on London's mass transit system about US$2,000.[1]

For the most part, terrorist attacks are relatively inexpensive, which appeals to resource-scarce terrorist cells. Like any organization, terrorist groups have operating costs. They require funds not only for attacks but also for general costs and support of their members. The challenge for terrorists is to ensure a regular flow of income. What is apparent is the large number of sources, both legal and illegal, that are available to terrorists.

This chapter examines some of the techniques and methods used by terrorists to raise money and find funding sources. Technology, specifically the Internet, has facilitated a proliferation of direct fundraising opportunities, such as crowd-funding endeavors. Virtual currencies have also made obtaining funds easier. Equally evident is a greater connection between organized crime and terrorism. Finally, a common and effective source of funding comes from nation-states. Both national and international state-sponsored terrorism remain the most lucrative form of raising money.

Fundraising

Fundraising refers to deliberate requests for money for terrorist activities. It is a process that finds funding for terrorist campaigns with the donors having knowledge of the end purpose of their money. With the rise of social media, fundraising has become easier because of the transnational reach of these online services. Using social media forums, fundraisers openly ask for money to supply weapons and equipment. Brazen individuals post calls for funding a variety of jihads, explaining how much money the group needs to purchase essential items. For example, a "sniper weapon ($6,000), a grenade thrower RPG ($3,000), and PK machine gun ($5,500)."[2] While social media administrators make attempts to remove such posts and close accounts, these preventive steps can be circumvented by reposting the notices under new accounts. Prospective providers of funding are also advised to contact the fundraiser via other social media websites that are better encrypted and provide greater security, so donors can receive information about how to make payments.

Austrac, Australia's financial intelligence agency, has identified fundraising for illicit purposes through the Internet as a growing concern. Within the Southeast Asian region, Austrac has provided several threat assessments on the possibility of terrorist groups or sympathetic individuals using social media or crowd-funding and the likelihood of the country they would operate from.

Terrorist fundraising via the Internet poses a medium-level threat in Australia, Thailand, and the Philippines. But Indonesia and Malaysia have been identified as having a high-level threat. Austrac also recognizes that fundraising on social media and crowd-funding platforms is essentially reliant on the efforts of supportive individuals rather than organized terrorist groups. Another problem identified by Austrac is that fundraising via the Internet is so vast that it is often difficult to determine legitimate activities from the illegitimate.[3]

Criminal-Terrorist Nexus

There is a growing connection between terrorist groups and organized crime. Terrorist groups often move into organized crime activities to fund their missions. Armed robbery, kidnapping, and extortion have become common practices to fund terrorist activities.

There are some similarities in the operational models of terrorist groups and organized crime gangs that provide the foundation for cooperation. Naturally, both have an aversion to state authority. However, where the terrorist group may be seeking to bring down a society, an organized crime group may benefit from a stable state. Stability of a state provides the opportunity to make money from illicit activities.[4] Although both will use violence, this activity has different objectives.

Increasingly, there are transnational tactical alliances between terrorist groups and organized crime. In this sense, a tactical alliance refers to short-term cooperation whereby one group will provide the other a skill or resource for mutual benefit. For example, a terrorist group may provide expertise in bomb manufacturing while an organized crime group may provide a trafficking route or money-laundering services.[5] As another example of the cooperation between organized crime and terrorist groups, in the Middle East, "there is evidence of Hezbollah establishing a strong base in Latin America over the past decade or more and working with Mexican [drug-trafficking organizations] to launder money, finance terrorism and smuggle people."[6]

Drug Cartels

Terrorist organizations are associated with the drug trade and in some instances appear to be operating as drug cartels. The nexus between terrorism and the drug trade has led to the term *narco-terrorist*. Narco-terrorism is terrorism that is financed by the drug trade. The drug trade provides an independent opportunity to raise large sums of money to support terrorist activities.

Initially, terrorist organizations may have benefited from the drug trade by allowing transportation through their territories for a fee. But terrorist organizations are also involved in the cultivation, production, and distribution of drugs. Perhaps the most infamous terrorist organization operating as a drug cartel is the Revolutionary Armed Forces of Colombia (FARC), a group that has been actively combating ruling governments and committing terrorist activities in

Colombia since the 1960s. Its ideology is Marxist-Leninist, but it is also known as one of the region's most active drug cartels shipping cocaine through Africa and into Europe. FARC denies direct involvement in the drug trade but does admit to "taxing" components of the cultivation, production, and transportation of cocaine. One estimate suggested through its taxation system, FARC was earning US$450 per kilogram of cocaine cultivated, produced, or transported through its territory, amounting to at least US$50 million per year.[7] Much of FARC's longevity can be attributed to its estimated wealth.

In Afghanistan, the Taliban was allegedly supplying half of the world's heroin. It is suggested that the Taliban was making about US$400 million annually from the heroin trade. Interestingly, it is the destabilization of the region that appears to encourage an increase in heroin production. Early in 2001, the Taliban regime had begun to ban opium cultivation. However, after the United States commenced military action to overthrow the Taliban, it began to increase cultivation to fund its military campaigns.[8]

Where once they were separate problems, the link between the drug trade and terrorism is now well recognized by both law enforcement and intelligence agencies. There is an understanding that breaking the drug trade can have benefits for curbing terrorism. The two are no longer treated exclusively. The metamorphosis of terrorist organizations into drug cartels not only has implications for international security and law enforcement but also requires a new understanding of terrorist motivations. No longer can the actions of terrorist groups with links to the drug trade be interpreted as solely an ideological or political struggle. What appears on the surface as a political act may be a strategic move to increase a terrorist dominance over the drug trade. Further, as terrorist groups move into the drug trade, their ideological or political motivations become secondary to making money. The involvement in the drug trade or other illicit activities can also be damaging to terrorists' support base. Supporters may perceive a contradiction in the ideologies or religious beliefs espoused by the groups and their role in the drug trade.

Human Trafficking

Trafficking people into forced labor or sexual exploitation is a commonly used method by terrorist organizations, but not solely for financial gain (see Figure 6.1). The Taliban, ISIS, Boko Haram, and

Marxist guerrillas in Nepal are known to have used trafficking to raise money. Allegedly, teenage girls in Iraq have been sold on the black market for between US$2,500 and US$5,000. In parts of Africa and Asia a girl between ten and fifteen years of age can be sold for US$600.[9] While not as lucrative as drug trafficking, human trafficking is mostly used by terrorist organizations for its fear value. Taking women and children from an occupied area or village creates fear and demoralizes the population. The funds raised from trafficking those women and children tend to be secondary to the benefits of creating fear in populations.

Human trafficking includes kidnapping. This is a common tactic used by the Abu Sayyaf group in the Philippines, which targets tourists as a way of ruining the local economy and generating some income in ransom demands. In hostage cases, the ransom price can be in the millions of dollars, which is seldom achievable for the families of hostages. It is not uncommon for hostages to be beheaded.

State-Sponsored Terrorism

State-sponsored international terrorism has been in decline since the end of the Cold War in 1989. However, there are still states willing to assist terrorist groups. According to the US State Department, nations like

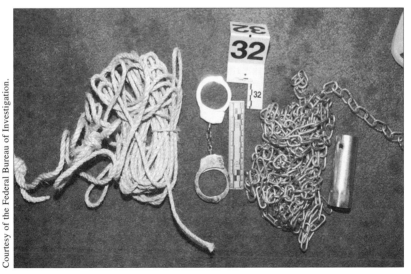

Courtesy of the Federal Bureau of Investigation.

Figure 6.1 Evidence of human trafficking.

Cuba, Iran, North Korea, and Syria have been suspected of sponsoring terrorist activities.[10] Contentiously, others may suggest that Saudi Arabia and Pakistan have been associated with sponsoring terrorist groups.[11] However, it is not at a state level that these nations support terrorism—rather, criticism is levied at those states because they do not adequately prosecute their individual citizens who support terrorists.

States sponsor terrorist organizations for a variety of reasons. States may be motivated to support a terrorist group because they share the same ideological, cultural, or religious backgrounds. Other reasons may include causing destabilization in another state or simply the geopolitical adage "the enemy of my enemy is my friend." In other instances, some nations may have little confidence in using organizations like the United Nations as a mechanism for resolving problems or furthering their political and economic interests. Those states are likely unable to wage open warfare and so use terror to pursue their political interests.

State-sponsored international terrorism functions by supplying assistance to carry out terrorist activities. The most common support that states offer is a safe haven—a place to conduct training, recruitment, and allow the terrorist organization to operate. Yet states can also provide other forms of assistance such as false passports, facilitate financial transactions, purchase weapons and explosives, provide diplomatic protection, and organize transportation.

Some notable examples of state-sponsored terrorism are evident Libyan-supported terrorist attacks. The actions of Libya during the 1980s illustrate the notion that states will resort to terrorism if they are unable to wage open warfare on a larger enemy, or in contempt of organizations like the United Nations. The now deceased Libyan dictator Muammar Qaddafi had been a staunch critic of the West and the United Nations. He likely sanctioned several terrorist activities that took place during the 1980s. Most notably, in 1986, Libya supported bombing a Berlin disco popular with US military service people. In 1988, Libya planted a bomb on Pan Am flight 103—infamously known as the Lockerbie bombing. Two Libyan intelligence officers were indicted and eventually Qaddafi surrendered to stand trial in The Hague in the Netherlands. Again in 1988, Libya was accused of detonating a bomb on UTA flight 772, which exploded over the Sahara Desert.

Pre–civil war Syria also had an association with sponsoring terrorism and allowed terrorist organizations to operate their headquarters from Damascus. The government also assisted several pro-Palestine terror groups such as Hamas. For a period, Sudan was also considered a terrorist haven when it gave asylum to Osama bin Laden after he was expelled from Saudi Arabia in 1991. In the late 1990s, Sudan signed several anti-terror international agreements. Subsequently, Sudan was removed from the US list of nations sponsoring terrorists.

Other nations may not be as supportive of terrorist groups as Syria, Libya, or previously Sudan, but they are still seen as vital sources of funding. Qatar, Kuwait, and the United Arab Emirates (UAE) have been identified as sources of terrorist funding.[12] It is not necessarily the governments that are actively providing funding but rather wealthy citizens or "front" companies established in those states.

It is not uncommon for fundraisers from terrorist groups located in Afghanistan or Pakistan to be masquerading as businesspeople or foreign workers in the Middle East while raising money and taking large sums of cash back to their respective organizations. In more extreme circumstances terrorists kidnap for ransom wealthy Pakistani or Afghani businesspeople residing in countries like the UAE. In Saudi Arabia it is alleged that terrorist fundraisers arrive during the period of hajj to solicit donations and then return with cash to their home countries. The significance of arriving during this period is the relaxed immigration policy officials have for pilgrims making their hajj.[13]

Public Donations

There are many ways terrorist groups may access public donations. It is not unusual for terrorist organizations to use charity organizations as fronts to receive donations from unsuspecting members of the public. Terrorists may create a fake organization and use all donations for their terror activities or as a means to launder money made through illicit activities. In other instances, a charity may be completely unaware it is assisting terrorist activities. A charity may have set up a partnership with an affiliate overseas group to conduct programs without knowing the complete background of that overseas group. The overseas group may then use part of that charity's funds to finance terrorist acts. Terrorist groups may also use a charity's assets such as vehicles for their own transport needs or warehouses to store weapons. In some cases, a terrorist group may use the name of a charity organization and its status to raise funds without the charity knowing. Other methods include infiltration of the charity by terrorist groups. Members of a terrorist group may infiltrate a charity group and pose as employees, embezzling money that is then funneled to the terrorist organization.[14]

The impact on the reputation of a charity organization that has been associated with terrorism has lasting effects. After the 9/11 attacks the International Islamic Relief Organization (IIRO) was alleged to have had links to al-Qaeda and Hamas.[15] Established in 1978 and located in Saudi Arabia, the IIRO provides aid and relief to countries around the world. While denied by the IIRO, it was alleged the organization had financed terrorism between 1986 and 2006. The accusations and arrests of some of its employees led to the organization being listed by the UN, European Union, United Kingdom, and United States as a group that aids terrorists. It was only after the IIRO appealed to the UN in 2014 and 2016 that it was delisted by the UN, the United Kingdom, and the United States as an organization financing terrorism.[16]

Crowd-funding as a means of appealing for public donations has been on the rise. Websites will take a percentage of what has been raised in return for use of their Internet forums. It is relatively easy to establish an account, and funds can be raised in the name of almost any entity. Unsurprisingly, public donations to crowd-funding ventures are susceptible to deception and fraud. Some examples of deceptive crowd-funding include using copycat websites—that is, websites made to look like a legitimate fundraising campaign—to divert funds. More simply, a lone terrorist can create a false campaign, raise money, and then disappear with the funds to implement their terrorist plan.[17] Nevertheless, financial intelligence agencies pay close attention to the role of crowd-funding and public donations, and their link to terrorism. The US Treasury Department's Financial Crimes Enforcement Network and Australia's Austrac recognize that many crowd-funding websites have little regulation, so these agencies have been monitoring crowd-funding campaigns.

Money Laundering

Money laundering is the process of making money that has been generated through illegal activities appear as if it has been obtained through legal means. For terrorist organizations, they are also faced with what can be called reverse money laundering. Reverse money laundering is the taking of money from legal sources, such as legitimate businesses or charities, and using it for illegal purposes.

Transferring funds from illegal activities such as drug trafficking into the mainstream financial system usually has three phases. The first phase is getting the funds into the banking and financial system. This is the most difficult part for covert organizations, because banks are required to report unusual deposits of cash. The second phase in the process involves the actual laundering. In this phase, money is put through many transactions using offshore accounts and false payments through dummy invoices and loans. The idea is to create a complicated and extensive trail that becomes difficult to follow. The final stage in the process is transferring the funds into the mainstream economy. This is achieved through expensive purchases or investment in company stock or real estate. Further, investments in businesses such as casinos, race tracks, bars, and restaurants that have a high number of cash transactions are favored, because it is easier to launder cash through such enterprises.[18]

Terrorist groups will also seek funds from legitimate sources. Donations and gifts are solicited from supporters. However, often people donating to charities could unknowingly be funding terrorist operations. Gifts or donations can be used to conduct terrorist acts. Using "clean" money for illicit activities can be just as difficult to trace as regular money laundering. The 9/11 attacks were financed through normal bank transfers and cash. Funds were sent from the UAE into a New York account and then to the terrorists in Florida. Other hijackers simply brought cash into the United States.[19]

Charities are ideal fronts for raising money. The Australian Charities and Not-for-Profits Commission published several guidelines to ensure organizations do not unwillingly help terrorists. These guidelines call for greater recording of transactions and more effective due-diligence of charities providing overseas aid. They also call for charities to check with the Australian Department of Foreign Affairs to ensure they are not aiding countries that have had financial embargoes placed upon them. For example, in 2012 the Australian government banned transferring funds of greater than A$20,000 to Iran.[20]

Cash

Cash payment through cash couriers is a common mechanism to move funds between terrorists. Consequently, governments have imposed controls and reporting requirements to monitor the transfer of cash. Cash is preferred by terrorists because it is difficult to trace. This is particularly the case when cash is raised within the targeted nation. The 2005 London bombings serve as an example of domestic terrorists raising funds locally to commit acts of terror.

Most nations now have a limit on the amount of cash that can be moved across their borders without a declaration to customs authorities. To be more effective, nations are now going further. In April 2017, the European Union Parliament passed a proposal for more regulations and controls on cash entering or leaving the European Union. India has put a limit on any cash transactions within its own borders greater than approximately US$3,000. In Australia there are discussions aimed at putting a limit of A$10,000 on cash transactions, and in the United Kingdom some banks will not accept large cash deposits without some proof of how the money was obtained.

Online marketplaces also provide a means to transfer cash both into other countries and within countries. In 2017, the Federal Bureau of Investigation uncovered the transfer of money to an Islamic State operative in the United States via fake eBay transactions.[21] Another similar method is to use webcam sex sites. Models are given money for shows by consumers from across the world. Terrorist operatives posing as customers pay the models for the shows. While the payments are made in virtual coins, these payments are redeemed for cash (often in US dollars) by the webcam model in the nation where the model resides and then the money is passed on (in cash) to the terrorist group via the model.

Gift and Travel Cards

Gift cards have to some degree replaced the traditional cash gift. Purchased through banks or stores with relative anonymity, these cards can easily be transferred internationally, because a person's wallet is seldom checked by customs and immigration officials. Further, with prepaid cards linked to cell phones, it is possible to transfer funds from that card to another cell phone located anywhere in the world.[22]

Is it suspected that cash travel cards are also used by terrorist groups. It has been reported by Australian authorities that hundreds of thousands of dollars have been deposited on these travel cards, and then redeemed in countries bordering Syria where clandestine terrorist camps and underground supporters are known to be hiding, including areas of Turkey, Jordan, and Lebanon.[23]

Crypto-Currencies

In 2018, crypto-currencies were still in their infancy, but their potential risks to national security have become apparent. Like the Internet during the early 1990s, crypto-currencies are so far mostly ungoverned, unregulated, and open for everyone to use. At the time of writing, there were calls to regulate crypto-currencies, with many policy analysts concerned about the opportunity these currencies create for illegal transactions.

Crypto-currencies are digital currencies that are largely anonymous. Crypto-currencies can be transferred internationally between people without using a bank or regulated exchange facility. Accounts cannot be frozen by authorities and there are no limits on transfers. Crypto-currencies can be exchanged for other traditional currencies and are kept in what is called a digital wallet, on either a computer or a mobile device. Crypto-currencies can be easily exchanged for a variety of goods and services.

These systems are overseen by what are called miners, who receive crypto-coins for verifying transactions. After the transaction is verified, it is recorded in a public register. It is unclear how payment verifications may be manipulated, such as through establishing accounts in false names. It seems possible to establish a digital wallet using a false name, but to purchase crypto-coins with traditional currency usually requires identification. The overall attraction of crypto-coins is the absence of fees and oversight from banks and government authorities.

Some advocates of crypto-currencies maintain that there have been only a few instances of terrorist organizations using these currencies, and question whether such currencies will ever be favored by terrorist organizations given the array of other funding mechanisms available. Advocates cite the use of the public register as the greatest inhibitor to keeping transactions hidden. However, others, such as the Rand Corporation, view the growth of crypto-currencies as a potential enabler of terrorist activities.

Research at Rand suggests that with the crackdown on existing fundraising and money laundering, the anonymity offered by crypto-currencies could prove irresistible.[24] Given that many nations are introducing limits on cash transactions and banks are required to notify government regulators of suspicious transactions, we can appreciate why terrorist organizations might venture into using crypto-currencies.

Despite having a public register, crypto-coin transactions could possibly be disguised through fake dealings in the way eBay was used to funnel money to terrorist cells in the United States.[25]

Hawala Money Transfer

Hawala money transfers are performed through a network of participants known as hawaladars. The process dates to the eighth century and is still used today, mostly in the Middle East, Southeast Asia, and Africa. Hawala money transfers do not necessarily involve sending cash directly from one person to another. Rather, a person may approach a hawaladar and request money to be sent to another party. The hawaladar will contact a hawaladar in the area where the other party is located and that hawaladar will pay the amount requested by the initiator. The hawaladar who makes the payment to the party will take a small commission and seek reimbursement from the hawaladar brokering the payment.

The attraction to using hawala money transfers is its ingrained cultural acceptance and its ability to bypass state-regulated banks, as well as its reduced fees. There are also no limits on the amounts that can be transferred.

Investigations by law enforcement and intelligence agencies regarding hawala money transfers reveal three types of transfers. There are the legitimate transfers, often used by migrant workers for transferring funds to families. Second, hybrid transfers occur when hawaladars are unaware that they are transferring funds to a terrorist group. Third, there are those using the network for criminal or terrorist purposes.[26] The overall concern is the lack of supervision by governments where hawala money transfers are practiced. The common concern is the lack of regulatory oversight in the process. There appears to be no formal registration of those involved in hawala transfers in some countries, which makes tracking the funds a difficult task.

The Financial Action Task Force is an independent organization with a thirty-eight-country membership aiming to develop measures to combat money laundering. It considers the greatest problem in assessing the hawala network to be trying to secure international cooperation and a lack of understanding of hawala money transfers and how they are used to fund terrorist actions.[27] Another challenge for investigating these transfers is the tendency for some hawaladars to barter rather than use cash. Redemption from one hawaladar to another may involve lottery tickets, cell phones, travel or gift cards, and, in the case of the United States, food stamps,[28] all of which are difficult to trace.

There are only a few known examples of hawala money transfers that have sponsored terrorist activities. According to Spanish intelligence, the hawala system has been operating through Spanish cities with sums of money being sent to those fighting in Syria. It has been estimated that approximately 250 hawala establishments were operating in Spain in 2015. To date, it is only Spain that has identified the connection between hawala fund transfers and terrorism in Europe.[29] According to the US State Department, hawala fund transfers have been used to finance terrorist attacks in India and consequently it has called upon Indian leaders to introduce measures to encourage greater transparency of the informal funds-transfer network.[30]

Hawala money transfers are embedded in the cultures of the Middle East and Southeast Asia. The cultural differences between these regions and the West make understanding the networks, payments, and records kept by hawaladars difficult to identify and interpret. Because hawala money transfers rely on noninstitutionalized networks, they are therefore difficult to trace. While at the time of writing there were only a few instances of hawala money transfers being used for terrorist activities, they may in the future prove more popular. Like crypto-currencies, the appeal is avoiding the required reporting of funds transfers that banks currently obey.

Study Questions

1. Describe the financial relationship that exists between terrorism and organized crime.
2. List three states that are considered to have been sponsors of terrorism and explain how these nations allegedly assist terrorists.
3. Explain two ways money can be laundered to fund terrorist activities.
4. Discuss how social media forums can be used to aid terrorist fundraising.

Learning Activity

Draw a diagram that you could use to explain the hawala money-transfer network. Using the Internet, compile a SWOT analysis of crypto-currencies from a counterterrorist perspective. Examine what safeguards your country uses to limit cash payments or the importation of cash. Provide a short summary of what those safeguards are, and comment on whether the evidence indicates that they have been effective.

Notes

1. Eben Kaplan, "Tracking Down Terrorist Financing," Council on Foreign Relations, April 4, 2006, https://www.cfr.org/backgrounder/tracking-down-terrorist-financing.

2. Abha Shankar, "Social Media Emerges As a Valuable Terrorist Fundraising Tool," April 20, 2016, https://www.investigativeproject.org/5314/social-media-emerges-as-a-valuable-terrorist.

3. Austrac, *Regional Risk Assessment on Terrorism Financing 2016: South-East Asia & Australia* (Canberra: Commonwealth of Australia, 2016), 26.

4. Peng Wang, "The Crime-Terror Nexus: Transformation, Alliance, Convergence," *Asian Social Science* 6, no. 6 (June 2010), 13.

5. Wang, "The Crime-Terror Nexus," 14.

6. Steven D'Alfonso, "Why Organized Crime and Terror Groups Are Converging," 2014, https://securityintelligence.com/why-organized-crime-and-terror-groups-are-converging.

7. Jeremy McDermott, "The FARC and the Drug Trade: Siamese Twins?" September 2014, http://www.insightcrime.org/investigations/farc-and-drug-trade-siamese-twins.

8. Hashim Wahdatyar, "How Opium Fuels the Taliban's War Machine in Afghanistan," *The Diplomat,* October 28, 2016.

9. Havocscope, "Human Trafficking Victims Prices, 2017," http://www.havocscope.com/black-market-prices/human-trafficking-prices.

10. US Department of State, *Patterns of Global Terrorism,* report of the Office of the Coordinator for Counterterrorism (Washington, DC, April 29, 2004).

11. Adam Weinstein, "The Real Largest State Sponsor of Terrorism," *Huffington Post,* March 16, 2017, https://www.huffingtonpost.com/entry/the-real-largest-state-sponsor-of-terrorism_us_58cafc26e4b00705db4da8aa.

12. Eric Lichtblau and Eric Schmitt, "Cash Flow to Terrorist Evades U.S. Efforts," *New York Times,* December 6, 2010; David D. Kirkpatrick, "Qatar's Support of Extremists Alienates Allies Near and Far," *New York Times,* September 8, 2014.

13. Declan Walsh, "WikiLeaks Cables Portray Saudi Arabia As a Cash Machine for Terrorists," *The Guardian,* December 6, 2010, https://www.the guardian.com/world/2010/dec/05/wikileaks-cables-saudi-terrorist-funding.

14. Australian Charities and Not-for-Profits Commission, "Protecting Your Charity Against the Risk of Terrorism Financing," https://www.acnc .gov.au/ACNC/Edu/ProtectTF.aspx?TemplateType=P.

15. Testimony of Steven Emerson before the House Committee on Financial Services, Subcommittee on Oversight and Investigations, "PATRIOT Act Oversight: Investigating Patterns of Terrorist Fundraising—Fund-Raising Methods and Procedures for International Terrorist Organizations," Washington, DC, February 12, 2002, 4.

16. US Department of the Treasury, *Federal Register* 81, no. 190 (September 30, 2016).

17. Becky Yerak, "'Suspicious' Crowdfunding Activity on the Rise, U.S. Watchdog Says," *Chicago Tribune,* October 15, 2015, http://www.chicagotribune .com/business/ct-crowdfunding-fincen-sars-1015-biz-20151015-story.html.

18. Jean-François Thony, *Money Laundering and Terrorism Financing: An Overview, 2002* (Versailles: French Court of Appeals, 2000), 3.

19. Stefan D. Cassella, "Reverse Money Laundering," *Journal of Money Laundering Control* 7, no. 1 (Summer 2003), 92.

20. Australian Charities and Not-for-Profits Commission, "Protecting Your Charity Against the Risk of Terrorism Financing."

21. Mark Maremont and Christopher S. Stewart, "FBI Says ISIS Used eBay to Send Terror Cash to U.S.," *Wall Street Journal,* August 10, 2017, https:// www.wsj.com/articles/fbi-says-isis-used-ebay-to-send-terror-cash-to-u-s -1502410868.

22. Jeremy M. Simon, "The Credit Card–Terrorism Connection: How Terrorists Use Cards for Everyday Needs and to Fund Operations," May 15, 2008, https://www.creditcards.com/credit-card-news/credit-cards-terrorism -1282.php.

23. "Terrorists Are Using Gifts Cards to Fund Attacks," *The Australian,* May 2, 2017, https://www.theaustralian.com.au/news/nation/terrorists-are-using-gifts -cards-to-fund-attacks/news-story/08bd153666332a62801184606b9261da.

24. David Manheim, Patrick B. Johnston, Joshua Baron, and Cynthia Dion-Schwarz, *Are Terrorists Using Cryptocurrencies?* (Santa Monica: RAND, 2017).

25. Maremont and Stewart, "FBI Says ISIS Used eBay to Send Terror Cash to U.S."

26. Financial Action Task Force, *The Role of Hawala and Other Similar Service Providers in Money Laundering and Terrorist Financing* (Paris: Organization for Economic Cooperation and Development, October 2013), 10.

27. Financial Action Task Force, *The Role of Hawala,* 11.

28. Dean T. Olson, "Financing Terrorism," *Law Enforcement Bulletin* 76, no. 2 (February 2007), 1–5.

29. Jack Moore, "Hawala: The Ancient Banking Practice Used to Finance Terror Groups," *Newsweek,* February 24, 2015, http://www.newsweek .com/underground-european-hawala-network-financing-middle-eastern -terror-groups-307984.

30. "Hawala Link to Terrorist Financing: U.S.," *The Hindu,* November 18, 2016, http://www.thehindu.com/todays-paper/tp-international/Hawala -link-to-terrorist-financing-U.S./article16627584.ece.

7

Media Coverage

The news media have been described as the "fourth estate"—a part of society that has indirect influence over public opinion and hence is used to shape the public consciousness. In democratic societies, the media fulfill several important roles, including informing the public about events that affect their everyday lives; stimulating public debates about issues small and large; exposing political abuse; drawing attention to human injustices and events that require humanitarian assistance; and promoting political pluralism with the aim to strengthen social cohesion.

News Reporting of Terrorist Events

News reporting of terrorism is a tightrope walk. The choice of language used in reports can be laden with value judgments. Even referring to someone as a "terrorist" creates some level of bias, as do the terms "freedom fighter" or "mujahidin" (the holy knights of Allah), among others.

The media's interpretation of a terrorist act and its motivation can also at times be fraught with error. Typically, radical Islamic terrorism is characterized as the dominant form of terror, but the challenge for the media is to report each incident without framing it—that is, without preconceived ideas or explanations. Historically, some assumptions about terrorist attacks made by the media have later proven to be erroneous. For example, early reports of the Oklahoma bombing in 1995 suggested it was an Islamic or Middle Eastern–inspired attack. Only later was it discovered to be domestic terrorism.[1]

The role of the media in reporting terrorist events is complex and, in some ways, can contribute to people's radicalization or deradicalization. People can be swayed by media opinion and often react emotionally to the stories portrayed. The complex nature of media and terrorism stems from media providers being called upon to adopt a number of roles, from assisting in providing public safety warnings and reporting on the events as expected in traditional journalism, to playing a part in the ideological struggle between radical and moderate politics. The greatest criticism leveled at the media concerns the way they present news stories about terrorism.

The journalistic formula of who, what, when, where, why, and how is no longer as pertinent to news as it once was, with greater emphasis now placed on commentary, analysis, and opinion. Today, news stories tend to be framed. Framing is in part the news agenda—that is, the choice of stories to present to audiences. Framing also aims to provide meaning to a news event, encouraging the audience to adopt a particular viewpoint.

Framing can be problematic if it prevents the audience from understanding the true nature of an event. Often a terrorist attack is examined for its own value, not its wider significance. The wider significance may include examining the issues that are motivating terrorists or highlighting the complex sociopolitical aspects of their grievances. Many news agencies (especially Western) will not interview terrorists for security reasons and a wariness about providing them a public platform. There is a perception that telling the terrorist side of a story may encourage the radicalization of individuals.

There has also been criticism that news reporting of terrorism tends to dramatize these events—whether intentional or unintentional—and poses a threat to national security. Phrases like "terrorism is a threat to Western democracy" are sometimes used by the media. The use of such emotive language could encourage terrorists by instilling a hypersensitivity across society. Some scholars have argued that when media capitalize on that fear, they are assisting terrorists in their mission.[2]

Media Coverage

Media coverage of a terrorist attack can sometimes resemble the fog of war (see Figure 7.1). That is, amid the chaos, reporters may not be able to see the event for what it is, or they may inadvertently be hindering those needing assistance. Broadcasting live can mean journalists are able to put together information only one piece at a time. Unwittingly, they may be reporting a mixture of fact and rumor with little opportunity to distinguish between the two.

Given the quick pace of live broadcasting, experience shows the necessity of establishing guidelines for relaying information. Broadcast news networks follow established rules that guide journalists. For example, what value will be placed on using social media as a source, given that social media are not always credible? What images will be used?[3] Should reporters relay not just what they do know, but also what they do not?[4] Outlining what is not known is not a weakness of journalism but rather an acknowledgment that early reporting

Figure 7.1 The media are omnipresent. US Army photograph taken near Ayn Issa, Syria, February 14, 2018, by Staff Sgt. Ambraea Johnson, part of the global coalition to defeat ISIS in Iraq and Syria.

is fluid as well as an acknowledgment that there is a responsibility to avoid conjecture and thus help to avoid hindering a subsequent investigation.

These guidelines also assist the associated security issues of news reporting. Those in media broadcasting are mindful that what they televise will likely be seen by the terrorists. Therefore, journalists see it as important that their media reports do not specifically describe the tactics or strategies of law enforcement or security forces, or of intelligence agencies.[5]

Media and the Terrorist Mystique

Since 9/11, terrorism has been given a certain mystique by predominantly Western media. The dramatization of terrorism in film and television depicts groups as radical, but also often as sophisticated, well-funded, organized networks of cells playing a cat-and-mouse game with national security agencies. Fictional accounts can contribute to a number of stereotypes and reinforce fears of the Middle East and Islam. Since 9/11, films with a terrorist narrative have often portrayed the terrorist as calculating and driven by evil. Few films show the complexity of motivation or the underlying causes of those committing terrorist acts.[6] Instead, fictional accounts are often fed by mainstream media interpretations of terrorism, viewed through an oversimplified lens of good versus evil. For the most part, terrorism, specifically radical Islamic terrorism, is viewed as almost homogeneous. Media reporting gives a sense that there is only one terrorist goal (to destroy the West) and that all terrorists are united in that goal. Media, in works of both fiction or fact, have contributed to a fundamental view of terrorism that does not reflect the reality and complexity of terrorist groups or acts.[7]

Social Media Reporting

Social media adds an interesting dimension to news reporting because of the unique problems it generates regarding terrorist events. There are many social media platforms that allow anyone with a smart phone to report news as it happens. In some respects, social media news is instant, raw coverage by nonjournalists. It is instant because news can be immediately uploaded from anywhere in the world and distributed globally within moments. The news is raw because it has not gone through journalistic checks of sources nor been held to editorial standards.

Nevertheless, in the rush to broadcast, even mainstream media have used social media images without proper verification. Instead, media will use a simple disclaimer that the images are unverified, but often there is little or no follow-up investigation of the images' authenticity because the media are constantly moving on to new stories. This results in a propensity for social media news to be inaccurate and biased.

Certainly, in the context of media literacy, social media are still in their infancy. They are full of misinformation and disinformation. However, in the long term, they offer great prospects to encourage moderate and broad-ranged views. As previously highlighted, within the mainstream media there is a propensity to focus on the extremes of an issue and dominate the framing. Social media can be a platform for alternative news sources that can look at the complexity of issues. Yet it may take significant time to develop that level of user literacy.

Terrorists and Social Media

Within this realm of instantaneous coverage, unfettered by editorial standards, terrorist groups have made use of this opportunity to promote their cause: "No one doubts that whoever controls the press wields power."[8] Speaking directly to social media subscribers, terrorist groups have highlighted their causes and glamorized their struggles. Social media images of terrorists fighting or depicting the lifestyle of a so-called freedom fighter contribute to terrorist groups' propaganda strategy.

As an example, ISIS understands the power of social media. It has used several social media platforms including Twitter, YouTube, and Facebook to encourage recruits and obtain financial resources. Combating the vast volume of posts, tweets, and uploads of ISIS propaganda is the responsibility of the Center for Strategic Counterterrorism Communications (CSCC), established in 2011 and housed at the US State Department. According to the CSCC, during the period 2014 to 2015, ISIS produced 1,800 videos.[9] The enormous amount of propaganda made it impossible for security agencies to monitor this propaganda, let alone effectively produce counter-propaganda. In many instances liberal democratic governments rely on the platform provider's support to assist in monitoring and removing material that appears to incite terrorist action or communicate terrorist ideology.

It seems terrorist ideology spreads easily throughout the online environment. But it is contentious whether the ideology actually transforms into direct action—actual terrorist boots on the ground. In 2018, the numbers of fighters joining ISIS are declining. While there is strong evidence that propaganda informs lone-actor attacks, this should be tempered with other factors such as the psychological state of the terrorist as well as any social or economic influences at play.

Another facet to terrorist organizations' use of social media is to promote their own version of events. As Brigitte Nacos has argued, "Regardless of their grievances, goals, size, and secular or religious convictions, literally all terrorist groups strive to maximize their media impact."[10] A study conducted by James Sheehan of the National Consortium for the Study of Terrorism and Responses to Terrorism (START) examined the content of the Twitter activity of al-Shabaab. The study found that most tweets concentrated on telling the terrorists' side of the story or highlighting their operational capacity.[11] Al-Shabaab appeared less concerned with inciting lone-wolf attacks and more with legitimizing its actions.

Understanding Terrorist Media Content

Examining online terrorist media requires a degree of content analysis. A rudimentary approach to that analysis begins with using Ole Holsti's model of the six elements of communication:[12]

- Who is the source of the message?
- What is the message?
- Who is the audience?
- How and through what channels is the message communicated?
- What is the purpose of the message?
- What is the effect of the message?

Knowing who are the creators of a website or social media message provides an opportunity to connect them to other organizations, past events, and activities. A close examination of what the message says leads to a better understanding of the intended audience.[13] Another clue to the intended audience is the medium used. For example, efforts to reach a younger audience may mean using a more contemporary social media platform. Understanding the purpose of the message has the natural advantage of knowing the aim of the communication and its objective. Measuring the effect of the message requires further analysis and relies on identifying the intended audience. Knowing the intended audience allows an opportunity to evaluate a message's impact.

Self-Regulatory Guidelines for Mainstream Media

Given the complex role the news media play in reporting terrorism and the criticism they have at times received for their coverage, it is not surprising that there have been several guidelines developed to ensure ethical, balanced, and socially responsible coverage of terrorist events. Regulation of media coverage of terrorism is left to the news organizations to ensure journalistic freedoms. However, there have been independent guides written to provide some principles for correspondents, journalists, and editors.

Media working within democratic nations have freedoms not enjoyed in nondemocracies. Specifically, they expect a right to access official information, the ability to protect confidential sources, the right to cover all those involved in a conflict, assurances that journalists will not be prosecuted for publishing (leaked) classified information, and a right to reject publishing propaganda on behalf of governments. Yet these rights must be tempered with responsibilities: differentiate between fact and opinion; explain without sensationalizing; publish corrections when errors have been made; and not publish state secrets if there is a risk to national security or to people's lives or well-being.

The traditional terrorist approach is that "you don't have to win the war, just break the opposition's will." The mechanism for doing this is to seek media coverage of any physical attack so that fear and anxiety are spread throughout the target population.[14] It is acknowledged that the ability of terrorists to garner media attention is pivotal to the success or failure of their mission. As Margaret Thatcher expressed succinctly while prime minister of Britain, democracies "must try to find ways to starve the terrorist and the hijacker of the oxygen of publicity on which they depend."[15]

Using the metaphor of a volume-control dial on an audio system as a means of demonstrating the impact the doctrine of "kill one, frighten ten thousand" might have on a public audience, the "message"—in the form of a violent terrorist act—will still be "heard," but will be heard at a greater distance and heard by more people. As noted earlier in the book, "many of today's terrorists want a lot of people watching *and* a lot of people dead."[16]

The fact that people are killed infuses a degree of shock; whether one victim or a hundred, a large number of fatalities has the potential to wield all the political influence of "killing one," but to a greater

Study Questions

1. List some of the advantages and disadvantages of social media when broadcasting a terrorist event.
2. Should the side of the terrorist be told in news broadcasts? Explain why or why not.
3. Explain in what ways the broadcasting of terrorist events could be shaped to avoid creating fear.
4. Using the Internet, examine the way Western media outlets cover a terrorist event in comparison to media outlets in the Middle East. List any differences in the way the stories are framed.

Learning Activity

Based on your understanding of the challenges facing the reporting of terrorist attacks, list five principles that you would like journalists to follow. Explain why you have chosen those principles.

degree. Large-scale terrorist attacks have the potential to reach more people and inflict greater fear and anxiety.

Notes

1. United Nations Educational, Scientific, and Cultural Organization (UNESCO), *Terrorism and the Media: A Handbook for Journalists* (Paris, 2017), 20.

2. Nathan Stitt, "Terrorism Media Coverage Playing into Extremists' Hands, Academic Warns," March 24, 2017, http://www.abc.net.au/news /2017-03-24/terrorism-media-coverage-is-helping-terrorists-academic-warns /8381780.

3. UNESCO, *Terrorism and the Media*, 70.

4. UNESCO, *Terrorism and the Media*, 45.

5. UNESCO, *Terrorism and the Media*, 70.

6. Carl Boggs and Tom Pollard, "Hollywood and the Spectacle of Terrorism," *New Political Science* 28, no. 3 (2006).

7. Philip Seib, "Mainstream Media Outlets Are Dropping the Ball with Terrorism Coverage," *The Conversation,* June 1, 2017, https://theconversation .com/mainstream-media-outlets-are-dropping-the-ball-with-terrorism-coverage -78442.

8. Roger Hilsman, cited in Brigette L. Nacos, *Terrorism and the Media* (New York: Columbia University Press, 1994), 16.

9. David Patrikarakos, "Social Media Networks Are the Handmaiden to Dangerous Propaganda," *Time Magazine,* November 2, 2017, http://time .com/5008076/nyc-terror-attack-isis-facebook-russia.

10. Brigitte Nacos, *Terrorism and Counterterrorism,* 5th ed. (New York: Routledge, 2016), 356.

11. James Sheehan, "Violent Jihadism in Real Time: Al-Shabaab's Use of Twitter," January 2013, https://www.start.umd.edu/sites/default/files/files /publications/research_briefs/STARTResearchBrief_AlShabaabsTwitter Use.pdf.

12. Philip Seib, Dana M. Janbek, and Andrew Hoskins, *Global Terrorism and New Media: The Post–Al Qaeda Generation* (London: Routledge, 2010), 44–45.

13. See Hank Prunckun, *Scientific Methods of Inquiry for Intelligence Analysis,* 2nd ed. (Lanham, MD: Rowman and Littlefield, 2015), 161–168.

14. This and the following discussion are taken, with the author's permission, from Henry Prunckun, "The First Pillar of Terror—Kill One, Frighten Ten Thousand: A Critical Discussion of the Doctrinal Shift Associated with the 'New Terrorism,'" *Police Journal: Theory, Practice, and Principles* 87, no. 3 (2014).

15. Margaret Thatcher, "Speech to the American Bar Association," Albert Hall, South Kensington, London, July 15, 1985.

16. Brian Michael Jenkins, "The New Age of Terrorism," in David G. Kamien, *The McGraw-Hill Homeland Security Handbook* (New York: McGraw-Hill, 2006), 119, emphasis added.

8

Victims of Terrorism

For terrorism to be a vehicle for social or political change, it must have a significant adverse impact on the target population. Deaths, destruction, and widespread fear within a population are all measures of an effective terrorist campaign. But adverse impacts are not solely about the volume or size of destruction. The scale of brutality and the ability to disseminate images of fatalities and casualties also play an important part in instilling fear.

What terrorists do to promote their cause has consequences for the people that are their target as well as for society. This chapter examines some of the effects terrorism has on its victims by placing fatalities and casualties into a global context. It illustrates the impact terrorism has had on survivors and some of the psychological damage inflicted. A victim of terrorism if often simply dismissed as "one of the dead or injured." But there is increasingly a need to recognize the impact terrorism has on victims to better understand its effects.

Typology of Victims

There is a typology of terrorist victims. This typology is broad so that it incorporates a wide interpretation of victims, acknowledging the range of people affected by acts of terrorism.[1] There are two categories in this typology. Simply, they are known as primary victims and secondary victims. A primary victim is one killed, injured, or mentally tortured by terrorists. These primary victims can also be injured or killed during a counterterrorist operation or injured physically or mentally after directly witnessing a terrorist attack.

A secondary victim is a person close to a primary victim, such as family or friend. A secondary victim may also be someone who fears for their life after they have been subjected to a terrorist threat. A secondary victim can also be a first-responder to a terrorist incident or someone who has lost income or property due to terrorism. Finally, a secondary victim can be someone who has had their lifestyle changed in a negative way by terrorism or a counterterrorism operation.[2]

Fatalities and Casualties

Since the 9/11 attacks, an estimated 167,300 deaths have occurred worldwide through acts of terrorism.[3] The regions most affected are the Middle East, South Asia, Southeast Asia, and Central Asia. In 2016, Iraq had the highest rate of terrorist attacks, followed by Afghanistan and then India.

Worldwide, casualties of terrorism peaked in 2014 and as of 2017 have been in decline.[4] Between 2000 and 2014, ISIL/ISIS, Boko Haram, and the Taliban were identified as being responsible for most terrorist attacks. Since 2001, the main weapons for terrorist attacks have been suicide bombings, incendiary devices, and vehicle-improvised explosives (see Chapter 9).[5] These weapons cause injuries including burns, amputation of arms and legs, ruptured ear drums, brain injuries, and lacerations from shrapnel.[6]

Treating Casualties

Treating casualties of terrorist attacks can test the management and organization of emergency services, particularly when there is a mass casualty event. Most countries have mass casualty plans in place and conduct regular simulations, drills, or exercises. These training maneuvers often involve first-responders attending a mock mass casualty situation, testing their ability to effectively allocate casualties to hospitals, and evaluate hospital capacity to deal with the event.

Individual nations have tended to develop emergency plans that focus on certain types of mass casualty events based on a risk assessment (see Chapter 13), thus paying a smaller amount of attention to less likely events. A short comparison of the United States and United Kingdom illustrates these practices.

Hospitals and medical centers in the United States are mandated to have an action plan in place for possible terrorist attacks. Interestingly, most of the planning is centered on mass casualty events involving a nuclear, biological, chemical, or radiological attack. The purpose of such an action plan is to be able to recognize and respond to the radiation fallout, or the type of disease, or the kind of chemical from the attack, and to have the capability to identify the areas of contamination and establish places to treat those contaminated.[7]

Chemical attacks have been more prominent in Iraq, Syria, and Afghanistan. Pesticides and chlorine have been the most common types of chemicals used in these attacks. As of 2017, the United States had not had a chemical or biological attack since 2001, when a series of anthrax-coated letters were sent to several individuals. Despite there being only a few chemical attacks on US soil, the United States seems predominantly concerned with nuclear, chemical, biological, and radiological attacks, and the associated human impact these types of attacks would have. Containment and treatment readiness for such attacks form the focus of its terrorism preparedness. (Canada also has an emphasis on planning for pandemics, as well as nuclear, chemical, biological, and radiological attacks rather than other possible mass casualty events such as bombings or mass shootings.)

In the United Kingdom, the National Health Service has taken a slightly different approach from that the United States. It has focused more on historical acts, using events such as the Manchester bombing and London Bridge attack in 2017 to steer its planning. The UK has adopted a system-learning approach, which means understanding and gathering information about each part of the health system's role in dealing with a mass casualty event. It relies on understanding what lessons can be learned from these events through a process that includes debriefing personnel from many health organizations. The UK commonly undertakes simulation exercises to test its systems and the preparedness of its staff.[8]

Psychological Damage

The psychological impact of a terrorist attack upon its victims is complicated. In some ways the psychological impact has a wider effect on society—spreading beyond primary and secondary victims and into the consciousness of a nation. Recall the first pillar of terrorism: "kill one, frighten ten thousand."

On an individual level, the most well-known psychological impacts are the Stockholm and the Lima syndromes. The Stockholm syndrome occurs when the hostage develops a sense of care about and connectedness to the captor.[9] The Stockholm syndrome was first described in 1973 when four hostages were taken during a bank robbery in Stockholm, Sweden. After the hostages were released they refused to testify against their captors.

Another example of this kind of syndrome was the abduction of Patricia (Patty) Campbell Hearst on April 15, 1974. Taken by the US domestic terrorist group the Symbionese Liberation Army, Hearst joined the group and took part in a bank robbery (see Figure 8.1).

The Lima syndrome is the opposite of the Stockholm syndrome. It is when the captor develops sympathy for the hostages. It is called the Lima syndrome after a Japanese ambassador to Peru was released by his captors when they had reportedly developed sympathy for him. The Lima syndrome can occur for many reasons, including the

Courtesy of the Federal Bureau of Investigation

Figure 8.1 Surveillance camera photograph of the San Francisco bank robbery by Patty Hearst (right), assault rifle in hand, with Symbionese Liberation Army member Donald DeFreeze (left), on April 15, 1974.

captive developing feelings for the hostage or simply losing the desire to inflict suffering on the hostage.

Most studies on the psychological impacts on terrorism victims agree that the influence of these human-caused disasters results in altering the victims' worldview. It is suggested that a terrorist event can change a person in many ways. According to research, a terrorist attack challenges the victims' beliefs about themselves and the world around them.[10]

A study undertaken by Mahwish Sabir and Naeem Aslam into the psychological impact of suicide terrorist bombings on victims found that 80 percent no longer liked crowded places and considered such situation a threat to their safety. Of those sampled, 58 percent lost interest in enjoyable activities. Others had repetitive thoughts about the suicide bombing. The underlining theme of the study was that these victims suffered post-traumatic stress disorder and other forms of anxiety that were not present before the attack.[11] Post-traumatic stress disorder is caused by a traumatic event. The symptoms may include flashbacks of the event, guilt or loneliness, insomnia, and unwanted thoughts, along with emotional detachment from others.[12] Other psychological injuries may include victims viewing themselves as pawns in a larger power-play between the government and militant organizations. It is a perception that fits within a greater sense of powerlessness many victims of terrorism feel.

While mass casualty events serve the terrorists' objective by instilling fear for political gain, smaller but more brutal attacks also meet this objective. In this instance casualties do not have to be high in number, but rather it is the manner of victims' injury or death that has significant impact. Videos of beheadings, throats being cut, individuals locked in cages and set on fire, or wearing necklace bombs show that even an event involving a single victim still has the ability to inflict psychological stress on a wide population.

Malicious executions conducted by terrorists impact not only a local area but also the global community. In some respects, the scale of physical attacks does not have the same level of impact as a brutal beheading seen internationally. The tactic of distributing these brutal images leads the group toward meeting its objective of forcing a population to question their government's ability to protect them from a similar gruesome death. If a terrorist act can make a population question its government's ability to provide security, then the terrorists are on the road to achieving their aim of destabilizing society.

Global Perspectives

One of the more significant challenges to treating victims of terrorism is establishing an internationally balanced approach. Such an approach should recognize the rights and needs of terrorism victims irrespective of their nationality. The United Nations has been instrumental in developing such an approach, one that focuses on the social, physical, and psychological needs of victims.

Under the UN's guidance, international conventions have been developed to provide victims of terrorism with the same rights and protections afforded to victims of crimes in general. As a precursor for acknowledging the rights of terror victims, the UN had to ensure that nations recognized terrorism as a crime. The UN's declaration Basic Principals of Justice for Victims of Crime and Abuse of Power[13] set the standard. The declaration established principles for treating victims of crimes that member states were encouraged to adopt. From that initial set of principles grew an acknowledgment that victims of terrorism may require additional support, greater than victims of general crime. These included medical treatment with specialized psychological therapies, relocation where required, along with economic compensation and institutional support.

Terrorist acts have a strong international component. Consequently, victims of terrorism can be widespread. However, most states do not make a distinction between national and foreign victims of terror. In many instances, they fail to appreciate that some victims will not understand the state's judicial systems and the way a state may investigate a terrorist attack. States also have divergent approaches to addressing the rights of victims. The corollary is that information is important for foreign victims of terrorism regarding victim support services and the judicial processes that follow.

Solidarity as Institutional Support

A difference between victims of a terrorist attack and victims of crime is the strong public displays of solidarity that occur after a terrorist attack. The United Nations has identified this as an important part of institutional support and has called for more expressions of global solidarity when supporting victims of terrorism. Expression of solidarity can be made through commemorating victims. Institutional support can also be extended by improving media coverage of terrorist attacks.

Traditionally, there has been a perception that media coverage tends to almost myopically focus on the acts of the terrorist and governmental responses. Victims tend to be more of a statistic, and the human face of victims is not always given importance. Nevertheless, this has changed. Bodies like the UN are encouraging the media to rethink their training of journalists, and how they approach coverage of terrorist attacks,[14] to emphasize the human aspects of victimization.

Victims and Perceptions of Bias

While statistics on victims of terrorism fail to show the humanity of attacks, they do have the benefit of highlighting realities of what could be described as mass hysteria. Within the Western world, there is an exaggerated concern about the possibility of terror attacks, but for the most part this concern does not reflect the real risks. Statistics published by the Global Terrorist Database, which is part of Maryland University, suggest that terrorist attacks in Western Europe account for less than 1 percent of total terrorist victims. Of the approximately 35,000 deaths from terrorism in 2016, 269 were in Western Europe, compared to about 19,000—or 55 percent—of victims who resided in the Middle East and North Africa.[15] Global Terrorist Database statistics also highlight that most terrorist attacks take place in Muslim countries. From 2001 to 2015, 75 percent of terrorist fatalities occurred in just twenty-five Muslim countries.

Other university studies suggest that media reports of terrorist activities are more extensively publicized when the perpetrator is Muslim. A university study found that between 2011 and 2015 there was a 449 percent increase in media attention for a terrorist attack taking place in the United States when the terrorist was identified as a Muslim.[16] Further, the study found that during the period 2011 to 2015, Muslims were responsible for only 12.4 percent of terrorist attacks in the United States, but attracted 41.4 percent of news coverage.[17] According to the study, there was a preoccupation with Muslim-associated terrorism and a failure to apply the same level of media attention to non-Muslim terrorist attacks.

Underpinning some of the media commentary on victims is a view that there is a bias toward (or newsworthiness toward) white or European terrorist victims rather than those in Africa and the Middle East. Whether it is racial bias, the unusualness of attacks in the United States and Western Europe, or the cultural connections between the victims and Western society, it remains a phenomenon worth noting. As an example, in 2017 a car bomb killed 300 Somalis in Mogadishu, but there was not the same level of solidarity after the Somali bombing as there was after previous terrorist attacks that had taken place in Europe and the United States. After the attack in Nice, France, Facebook and other social media sites displayed the French national flag in global solidarity. Such sentiment was not replicated after the Mogadishu bombing, which claimed more lives.

Survivors and Compensation

The need to compensate victims recovering from a terrorist attack has become an important policy position. Governments have responded to victims' needs by establishing victim funds and legislative frameworks to foster civil action against terrorist organizations as well as their supporters. In Australia, victims of terrorism, both domestically and abroad, can apply for compensation from the federal government. Payments of up to A$75,000 are made to Australians who have been victimized by a terrorist attack.

Until 9/11, the United States did not have specific compensation schemes. Prior to 9/11, victims such as those of the Unabomber and the Oklahoma Bomber were not given access to government compensation; it was left to insurance companies to address. However, after the 9/11 attacks, there was an outpouring of support, with one in three Americans sending donations for victims and their families. This led the US government to introduce the September 11 Victim Compensation Fund, the first government program established to compensate the victims of terrorism.[18]

Since then the United States has introduced a fund for victims of state-sponsored terrorism that provides compensation for this type of attack. According to fund administrators, as of 2017 approximately US$1 billion has been given to victims. In the UK, victims of terrorist attacks can apply for compensation through the regular process for victims of crime. The UK Red Cross has also established a Solidarity Fund, designed to assist victims of terrorism in that country.

Meanwhile, in Canada there is a scheme that is implemented through the nation's Justice for Victims Act. The act allows for lawsuits to be brought by victims against terrorist groups and those supporting terrorism.

Event-Based Terrorism and Societal Victimization

Event-based terrorism comprises acts that destroy an important piece of infrastructure or cultural heritage. The impact can have a profound psychological effect on people, not just around the destruction site, but also farther afield. For example, in 2001 the Taliban in Afghanistan destroyed a 1,700-year-old sandstone statue of Buddha using explosives. The destruction of the Buddhas of Bamiyan was ordered by a Taliban leader who had directed that all non-Islamic statues be destroyed.

In 2016, Islamic State of Syria made a similar directive for similar reasons and wrecked the remains of a 3,000-year-old Mesopotamian city's statues and temples in Iraq using explosives, hammers, and bulldozers. The rationale for such destruction is not simply a reaction against religious idolatry. It has deeper significance. By removing cultural and historical artifacts, terrorists are attacking the identity of communities.[19]

Attacking critical infrastructure (even without loss of life) also has a psychological impact on society. Targeting power stations, gas supplies, and water reservoirs not only disrupts everyday life and economic activities but also leaves victims with a sense of fear and anger. Terrorism is effective when it causes people to be concerned about their security. When that concern manifests itself into changes in government policies that impact people's way of life—or makes society more hypervigilant—then terrorism has achieved its goal.

Cyber-terrorism is an example of politically motivated attacks that can instill fear and anger without taking life. Some studies suggest that the anxieties generated from a cyber attack (even without casualties) are only marginally less than from a physical terrorist attack with casualties.[20]

Victim Politics

The political effects of terrorism on victims may appear contentious but still require acknowledgment. There are two distinct yet related aspects: political views or rhetoric of victims, and politicians. First is a change in political outlook experienced by the victims of terrorism and their families. Psychological studies have documented this changed attitude, identifying that victims tend to support more authoritarian policies to counter terrorism after experiencing an attack[21] even if it is at the expense of civil liberties or personal free-doms. The second aspect is the manner in which politicians describe terrorist victims; it is suggested that such descriptions are emotive to galvanize support for other political agendas.

Victims' Change in Political Outlook

A 2012 study by Eitan Hersh of Yale University examined changes in the political outlook of survivors and relatives of the 9/11 terrorist attacks. The study found an increase in political participation, includ-ing donations made to favored candidates, and an increase in sur-vivors or families taking part in the candidate nomination process. The study also found that survivors shifted toward voting for a more conservative leadership.[22] The swing was described as the conserva-tive shift hypothesis—meaning a shift toward religiosity, patriotism, and even militarism.[23] The conservative shift is also evident in the way many Americans accepted increased security measures that were often in opposition to liberal democratic ideals.

Victims Galvanize Support

Politicians have been accused of using terrorist victims to further their own agendas. Social critics and media opinion have explored this issue. It is a twofold observation. First, politicians have used an event to pursue an existing issue—for example, they may suggest that unchecked immigration has led to people with radical beliefs entering the country and committing terrorist acts, or that with more guns in citizens' hands a terrorist act could have been prevented.

Underlining the politicization of victimization is the schism created within society because people either support the premise or reject it. This naturally divides society, which incidentally is also the objective of terrorism. More important, using victims to promote a political position takes attention away from the impact of terrorism on the victim.

The second observation about the politicization of victims is the way this can be used to quash dissent. Again using 9/11 as an example, legislation like the Patriot Act and the various surveillance acts were passed into law with little opposition. Any debate about the long-term ramifications of these laws was viewed in the direct aftermath of the attacks as unpatriotic and associated with being unsupportive of victims as well as first-responders who risked their lives to save those injured.

Study Questions

1. Discuss several ways terrorists adhere to the pillar "kill one, frighten ten thousand" in their acts.
2. Describe what is event-based terrorism.
3. Describe the types of psychological disorders that can be experienced by people who are apprehensive about a terrorist attack.
4. List some of the key ideas put forth by the United Nations to improve the standing of victims of terrorism.

Learning Activity

Examine compensation legislation in your country for victims of terrorism. Provide a written critique that includes background for the compensation (include what victims are entitled to), the governing legislation, and the requirements victims must demonstrate to be eligible.

Notes

1. Alex Schmid, "Strengthening the Role of Victims and Incorporating Victims in Efforts to Counter Violent Extremism and Terrorism," (The Hague: International Centre for Counter-Terrorism, August 2012), 2.

2. Schmid, "Strengthening the Role of Victims," 2.

3. Global Terrorism Database, http://www.start.umd.edu/gtd.

4. Statista, https://www.statista.com/statistics/271514/global-terrorism-index.

5. James L. Regens, Amy Schultheiss, and Nick Mould, "Regional Variation in Causes of Injuries Among Terrorism Victims for Mass Casualty Events," *Front Public Health* 3 (2015), 198.

6. Regens, Schultheiss, and Mould, "Regional Variation in Causes of Injuries Among Terrorism Victims."

7. Federal Emergency Management Agency (FEMA), *Managing the Consequences of Terrorist Incidents: Interim Planning Guide* (Washington, DC, July 2002), 10–14.

8. C. Moran, K. Brohi, M. Smith, and K. Willet, "Lessons in Planning from a Mass Casualty Event in U.K.," *British Medical Journal* 359 (2017).

9. Michael Adorjan, Tony Christensen, Benjamin Kelly, and Dorothy Pawluch, "Stockholm Syndrome as Vernacular Resource," *Sociological Quarterly* 53, no. 3 (2012).

10. M. Sabir and N. Aslam, "Impact of Suicide Bombing on the Cognitions of Victims," *Journal of Behavioural Sciences* 21, no. 1 (2011).

11. Sabir and Aslam, "Impact of Suicide Bombing."

12. S. Regal and S. Joseph, *Post-Traumatic Stress* (Oxford: Oxford University Press, 2010), 1.

13. Cited in United Nations, *The Criminal Justice Response to Support Victims of Acts of Terrorism,* rev. ed. (New York, 2012).

14. United Nations Secretary-General, *First Global Symposium on Supporting Victims of Terrorism* (New York, September 9, 2008).

15. Global Terrorism Database, http://www.start.umd.edu/gtd.

16. Erin Kearns, Allison Betus, and Anthony Lemieux, "Why Do Some Terrorist Attacks Receive More Media Attention Than Others?" March 5, 2017, https://ssrn.com/abstract=2928138.

17. Kearns, Betus, and Lemieux, "Why Do Some Terrorist Attacks Receive More Media Attention Than Others?"

18. L. Dixon, "Compensation Policies for Victims of Terrorism," *RAND Review* (Summer 2002).

19. H. Silverman and D. Ruggles, *Cultural Heritage and Human Rights* (Singapore: Springer Singapore, 2008), 3–29.

20. M. L. Gross and D. R. Vashdi, "The Psychological Effects of Cyber Terrorism," *Bulletin of the Atomic Scientists* 72, no. 5 (2016).

21. E. D. Hersh, "Long-Term Effect of September 11 on the Political Behavior of Victims' Families and Neighbors," *Proceedings of the National Academy of Sciences of the United States of America* 110, no. 52 (2013).

22. Hersh, "Long-Term Effect of September 11."

23. George A. Bonanno and John T. Jost. "Conservative Shift Among High-Exposure Survivors of the September 11th Terrorist Attacks," *Basic and Applied Social Psychology* 28, no. 4 (2006).

Part 2
Counterterrorism

9

Counterterrorism and the Rule of Law

At the end of the nineteenth century, the world faced a challenge to the authority of the state—anarchism. The movement began in tsarist Russia and then spread across Europe. The anarchist philosophy was underpinned by violence under the guise of "propaganda by deed." The 1880s saw a series of assassinations and bombings that were designed to terrorize the ruling classes of society, for example, the 1881 assassination of Tsar Alexander II.

The turning point appears to have been the December 9, 1893, bombing of the French Chamber of Deputies by anarchist Auguste Vaillant, which injured twenty deputies. This resulted in what could be argued were the first anti-terrorism laws. These laws restricted freedom of expression, which was viewed as the mechanism to the incitement of violence.

From Europe, anarchists took their movement to the United States. Yet, having seen what was taking place across the Atlantic, the United States was keen to avoid the same civil unrest. In the early 1900s, the government instructed immigration inspectors to question those arriving from Europe whether they were anarchists. If a potential immigrant answered yes, they likely were sent back to their country of birth.

However, it was not until 1934 that a global approach to the issue was instigated. That year, the League of Nations developed a convention on terrorism that was later adopted in 1937 (but never entered into force). Known as the Convention for the Prevention and Punishment of Terrorism, it was the first international attempt to apply legislative controls to the problem.[1] At present, there are nineteen conventions that address various aspects of terrorism.

International Conventions

The term *convention* covers several legal instruments, such as agreements, contracts, pacts, and treaties. When international parties want to agree on a course of action, or when inaction is warranted, or when they want to codify the situations that they seek to avoid or to have happen, some form of legal agreement is drafted. When the parties are nation-states, a convention is the instrument they use.

Since 1963, under the auspices of the United Nations and the International Atomic Energy Agency, nineteen conventions have been formed to specifically address acts of terrorism. These conventions can be categorized by the terrorist activity that they aim to prevent: (1) harm to civil aviation; (2) harm to protected persons; (3) the taking of hostages; (4) acquisition of nuclear material, and harm to nuclear facilities; (5) harm to maritime navigation; (6) untraceable plastic explosives; (7) harm to the public from bombings; and (8) financing of terrorist operations.

The conventions relating to civil aviation address such issues as offenses committed aboard an aircraft, the seizure of an aircraft (air piracy), and jeopardizing onboard safety. In order of their passage, they are

- The 1963 Convention of Offenses and Certain Other Acts Committed On Board Aircraft.
- The 1970 Convention for the Suppression of Unlawful Seizures of Aircraft.
- The 1971 Convention for the Suppression of Unlawful Acts Against the Safety of Civil Aviation.
- The 1988 Protocol for the Suppression of Unlawful Acts of Violence at Airports Serving International Civil Aviation (a supplement to the preceding 1971 convention.
- The 2010 Convention on the Suppression of Unlawful Acts Relating to International Civil Aviation.

- The 2010 Protocol Supplementary to the Convention for the Suppression of Unlawful Seizure of Aircraft.
- The 2014 Protocol to Amend the Convention on Offenses and Certain Other Acts Committed On Board Aircraft.

Of the four conventions relating to maritime terrorism, two address fixed ocean platforms. This is understandable given the vulnerability these installations pose, as well as the world's reliance on the energy they supply and the environmental damage that would result from an oil spill—for example, the 2010 Deepwater Horizon oil spill in the Gulf of Mexico resulted in an uncontrolled discharge of an estimated 210 million gallons of oil. Another convention addresses acts of piracy in a similar way that the aviation conventions address air piracy. The fourth convention criminalizes the use of a ship as a means of committing an act of terrorism (see Figure 9.1) or using a vessel to transport material used for terrorism or persons engaged in terrorism.

Courtesy of the US Navy.

Figure 9.1   The USS *Cole* was attacked by suicide terrorists using a small fiberglass boat to deliver their bomb. The explosion crippled the vessel and killed seventeen sailors while it was in Aden harbor, Yemen.

The four maritime-related conventions are

- The 1988 Convention for the Suppression of Unlawful Acts Against the Safety of Maritime Navigation.
- The 1988 Protocol for the Suppression of Unlawful Acts Against the Safety of Fixed Platforms Located on the Continental Shelf.
- The 2005 Protocol to the Convention for the Suppression of Unlawful Acts Against the Safety of Maritime Navigation.
- The 2005 Protocol to the Protocol for the Suppression of Unlawful Acts Against the Safety of Fixed Platforms Located on the Continental Shelf.

Three UN conventions provide for the protection of nuclear material. One criminalizes the theft of nuclear material or its transfer to groups who could use it to cause death or injury, or to destroy property. It also criminalizes groups possessing nuclear material. The second convention (which is a set of amendments) requires states that have nuclear material to ensure that it is safeguarded, in this way making it more difficult for terrorist groups to steal or bribe, blackmail, coerce, or otherwise facilitate the transfer of this material to themselves. It also requires states to cooperate in quickly locating and recovering any material that is stolen or smuggled. The third convention addresses a range of potential terrorist acts and targets, including nuclear power plants and nuclear reactors. These three nuclear conventions are

- The 1980 Convention on the Physical Protection of Nuclear Material.
- The 2005 amendments to the 1980 convention with title change that reflects a new emphasis: Convention on the Physical Protection of Nuclear Material and Nuclear Facilities.
- The 2005 International Convention for the Suppression of Acts of Nuclear Terrorism.

The other five United Nations conventions that have been developed by the General Assembly address specific issues that are mirrored in their titles:

- The 1973 Convention on the Prevention and Punishment of Crimes Against Internationally Protected Persons.

- The 1979 International Convention Against the Taking of Hostages.
- The 1991 Convention on the Marking of Plastic Explosives for the Purpose of Detection.
- The 1997 International Convention for the Suppression of Terrorist Bombings.
- The 1999 International Convention for the Suppression of the Financing of Terrorism.

Over the decades, there have been many thoughts about creating an international counterterrorism strike force to deal with terrorist incidents. After the terrorist attacks of September 11, 2001, these thoughts were revived. The reality of forming an international operational force along the lines of the fictional United Network Command for Law and Enforcement of the 1960s (*The Man from U.N.C.L.E.*)[2] is mired in insurmountable political difficulties. Therefore, no such force has ever been established.

Although the UN General Assembly has passed nineteen conventions placing legal obligations on states to act in certain ways, there is no operational enforcement arm. To bridge this void, the UN Security Council passed two resolutions[3] that created the organization's Counter-Terrorism Committee. The Counter-Terrorism Committee supports United Nations member states in preventing terrorist acts within their borders, as well as internationally. It does not provide direct operational assistance but does facilitate briefings, meetings, consultations, and country visits, and distributes reports submitted by member states. For instance, the Counter-Terrorism Committee's operational arm is the Counter-Terrorism Committee Executive Directorate, which conducts country visits to assess member states' counterterrorism plans, processes, and procedures, and whatever technical assistance might be needed to maintain peace and security.

Of course, there are international treaties other than those passed by the United Nations. Take as an example the 2005 Protocol to the Council of Europe Convention on the Prevention of Terrorism, which makes certain acts criminal offenses. These acts include being part of a group engaged in terrorism, being trained in terrorist tactics, traveling overseas to participate in acts of terrorism, and financing such travel. The protocol also places an obligation on states to share counterterrorism information on a timely basis.[4]

In addition, there are regional conventions. To mention a few, there are conventions signed by the Commonwealth of Independent States,[5] the Organization of American States, the Organization of African Union, the League of Arab States, and the Organization of the Islamic Conference. The conventions signed by these parties address similar issues to those of the UN, but have a regional focus, underscoring regional cooperation.

National Laws and Domestic Policies

It would be difficult to provide an exhaustive discussion on all nations' counterterrorism laws and domestic policies. To better understand the scope of such laws and to appreciate how these legal approaches play their part in dealing with terrorism, an illustrative survey will suffice.

It is reasonable to say that every country has its own political system that is integral to its legal system. Regardless of individual variations, these systems recognize that terrorism is a form of violence that threatens to undermine the stability of societies. The political aspects of governing are often at the center of how national laws are crafted. When the term *political* is used, it is a catchall concept that can include political philosophy but also economic issues, religious issues, cultural and racial issues, historical events and grievances, and so on. It is a broad term covering many issues that impact societal power and influence.

There are important elements in law that provide insight into how countries view terrorism and how they have gone about crafting a legal framework for its prevention and treatment. To begin such a survey, it would be beneficial to look at these key legal elements from a regional perspective of selected countries from North America, Western Europe, and Australasia.

United States

The US political system is built upon a federation of fifty states comprising three branches of government in a check-and-balance arrangement: executive, legislative, and judicial. International treaties, like the UN's counterterrorism conventions, must be ratified by the Congress (the national legislature). Congress is the body that makes and passes laws, so it is at the heart of debating what laws need to be enacted and what form they should take.

The centerpiece of domestic law in the United States is the Uniting and Strengthening America by Providing Appropriate Tools Required to Intercept and Obstruct Terrorism Act of 2001, also known as the Patriot Act. The thrust of the legislation is to increase the nation's law enforcement and security services to prevent terrorism. The act does this in several ways by providing additional authority to the president, the military, and the Federal Bureau of Investigation when critical terrorist circumstances arise.

The legislation targets key issues that are crucial to terrorists' operations: identifying suspects and verifying their backgrounds; financing operations; funds transfer; communications between members; aiding of terrorists (e.g., safehouses, transport, false documentation, weapons, etc.); protecting critical infrastructure; and espionage. The act has also increased law enforcement agencies' ability to investigate suspected cases of terrorism and conduct investigation into terrorism incidents. By way of example, the US Secret Service has been granted authority to investigate criminal activity at the center of terrorism—financing. Under the act, the Secret Service can investigate a range of fraud activities, such as false identity documents, computer fraud, and fraud directed at financial institutions.

The act takes a wide view of what is needed to address terrorism by incorporating intelligence gathering and the ability of intelligence agencies to share these data with foreign partners (e.g., the Five Eyes countries—Australia, Canada, New Zealand, the United Kingdom, and the United States—as well as other allied nations). It also addresses several associated criminal issues that, although not specific to terrorism, have an overlay sufficient to warrant remedial legal redress: compensation to victims and victims' families, grants to first-responders to improve their capabilities, attacks on mass transport systems, racketeering, cyber-crime, and other issues.

Italy

Italy is an interesting case study. After the Allies defeated Mussolini's Fascist Party during World War II, the country experienced decades of moderate rule under the leadership of the Christian Democrats. However, the country was being pulled by extremist elements within government by the Communist Party and the Socialist

"There is an international disease which feeds on the notion that if you have a cause to defend, you can use any means to further your cause, since the end justifies the means. As an international community, we must oppose this notion, whether it be in Canada, in the United States, or anywhere else. No cause justifies violence as long as the system provides for change by peaceful means."

—*US president Richard M. Nixon,*
from a speech in October 1970[6]

Party, and outside government by groups associated with far-right and far-left politics.

During a fourteen-year period that stretched from 1968 to 1982, there was a wave of terrorist activity that became known as Anni di Piombo, or the Years of Lead. The term is said to have been coined because it was symbolic of the bullets that were fired on both sides of the conflict. The Italian government passed a number of terrorism laws during this time. Prominent were the laws that allowed the search and arrest of persons without the mandate of an investigative judge. This occurred under the Reale Act of 1975. The act's focus was on preventing incitement to racial violence and racist hatred, as well as public displays of symbols of racist organizations.

The other piece of legislation worth noting concerns preventive detention—custody in jail. Although law enforcement authorities could hold a person in preventive detention for up to two years if the alleged crime could attract a prison sentence of over twenty years, and up to one year if the sentence could attract jail time of less than twenty years, in 1970 the law was changed by a decree that increased the time a person could be held. In 1974 another law extended this to twelve years from first appearance to final judgment.

A number of circumstances were covered under these precautionary-custody functions. For instance, the state could hold a person if it was considered they were about to commit an act of terrorism. Or they could be held if their prior offenses were such that they posed a danger to society, or if after serving a sentence, there was evidence their release placed society in danger of future crimes.

These laws may seem to contravene Italian constitutional limitations, especially after the totalitarian experience of Mussolini's rule. However, the Italian legal system has a safeguard in what is known as the legality principle. It is a principle that examines the proportionality of actions by way of judicial review.

Australia

The Australian Parliament passed several important pieces of legislation in 2004 and 2005 that aimed to strengthen the nation's existing counterterrorism laws. In 2004, three bills passed into law that provided for the extension of a fixed period for conducting criminal investigations into suspected terrorism offenses and allowed law enforcement agencies to delay a suspect's questioning so that overseas inquiries could be made to obtain information. These amendments to the criminal and procedural codes came with several civil libertarian safeguards: (1) the right to legal counsel, an interpreter, or a consular representation; (2) the right to remain silent; (3) any admission or confession must be recorded; and (4) the right to have a copy of all interviews.

Two other bills followed. The first addressed several weaknesses in allied legislation by (1) making it an offense to associate with a member of a listed terrorist organization; (2) enhancing forensic procedural laws to help investigate a terrorist attack (see Figure 9.2); (3) giving powers to police and intelligence agencies to compel a person to surrender their Australian and foreign passports; and (4) allowing the attorney general to make certain terrorism-related decisions that were exempt from earlier legal provisions.

After the passage of these bills into law in 2005, the Australian Parliament passed the Anti-Terrorism Act. This act was drafted to hinder terrorists in the country. The enactment of this legislation stemmed from the London attacks of July 7, 2005, and provided law enforcement agencies the ability to intervene in the planning and execution stages of a terrorist attack. The 2005 legislation allowed authorities to use preventive detention to stop terrorist acts in progress and question suspects to obtain intelligence that might lead to disruption of further terrorist acts. The changes also allowed for control orders to restrict suspects from associating with others who might aid an attack. These orders can be viewed as "jails without walls" because they restrict liberties rather than deprive of liberties.

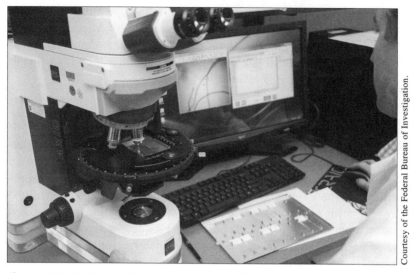

Courtesy of the Federal Bureau of Investigation.

Figure 9.2   Enhanced forensic procedural laws assist terrorist investigations.

Other amendments to Australian laws made funding terrorist activities an offense and allowed law enforcers to obtain detailed information about a suspect, such as travel details, telephone records, and financial transactions. These legislative changes made terrorist-inspired hoaxes more serious offenses because of the disruption they can cause to society.

Military Law and Doctrine

In war there are laws that govern armed conflict between nation-states. These laws are contained in the Geneva Conventions of 1949 and their Additional Protocols. Although detailed, the basic principles state that "the wounded and sick, POWs [prisoners of war] and civilians are to be protected; military targets must be attacked in such a manner as to keep civilian casualties and damage to a minimum; humanitarian and peacekeeping personnel must be respected; neutral or non-belligerent states have certain rights and duties; and the use of certain weapons (including chemical weapons) is prohibited, as also are other means and methods of warfare that cause unnecessary suffering."[7]

These laws adhere to the legal concepts of *jus in bello* and *jus ad bellum*. The former captures the legal arguments that govern the ways in which wars are conducted. The latter governs the reasons a country chooses to go to war. *Jus in bello* is synonymous with humanitarian law. *Jus ad bellum* is the precept that sets out the intentions for waging a war. Under *jus ad bellum,* a war cannot be initiated to annex territory or to facilitate a political regime change. However, this legal principle evolved after 9/11 to include what is termed *anticipatory self-defense.* Such actions include preemptive strikes. These tactics are similar to domestic law enforcement agencies' ability to intervene in the planning or execution phases of an attack. In the United States, this addition to *jus ad bellum*—justifying the use of preemptive war—is regularly referred to as the Bush Doctrine. The doctrine posits that states that support terrorists, or provide them sanctuary, are to be deemed criminal, like the terrorists themselves. In June 2003, then–vice president Dick Cheney stated, "Before 9/11, all too many nations tended to draw a distinction between the terrorist groups and the states that provided these groups with support. They were unwilling to hold these terror-sponsoring states accountable for their actions. . . . [T]he distinction between the terrorists and their sponsors should no longer stand."[8]

War between nation-states has a long and established body of law that guides conflict. But with nonstate actors, like terrorists, military units have had to develop a new body of principles to assist them in meeting their national security obligations—these principles are termed *military doctrine.*

Military doctrine is a set of principles that cover many aspects of military affairs. Like laws, these principles dictate how military forces should engage hostile challenges, under what circumstances, and to what degree. Regarding terrorism, military doctrine guides military units in their prosecution of the wider national security objectives. Doctrine can be viewed in several ways, but for simplicity it can be categorized as policies and procedures relating to tactics and techniques.

There are nine tenets of war: "objective, offensive, mass, economy of force, maneuver, unity of command, security, surprise, and simplicity."[9] However, when the military is tasked with confronting nonstate actors, these traditional canons need to be placed alongside *legitimacy.* In this sense, legitimacy is the set of legal and moral conditions that allow hostilities to take place. It also includes the authority of those directing the military as well as the military units themselves.

Integral to legitimacy are the tenets of balance and precision. Balance applies to military actions that are appropriate to the scale and type of threat being addressed. Precision refers to limiting collateral damage. Together these principles help strengthen the military's legitimacy.

Human Rights Issues Involving Terrorism

It might seem odd to discuss human rights in a chapter that deals with legislative approaches to counterterrorism. Human rights are the values inherent in every person. Human rights do not consider issues such as personal background or sexual orientation; country of birth; color of skin; what religion people do or do not believe in; or political views.

When we consider these personal values, it becomes apparent that human rights are intrinsically tied to counterterrorism laws. This is because terrorists directly target a range of human rights. The objective of terrorism is to undermine the legitimate authority of the state by unpredictable acts of violence against civilian populations. Therefore, terrorism undermines, first and foremost, the right to life. Terrorism also violates peoples' right to nondiscrimination because, for instance, they are citizens of a certain country, they are part of a religious community, or they are women and girls.

Terrorism violates other human rights: the right to a fair trial because of attacks on police, law courts, and lawyers. It challenges a person's freedom to express their beliefs through religion. It prevents people from feeling free to express themselves and share information. Because terrorism targets public spaces, it seeks to curtail a person's freedom to assemble and associate with like-minded people. And terrorism inhibits a person's right to participate in the political process.

The move to use legislative controls to address terrorism is a logical method for a civilized country that honors the rule of law. Nevertheless, legal steps to control terrorism are a double-edged sword; they may help prevent terrorism, but they may also jeopardize human rights. Take, as an example, a law that allows law enforcement officers to hold a suspect in preventive detention. If legislative safeguards are not enacted alongside such a provision, it could erode a person's right not to be subjected to arbitrary detention. More precarious is the issue of the right to freedom of expression. By limiting a person's ability to express their political thoughts, laws infringe on freedom of speech, thought, and expression. It is a fine line between allowing such a freedom and limiting a terrorist to incite hatred and inspire violence in the name of their cause.

Other issues that require legislators to think carefully before passing laws include the right of people to have freedom of movement, to have privacy, and not to be discriminated against (e.g., racial profiling). There is clearly a need for laws to protect a nation's population from security threats, but these laws need to be cognizant of human rights.

Study Questions

1. Explain what is meant by an international convention.
2. List three international conventions regarding terrorism and explain the intent of each.
3. Explain the difference between international conventions and domestic laws.
4. Explain what is meant by military doctrine in relation to terrorism.

Learning Activity

Research the domestic counterterrorism laws for a European country not discussed in the chapter (e.g., France, Germany, Poland, Spain, Denmark). Summarize the provisions of that country's central or prominent piece of legislation regarding terrorism and discuss how these provisions help inhibit terrorism. Also identify the safeguards written into the legislation to ensure human rights are not violated in the process of defending national security.

Notes

1. Lyal S. Sunga, *The Emerging System of International Criminal Law: Developments in Codification and Implementation* (The Hague: Kluwer Law International, 1997).

2. Jon Heitland, *The Man From U.N.C.L.E. Book: The Behind-the-Scenes Story of a Television Classic* (New York: St. Martin's, 1987).

3. UN Resolution 1373 (2001), which created the Counter-Terrorism Committee, and UN Resolution 1624 (2005), which condemned all acts of terrorism.

4. Council of Europe, *Convention on the Prevention of Terrorism,* Treaty Series no. 196 (Warsaw, 2005).

5. Also known as the Russian Commonwealth, which comprises the states that were once part of the Soviet Union before its dissolution on December 26, 1991.

6. Cited in Chairman of the Joint Chiefs of Staff, *Antiterrorism,* Joint Publication no. 3-07.2 (Washington, DC: US Department of Defense, 2010), II-1.

7. Adam Roberts, "Counter-Terrorism, Armed Force, and the Laws of War," *Survival* 44, no. 1 (Spring 2002), 8.

8. Richard (Dick) Cheney, cited in "Vice President Tells West Point Cadets 'Bush Doctrine' Is Serious," *Department of Defense News,* June 2, 2003.

9. Chairman of the Joint Chiefs of Staff, *Antiterrorism,* II-1.

10

Law Enforcement and the Military

To avoid the civil unrest caused by terrorism, continental Europe and the United States passed laws that restricted inciting violence. During the late 1800s and early 1900s lawmakers passed various legal statutes and in 1934 the League of Nations passed the first convention that heralded a global approach to the issue.

Laws are a necessary framework for civil governance. Nevertheless laws cannot prevent acts of violence or any other form of behavior on their own. Laws act to guide people in what is expected of a civil society. If a person decides to act in a contrary way, the mechanism for preventing, intervening, and bringing this person to justice is an enforcement agency.

Domestic law enforcement is performed by police, but there are many other agencies that have law enforcement, regulatory, and compliance responsibilities. Combined, these agencies prevent crime as well as investigate crimes that have occurred. International laws are enforced by law enforcement agencies working with overseas jurisdictions and the military—for example, interdiction at sea by naval forces. The way this is done can be categorized as defensive measures and offensive strategies.

The term *counterterrorism* is in widespread use and describes defensive countermeasures. For some reason, it is used instead of the term *anti-terrorism,* which strictly speaking is the correct term for this activity. Counterterrorism involves offensive measures taken to "prevent, deter, pre-empt, and respond to terrorism,"[1] so the more accurate term should be *anti-terrorism*.

Regardless, the term *counterterrrorism* is used in this book, as it is the most common term used by law enforcement and security agencies worldwide. Notwithstanding, the distinction between these two forms of activity should be kept in mind whenever discussing approaches to deal with terrorists.

Defense

Border Security

Although nations face terrorist threats from within, they also face threats emanating from outside their borders. Border *security* is used by countries to control people entering their country who harbor violent radical ideologies. This is done, in the main, by immigration agents and border security personnel.

Immigration is a process of vetting foreign nationals arriving at seaports, airports, and land border crossings. This process ensures compliance with visa and immigration laws and rejection of those in breach. It also ensures that those who have been approved to remain in-country are abiding by the laws of that nation.

Border *control* is related, but it involves patrolling and watching over the areas of the country that are not serviced by ports or official transit points. It is viewed as a national security function of government. Depending on the country, borders can be land as well as sea borders. In small countries with limited geographic areas to patrol, patrolling can be done with relative ease, but those with vast land masses that also have sea borders require a much larger force that includes land, sea, and air patrols.

The organization and composition of border security agencies vary but usually comprise a uniformed branch and an investigation branch. These branches are analogous to uniform and detective branches of police forces. Their objective is to control illegal immigration and to prevent and detect terrorists and terrorist weapons from entry. This is done by traditional police work and by using technology that increases the efficiency of detection methods. This type of technology includes electronic sensors and devices for remote monitoring. This technology is ever evolving and can be deployed in strategically fixed positions or on mobile and airborne platforms.

The chief strategy is deterrence—that is, prevention by deploying personnel, supported by equipment and devices. This is intended to send a signal to would-be illegals that if they attempt to enter the country, they will be caught. The surveillance devices that border guards use are part of this increased efficiency, but the building of infrastructure that facilitates quick response times is also important. Take for instance the building of all-weather roads in remote areas, the construction of remote airfields, as well as fencing and lighting.

Aviation Security

Next to car journeys, flying is probably the most popular form of travel. Estimates by the US Federal Aviation Authority show that in 2016 more than 2.5 million passengers flew in and out of US airports each day. The number of scheduled passenger flights in the United States that year exceeded 9.7 million. If this figure is extrapolated to include all commercial flights worldwide, it is no wonder that when it comes to terrorist thinking, aviation is an attractive target.

Given the volume of commuters, it is not an exaggeration to say that the world's trade would suffer catastrophic harm if aircraft could not fly. Safe air travel is an essential part of social as well as economic life. Air travel connects people, places, and commerce across the world in an interdependent network.

In the wake of the 9/11 attacks, law enforcement and national security agencies undertook a review of aviation security. Jurisdictions have enacted a variety of security measures, which take the form of what is known as security-in-depth. This strategy is designed to provide layers of security and is analogous to the layers of an onion. The theory suggests that the more security layers there are, the less likely criminals can exploit them all.

Initial reviews highlighted weaknesses in passenger screening and general access controls. With the enactment of new laws to enable security personnel to exercise greater power, these weak points were closed. However, as in a game of chess, for each defensive move, the opposition thinks of a new offensive maneuver. As terrorists devised ways around aviation security measures, the frailties in the systems were reviewed and countermeasures implemented. Take for instance the so-called Underwear Bomber. On Christmas Day 2009, Nigerian-born terrorist Umar Farouk Abdulmutallab attempted to detonate plastic explosives that he had hidden in his underwear while he was flying on Northwest Airlines Flight 253 that was en route from

Amsterdam to Detroit. Because of attempts like this, full-body scanners are now being used.

Body scanners are just one of many devices used in safeguarding the world's skies. But security in the skies involves more than just deploying security equipment; there need to be processes and procedures that guide how security-in-depth will be structured (e.g., passenger screening, baggage screening, and physical security of airports and aircraft); who is responsible for what; and when and how these security measures are carried out. Also, the responses to breaches need to be recorded in policies and standing orders—ranging from innocent acts by naive travelers to calculated deceptions perpetrated by terrorists. Moreover, the recruitment and training of security personnel are paramount considerations. Since 9/11, training programs have been created and standards for employee training have been set. However, anecdotal evidence suggests that some jurisdictions have been less than rigorous in conducting personnel screening of security staff. It is known that staff with criminal associations have been hired to fill some of these security-sensitive positions. As the aviation security systems mature, these types of weakness are being addressed through continuous review programs.

Security of Public Places

July 14 is Bastille Day in France. The country commemorates the Storming of the Bastille in 1789, which was a significant day that led to the unifying of the French people. In 2016, the citizens in the city of Nice celebrated along the popular Promenade des Anglais. During what was a pleasant and happy summer evening, a terrorist drove a stolen nineteen-ton truck into the crowds. He killed 85 people, including ten children, and injured another 201. Police identified the attacker as thirty-one-year-old Mohamed Lahouaiej-Bouhlel, a Tunisian citizen who was living in France. He was later killed by police in an exchange of gunfire. The incident was classified by Europol as a jihadist terrorist attack.[2]

The ability of people to assemble, move freely, openly associate, and express their thoughts in public constitute some of the most important attributes that define a civilized and enlightened society. Terrorists who target public places are trying to undermine these human needs. Protecting a population from indiscriminate political murder is a challenge. Governments are cognizant of their responsibility to afford protection, but are also aware that in doing so they must not overreach and turn the systems of protection into systems of oppression.

By their nature, public places are difficult to guard, simply because they are everywhere. A list of all types would be very long—streets, lanes, and boulevards; town centers and parks; shopping malls, sports stadiums, open-air music venues; and so on. With a finite amount of resources available, governments use a risk-based approach to identify areas where the highest levels of protection need to be provided. This usually takes the form of protecting crowded places, because of such attacks as those on the London Bridge and Borough Market in June 2017, the Manchester Arena attack in May 2017, and the Berlin Christmas market attack in December 2016. Crowded places are an attractive target for several reasons. They provide the potential for mass casualties and this enhances the indiscriminatory nature of terrorism and psychological impact on large numbers of witnesses (who will then post stories and photographs on social media). Crowded places also provide unrestricted access to terrorists in comparison to, say, a commercial airliner. These types of attacks also impact the surrounding businesses, causing a downturn in the local economy. And after all, these areas are symbolic—they represent the civility of society. For public areas to be at less risk, governments are using technology as a cost-effective alternative.

To protect venues, law enforcement agencies recommend a security-in-depth approach. The first layer is deterrence. This can include both physical structures and electronic devices that limit access—for instance, masonry road barriers or electronic access controls. Next is detection. This involves human observation as well as electronic surveillance and computerized detection algorithms—for example, facial recognition, human movement patterns, and suspicious shape and size alerts. The third layer is delay. Delay tactics include any type of process or device that slows down an attacker or frustrates their efforts should they get past the first two security layers. The final layer is response—a quick reaction by security forces to suppress the attack and stop it from continuing.

Export Control

Just as governments control the importation of prohibited items, they control what is exported too. Although this may seem odd at first, upon inspection we can see that a country—especially one with an advanced economy that manufactures sophisticated devices and generates intellectual property—can inadvertently export items that could then be used against that country by hostile third parties. These items are termed *dual-use munitions*.

The word *munitions* invokes images of stockpiles of explosives or weapon ammunition; munitions in the wider sense include software or technology that can be used not only in a commercial setting but also for military purposes. Of course, munitions encompass such items as certain types of weapons and ammunition, but also chemical warfare precursors, rocket fuels, space launch vehicles, carbon-fiber technology, surface and submersible vehicles of war, lightweight turbojet engines, certain types of telecommunications equipment, and hundreds of other items defined in registers such as the US Commerce Control List. These control lists are based on the Wassenaar Arrangement, which is an international convention established by more than forty countries to provide regional and international security through transparency of transfers of conventional arms and dual-use goods and technologies.

Export law enforcement officers protect national security, uphold a country's foreign policy objectives, and guard its economic interests. They do this by ensuring that sensitive exports do not reach hostile entities, especially terrorist organizations, by programs designed to prevent export, and by investigating those who try to purposely circumvent legislative controls. In the United States, export control is administered by the Office of Export Enforcement, the Office of Enforcement Analysis, and the Office of Antiboycott Compliance. Other countries have similar offices for oversight and enforcement.

Information Security

Information security is often conflated with computer security. Although aligned, these two fields of endeavor are different. The reason is simple: information exists in domains other than just computer data-storage systems. A quick look at the history of information security shows that information security grew from the need to share ideas, plans, schemes, and strategies. Today, information is created, stored, retrieved, and transmitted to others via computers over the Internet. This isn't the sole method, though perhaps it is the most used.

There is evidence that cyphers were used over 2,000 years ago to secure military messages. The first recorded use of such a method was by Julius Caesar, who used a substitution cypher to scramble the letters of words so that, if intercepted, the opposition could not read it.[3] Today, such a form of information security would be ineffective,[4] but at a time when the opposition was likely to be less literate, they might have thought such a message was written in a language unknown to them.

Code words are similar in purpose to cyphers, except a code word or phrase stands for an idea, plan, or action to be taken—or not to be taken. For instance, during the D-Day invasion of Nazi-occupied Europe, coded messages were broadcast to the French resistance over shortwave frequencies. The coded messages were meaningful to particular resistance cells that had specific missions. A coded message such as "dice are on the table" meant railway lines should be sabotaged, and "it's hot in Suez" meant telephone lines should be attacked. These were one-way transmissions directed at French partisans who would sit in front of a simple "crystal set" and listen to these personal messages on the BBC's French service, Radio Londres.[5]

Whether the information is in paper form, oral, or transmitted over radio frequencies or the Internet, some type of security is required if these data are to remain out of the hands of those who intend to use that data to cause harm. Shortened to the term *infosec,* information security is the science of denying opposition forces, including terrorists, sensitive information. It is also concerned with ensuring that data transmissions are not disrupted and that data are not changed, copied, or destroyed.

Security personnel approach these issues by a method that is encapsulated in the mnemonic *CIA*—that is, confidentiality, integrity, and availability. Although it might be tempting to apply strong security policies and practices to every piece of sensitive information, the aim of CIA is to provide a balanced approach that allows an organization to operate efficiently without hindering its business processes. In the field of intelligence work, this is known as counterintelligence; entire textbooks have been written on its theory and practice,[6] but in short, scholars and practitioners have developed procedures that encompass physical security, personnel security, and the security of the data. All three aspects work in unison to form a balanced approach.

As an example, take the information that exists in the cybersphere. The procedures start with classification of each data type or item and storing and transmitting each classification via methods that are appropriate for its classification—for example, confidential, secret, top secret. In terms of creating, accessing, and changing these data, or destroying information, security vetting of personnel is required to ensure that those who have access to the data are trustworthy. The physical premises where the data are processed need to have a commensurate level of security for the data being processed (confidential, secret, top secret)—this applies for both buildings and equipment as well as for the staff who oversee the facility. Data-cabling and microwave transmission modes also need to be protected from interception. Each aspect of the information development, use, and communication stages needs to be protected using the doctrine of security-in-depth, including through the use of passwords, antivirus software, firewalls, and encryption, as well as security training for information users and data administrators.

Offense

Law Enforcement Undercover Operations

Offensive operations against terrorists take two forms—internal and external to the nation. The latter are performed in the main by the military and intelligence agencies. Some law enforcement agencies, such as the FBI and the Drug Enforcement Agency (DEA) in the United States, are also authorized to work overseas, but in the main, law enforcement is confined to working within a nation's geographic boundaries.

What differentiates a defensive posture from one that is offensive is pursuit. Defense is a shield, whereas offense is a spear. Both approaches protect, but offense is an active means—it is intended to head off an attack rather than wait for the attack and try to defend against it. It has been said that offense is the best form of defense, and is one of the principles of war.

Because society is not at war with its own people, offensive law enforcement actions take the form of undercover operations. An undercover operative is a sworn law enforcement officer who would normally be in uniform, but because they mingle with people suspected of being criminals, they operate under a cover story; hence their designation as undercover operatives. The role of an undercover operative is different from that of a plainclothes detective. Detectives and other government investigators (e.g., those who work in regulatory and compliance fields) do not usually wear uniforms but identify themselves as officers by presenting their authority card or badge. Undercover operatives do not; instead they present a fictional story about who they are and what they are doing—this provides their cover.

By going undercover, an operative can penetrate a terrorist cell to obtain intelligence about their plans and activities, as well as collect evidence that will facilitate criminal prosecution. Unlike undercover operations into illicit drug trafficking, counterterrorist operations are more difficult. Drug dealers are usually known to police because there is a pattern of behavior, and there are known venues where sales take place—and, of course, the market is open for new buyers. Depending on the quantity of drugs for sale, these purchases take place monthly, weekly, or even daily. Operatives have a greater scope of opportunity to interdict drugs. However, with terrorism, terrorists operate in small groups—cells—who know one another, identify ideologically with a cause, and avoid patterns of behavior that will draw attention to themselves. So penetration is more difficult.

Nevertheless, there are approaches that law enforcement uses to attract terrorists to itself rather than trying to be accepted into a cell. For instance, a dangle can be used whereby the undercover operative pretends to have knowledge or resources, or access to these, that the terrorists need for their attack. Human nature being what it is, if a person approaches someone who is planning a criminal act, that person is likely to be on their guard. However, if that person is the one initiating the approach, especially after having observed the person to be approached for some time to ensure that the person to be approached is not a police officer, then he or she is more likely to feel ease. Of course there are other techniques that law enforcement agencies use, including sting operations, but the thrust of offensive operation is one of going after terrorists to prevent attacks or, after terrorists have attacked, to prevent them from conducting another attack.

Military Intervention

Offensive operations against terrorists call on the response of a nation's military. The adage that offense is the best form of defense is enshrined as one of the principles of war, and a nation's military is *the* organization that conducts war. A nation's intelligence agencies also engage in offensive operations against terrorists (see Chapter 11).

There is debate about the use of military forces in attacking terrorist targets under the legal doctrine of *jus in bello*—the legal thinking that governs the way in which a war is conducted. This section does not address this legal argument; it instead focuses on how military force is used offensively.

Small-scale deployment. In simple terms, a military force can be used in either a small-scale deployment or larger numbers. The size of the response is determined by the objective—take for instance retaliation for an act of state-sponsored terrorism as compared to a nation that is overrun by, and controlled by, terrorists. In the former situation a small-scale attack—direct action—is likely to suffice, whereas with the latter a large-scale intervention is needed.

The US Department of Defense defines *direct action* as "short-duration strikes, and other small-scale offensive actions conducted as a special operation in hostile, denied, or diplomatically sensitive environments, and which employ specialized military capabilities to seize, destroy, capture, exploit, recover, or damage designated targets."[7] A small-scale offensive strike can be seen in the case of the 1986 US air strike that targeted Libya's dictatorial leader at the time, Muammar Qaddafi. Codenamed Operation El Dorado Canyon, land- and carrier-based US aircraft struck targets in Tripoli in direct retaliation for Libya's role in a terrorist attack on US service personnel at the Le Belle discothèque in Berlin, Germany, ten days earlier.

The aim was to send a message to states that sponsored terrorism that they would be the target of punitive strikes. A subsequent study by Henry Prunckun and Philip Mohr found that following the Libyan air strike there was an increase in the number of terrorist attacks worldwide, though the severity of these attacks diminished.[8] The study showed that terrorist attacks that were classified as either high- or medium-level violent events decreased by a statistically significant amount. This meant that although the overall number increased, there was a shift to low-violence attacks. The study found that this reduction in the level of violence was a result of the small-scale direct military action by the United States.

In the United States, units that undertake unconventional warfare missions have been given an increased mandate for direct action against high-value targets. Such targets can be either a person or a resource that has been determined to be an essential component in an opposition's mission. Take for instance Osama bin Laden, who was the target of small-scale direct action by US Navy SEALs on May 2, 2011.[9]

Units that conduct these special operations also include the 75th Ranger Regiment and the US 1st Special Forces; in the United Kingdom there are the Special Air Service and the Special Boat Service; in Australia is the Special Air Service; in Canada are the Special Operational Forces; and in New Zealand also is the Special Air Service.

A couple of final examples of where small-scale direct action has been used against terrorist targets demonstrate the diversity of these missions. In 1976 was the famous Israeli commando raid on Entebbe, Uganda, to free 248 hostages held by the Popular Front for the Liberation of Palestine—External Operations after their Air France flight was hijacked. Another example is Operation Enduring Freedom, from 2001 to 2014, which involved hundreds of high-risk arrests of Islamic militants and Taliban leaders during the war in Afghanistan.

Large-scale deployment. On September 20, 2001, then president George W. Bush told a joint session of Congress: "We are a country awakened to danger and called to defend freedom. Our grief has turned to anger, and anger to resolution. Whether we bring our enemies to justice or bring justice to our enemies, justice will be done."[10] The president spoke in relation to the terrorist attacks of September 11. He explained: "Al Qaeda is to terror what the mafia is to crime. But its goal is not making money; its goal is remaking the world— and imposing its radical beliefs on people everywhere."[11] Therefore, the response needed to be different from the small-scale attacks of the past. These attacks required a large-scale deployment.

Although widely debated, the term *large-scale deployment* was initially used to describe the response of the United States and its allies to the US war on terror (also called the global war on terror). Such deployment has been described simultaneously as a "set of actual practices—wars, covert operations, agencies, and institutions" and as an "accompanying series of assumptions, beliefs, justifications, and narratives."[12] This doctrine launched Operation Enduring Freedom, the aforementioned large-scale military operation that targeted al-Qaeda and Taliban forces in Afghanistan from 2001 to 2014.

The United States and its coalition partners from over forty countries destroyed the leadership and infrastructure of al-Qaeda, thus denying the terrorist organization a safe haven that it used for training members, planning attacks, and conducting operations. On December 31, 2014, Operation Enduring Freedom concluded and Operation Freedom's Sentinel replaced it. The name of the mission

For an interesting insight into the war on terror, consider the positions of two scholars. Professor Michael Howard has questioned the use of a military model in addressing terrorism and suggests a law enforcement model may be more apt: "To declare war on terrorists or, even more illiterately, on terrorism, is at once to accord terrorists a status and dignity that they seek and that they do not deserve. . . . To declare that one is at war is immediately to create a war psychosis that may be totally counterproductive for the objective being sought."[13]

Attorney William G. O'Neill posited: "If the 'war on terrorism' truly is a 'war,' then the laws of armed conflict apply, both to the states combating terror and to the terrorists themselves. These laws, commonly known as the Geneva Conventions and their Protocols, prohibit acts of terror."[14]

was selected to signify an enduring security cooperation between the United States and the Afghan government so that the new government could work toward self-reliance.

Covert preemptive neutralization. In 1984, then president Ronald Reagan signed National Security Decision Directive 138. This directive addressed the need to use covert preemptive neutralization regarding terrorists. The directive authorized the CIA and the FBI to conduct covert operations. The thrust of this directive was to approve the use of military special forces to engage in what can be described as guerrilla-style war against terrorists. Some of the key authorizations stated in the directive include the use of preemptive operations as well as retaliatory strikes; expanded intelligence collection and dissemination of information warning terrorists; and to mandate, when required, to kill terrorists as an act of preemptive self-defense.

> The Director of Central Intelligence, in consultation with the Secretaries of State, Treasury, and Defense and the Attorney General, shall:
>
> • Develop a clandestine service capability, using all lawful means, for effective response overseas against terrorist acts committed against U.S. citizens, facilities, or interests.

- Provide a new Finding on combatting terrorism which includes, inter alia, lawful measures to:

  - Increase cooperation with the security agencies of other friendly governments.
  - Unilaterally and/or in concert with other countries neutralize or counter terrorist organizations and terrorist leaders.
  - Develop an information exploitation program, aimed at disrupting and demoralizing terrorist groups.[15]

By and large, these activities are conducted by the CIA's Special Activities Division. The division is responsible for conducting covert operations that have been authorized by National Security Decision Directive 138 and other such subsequent legal instruments. The division comprises a Special Operations Group and a Political Action Group. The former conducts combat operations against high-threat targets using operatives drawn from military units such as the US Army Special Forces, Delta Force, the 75th Ranger Regiment, the Marine Corps' Force Reconnaissance, the Navy's SEALs, and the Air Force's 24th Special Tactics Squadron.

The CIA's Political Action Group carries the responsibility for conducting psychological warfare operations (psyops), as well as exercising covert political influence, and conducting economic warfare. These are counterintelligence operations that are designed to change the target's values, beliefs, emotions, and reasoning to destroy their morale and depress their psychological state.

The techniques used in psyops are varied and numerous, but a few examples provide a glimpse of the types of methods used: airdropping pamphlets with instructions about how to surrender; projecting the perception that overwhelming force will be used (i.e., the doctrine of rapid dominance or shock-and-awe); radio propaganda broadcasts; and false and misleading Internet blog posts.

Economic warfare can use economic controls, diplomatic pressure, and the threat of military interdiction to exercise control over critical economic resources of an opposition. With terrorist organizations, this might mean exercising influence over states that provide support or safe haven, or supply knowledge or resources, to terrorists. The responsibility for targeting terrorists with these types of interventions is tasked to intelligence agencies.

Command-and-Control

Dealing with a terrorist incident is one of many situations that law enforcement and security agencies encounter. But unlike routine criminal matters, a terrorist incident requires the deployment of specialist resources to resolve the issue. To oversee these operations, a dedicated command-and-control arrangement is needed. Command-and-control refers to the authority to direct agency officers, and to permit them the use of particular types of equipment.

Command-and-control has nothing to do with the actual engagement of terrorists in either a law enforcement or a military sense, but without it engagement is reduced to haphazard tactics that have no connection to an overarching strategy. Therefore, law enforcement, national security agencies, and the military rely on command-and-control.

The principles of command-and-control are derived from two types of authority—legislative (or policy, or doctrinal), and the rank or position of personnel. The former provides the legal basis for issuing orders, and the latter makes those issuing orders personally responsible for the success or failure of an operation. This is known as accountability.

There is a difference between "command" and "control," though at one time control might have been viewed as an extension of command. That is, a commander issues commands to subordinates under his or her control. However, this is no longer the case. The prevailing thinking is that control is the feedback that commanders receive during an unfolding operation. This information can come from operatives engaging the terrorists, reconnaissance or surveillance operatives, intelligence reports, or any number of other sources. This feedback helps the commander control the situation as developments occur.

Command-and-control is a scalable enterprise. Take as an example an army command structure—the smallest group of soldiers operating collectively is usually called a fireteam and comprises three or four soldiers who are under the command of a corporal. The next higher unit of command is a squad or section, which comprises nine to twelve soldiers under the command of a sergeant. Following this is a platoon, comprising about thirty soldiers commanded by a lieutenant. Then there is a company, led by a captain or major, of between 90 and 150 soldiers. And so on through to battalion, regiment, division, corps, and field army. As can be seen, command-and-control is a scalable concept.

Study Questions

1. Describe what is meant by security in public places.
2. Discuss the difference between defensive and offensive security operations.
3. Describe what is meant by direct action and provide an example from a recent news account.
4. Explain what is meant by command-and-control.

Learning Activity

As a way of understanding how offensive law enforcement operations work, research several cases that have been reported in the world's media regarding the discovery of terrorist cells who were arrested before the members were able to act. From these multiple reports, extract themes that describe what makes a successful undercover operation. For example, do the reports mention how agents were able to penetrate the cell? Did the operation use surveillance to complement the work of the agents? If these news reports are silent on such details, perhaps expand your search to books to go into more details about historical cases. The end result of your research should be a descriptive analysis of the key elements of a successful law enforcement undercover operation.

Notes

1. US Department of Defense, *Department of Defense Dictionary of Military and Associated Terms,* Joint Publication no 1-02 (Washington DC, October 18, 2008), 132.

2. European Union, *Terrorism Situation and Trend Report* (The Hague: European Union Agency for Law Enforcement Cooperation, 2017), 23.

3. Laurence Dwight Smith, *Cryptography: The Science of Secret Writing* (New York: Dover, 1943).

4. David Kahn, *The Codebreakers: The Story of Secret Writing* (New York: Macmillan, 1967).

5. Perhaps the most famous coded message was *"Blessent mon coeur d'une langueur monotone"* (in English, "Wound my heart with a monotonous languor"). This was broadcast at 23:15 hours on June 5, 1944, signaling that the invasion would start within forty-eight hours, so sabotage operations should commence.

6. See Hank Prunckun, *Counterintelligence: Theory and Practice,* 2nd ed. (Lanham: Rowman and Littlefield, 2019).

7. US Department of Defense, *Dictionary of Military and Associated Terms* (Washington, DC, 2017), 67.

8. Henry W. Prunckun and Philip B. Mohr, "Military Deterrence of International Terrorism: An Evaluation of Operation El Dorado Canyon," *Studies in Conflict and Terrorism* 20, no. 3 (1997).

9. Mark Owen with Kevin Maurer, *No Easy Day: The Autobiography of a Navy SEAL* (New York: Dutton, 2012).

10. White House, "Address to a Joint Session of Congress and the American People," September 20, 2001, https://georgewbush-whitehouse.archives .gov/news/releases/2001/09/20010920-8.html.

11. White House, "Address to a Joint Session of Congress and the American People."

12. Richard Jackson, *Writing the War on Terrorism: Language, Politics, and Counter-Terrorism* (Manchester, UK: Manchester University Press, 2005), 8.

13. Michael Howard, "What's In a Name? How to Fight Terrorism," *Foreign Affairs* 8 (January–February 2002), 81.

14. William G. O'Neill, "Terrorism and International Law: Why Conventions Matter," *Daily Star,* October 28, 2004, cited in Alex Schmid, "Terrorism: The Definitional Problem," *Case Western Reserve Journal of International Law* 36 (2004), 376, emphasis added.

15. Excerpt from "Combatting Terrorism," *National Security Decision Directive 138* (Washington, DC: White House, April 3, 1984), 4.

11

Intelligence Collection and Analysis

The term *intelligence* refers to several things: a process, a product, a body of knowledge, and organizations that deal in secret knowledge.[1] *Intelligence analysis* refers to the process of producing a product within an intelligence organization to add to its body of secret knowledge. To do this, information is collected about a target that will help answer operational or tactical questions about current operations or to forecast future events. Intelligence analysis is used in several types of intelligence work, including national security, military, law enforcement, business, and the private sector.

On face value, one might be drawn to the conclusion that each of these types of intelligence is distinct, but they are not. Perhaps in the Cold War climate between 1947 and 1991 that argument might have held weight, but in the security environment that has evolved since 9/11 (referred to as the era of homeland security), there is an overlapping, and even a merging, of what might be considered different types of intelligence. This situation applies to the threat posed by terrorists. Terrorists not only are a threat to national security, but also present problems for the military, law enforcement, and business.

To understand how intelligence analysis is used to respond to acts of terrorism, this chapter looks at the kinds of information that an intelligence analyst uses to produce reports, briefings, and other forms of estimates for decisionmakers.

Open-Source Intelligence

Open-source information is information available to the public.[2] It requires no special legal authority, nor any special request to be made for access.[3] These sources are in direct contrast to covert and clandestine methods, which are arguably the methods most commonly associated with intelligence work. In the parlance of social science research, open-source information is categorized as secondary data, and covert and clandestine information are likened to primary data.

One might assume that because intelligence research into terrorists is conducted in secret, the sources of information used are also secret. However, as Harry Howe Ransom wrote in his watershed work on intelligence: 95 percent "of peacetime intelligence [comes] from open sources."[4] In his analysis of the national intelligence collection effort of the United States, Ransom stated that more than 80 percent came from "overt, above-board methods [that] would normally be available to anyone with a well-organized information gathering system."[5]

Between the end of World War II, when the Office of Strategic Services was deactivated, and 1947, when the CIA was created, the agency responsible for secret intelligence was the Strategic Services Unit (SSU). In conducting its intelligence research on the Soviet Union, the SSU used the Library of Congress as its main source of data.[6] All the Library of Congress data in relation to the Soviet Union were publicly available.

Regarding business intelligence, it has been estimated that 90 percent "of all information that you and your business need to make key decisions and to understand your market and competitors is already public or can be systematically developed from public data."[7] As an illustrative point from history, take the following Cold War example. Polish intelligence officer Colonel Pawel Monat was a military attaché in Washington, DC, who saved his communist government large sums of money, time, and effort by accessing open-source information about commercial aviation "secrets." He pointed out one experience in particular, involving *Aviation Week* magazine: "Very little of this information was of really classified nature. We could have dug up most of it ourselves from other sources. But it would have taken us months of work and required us to shell out thousands of dollars to various agents to ferret out the facts, one by one. The magazine handed it all to us on a silver platter [for fifty cents]."[8]

More recently, the late Tom Clancy was once queried about his infallible knowledge of some of the obscure technical and scientific details contained in his espionage novels. He denied having access to classified defense information but instead pointed out what others have discovered—it could all be found in the open-source literature.[9]

Today, intelligence analysts use the Internet to gather information about persons-of-interest as well as known terrorists using social media and information posted to websites. Analysts also access volumes of information from other publicly available sources of information.[10]

Sources of open information are extensive. This information can be obtained from newspapers, magazines, academic and professional journals, radio and television broadcasts, and the Internet. Arguably, until the 9/11 terrorist attacks, intelligence analysts used these sources of information as a means of supplementing classified information.

> "It is estimated that one weekday edition of today's *New York Times* contains more information than the average person in seventeenth-century England was likely to come across in an entire lifetime."[11]

The importance of systematically collecting open-source information did not become a priority for the intelligence community until after the 9/11 attacks. For instance, the effective mining of Internet-based information has enabled the intelligence community to better understand how Islamic radicals use the Internet's television capabilities, chat rooms, and news sites to recruit and train their members, as well as raise money.[12]

One of the concerns in collecting covert data is the safety of the officer or agent tasked to collect it. The risks are real, and the consequences of failure are grave—to both the operative and the security agency. However, open-source data collection does not pose the same risks, and the depth and breadth of the information are potentially vast. Still, the latter point can also be a drawback—sometimes a specific piece of information may be needed to provide insight into, say, a terrorist cell's operation, and hence the only way to gather it may be through an agent working undercover. In this regard volumes of information cannot be substituted for specificity.

Nevertheless, open-source information can facilitate a quick means of supplying data to answer intelligence questions and therefore help assess an unfolding situation. It can also be used to determine the missing pieces of information (i.e., the specificity just discussed) by highlighting what is required in an information-collection plan. Such a plan may, at that stage, point to the need to involve covert means.

Social Media

Because we live in an age where information is central to every aspect of life, an astonishing variety of obligations have been placed on individuals to record information about their affairs. The same applies to corporate bodies and governments. It is because of these record systems that society generates what has become known as a paper trail.

A paper trail can be described as all records and documents created by an individual or entity in the course of commercial and social interaction with other individuals, organizations, government departments, and businesses (both public and private). These records have the effect of leaving a trail detailing where the individual (or entity) has been, with whom they have had dealings, what goods and services they have purchased, what they own, what their likes and dislikes are, and more important, what their intentions may be.

To an intelligence analyst, this trail forms a composite picture of a terrorist target or a person-of-interest. Uncovering one part of the paper trail can lead the analyst to other sources of information. These sources are not limited to those on paper but also extend to interviews with friends, neighbors, and colleagues of the target, perhaps using a pretext as well as physical, optical, or electronic surveillance.

To law enforcement and national security agencies, the paper trail symbolizes a valuable set of leads. The value of this information in a collated and analyzed form can be seen in the arrests reported in the media from time to time of terrorists plotting attacks that were, until that point, unnoticed by the public.

But a paper trail does not need to be on paper. With social media, what used to be recorded in hard-copy documents now appears in electronic form. Any electronic media that records social interaction and is accessible by others satisfies this definition. Information about a person's ideology; interests; friendship groups; movements; past, present, and future activities; education; employment; and so on forms a long list of the types of data that electronic media record. Unlike the paper trails of the past, these electronic paper trails also hold audio files, videos files, and photographs that can be used by intelligence services.

The use of social media for intelligence analysis has great application. As people's lives, and the lives of many organizations, are captured every day and in many ways using social media, these data can be incorporated in what are called information collection plans. These data can be collected, collated, stored, analyzed, and then shared among intelligence services. Online harvesting of personal data via search engines can be done without the target's knowledge.

Social-networking websites can be used to conduct background investigations on persons-of-interest. Take, for instance, the situation where an undercover operative intends to pitch to a potential agent at a public event (e.g., the opening show of an artist's recent paintings). An intelligence analyst might therefore compile a background file on the potential agent using social media, including social networking. This information is then provided to the undercover operative, who synthesizes it into a cover story that allows this operative to strike up a conversation with the potential agent and have enough in common to win their favor.[13]

It would be fair to say that there are few people who do not resent the thought of being surveilled by their government. A Big Brother society where the state conducts surveillance on everyone conjures up notions of shadowy, sinister, secretive, and repressive regimes. Yet free people worldwide now collude with this type of surveillance by willingly posting personal information to social media outlets.

In some regards, today's world may have astonished George Orwell,[14] but social surveillance is accepted without concern by most of the population, and as such can be and is exploited by intelligence practitioners. Take as an example the notorious Jordanian terrorist Humam Khalil Abu Mulal al-Balawi, who began his activities in chat rooms on social media websites. It wasn't long before the world's intelligence services began monitoring him through these media and compiled a dossier on him and his activities.[15]

As rich as this source is for information, social media have limitations. One example that demonstrates this is the use of "sock puppets." A sock puppet is a false identity that is created as a deception so that the creator can manipulate the ideas posted on social media websites.[16] This is different from the use of a pseudonym, because a sock puppet purports to be another person—a real person, but no such person exists—the person is computer generated using algorithms crafted by a third party. These algorithms are usually based on narrative and statistical probability, as well as other methodologies. Software exists that allows the simultaneous control of numerous false identities.

If used by an intelligence agency, online operations officers (like case officers in field operations) can control these fake agents for the purposes of, say, penetrating extremist social media forums and sowing disinformation to prevent the objective of an intelligence project being realized. Such objectives can be wide-ranging—from simple disruptive activities aimed at a targeted terrorist support group to influencing future actions of the persons-of-interest in the same vein as would an agent provocateur. This is done by what has been described as personality-based social robots (often called simply bots). These bots use keywords that define the persona of the fake agent to automate the posting of computer-generated blogs to all the social media forums that exist.

The implication that intelligence services deal with is that they must be constantly mindful that terrorist cells could be running sock puppet agents online, so they do not mistake this disinformation for genuine information posted by the target group. Likewise, intelligence agencies must be conscious that intelligence officers from allied foreign nations may be doing the same, and that such websites may contain misinformation and disinformation. Further, social activists may be using these techniques, as well as those developed by marketers, to exploit the fundamental flaws in online journalism to manipulate public opinion.[17]

Social media websites are accessible not just by individuals and groups of the target group who may reside outside the geographic bounds of the intelligence analyst's country; citizens of his or her country may also be accessing and participating in these online discussions. As such, another unintended consequence is that the manipulation of this online information may affect wider public opinion. This issue has consequences in liberal democracies and it is not overlooked or discounted by law enforcement and intelligence agencies. History has shown us the ramifications of government officials who have not heeded this lesson.[18] There are also legal implications in terms of the perennial issue raised by defense counsels known in jurisprudence as entrapment.

Data Mining

The term *data mining* conjures the notion of an analyst "digging" into numerous datasets to extract "nuggets" of informational gold. In a way, this is what the process of data mining is about. At the core of this process, an intelligence analyst uses software applications to interrogate many relational databases to discover correlations or patterns in the data that will eventually lead to insightful conclusions.

Data mining is not new—it has been around for decades. However, it once was expensive to perform, and the datasets used were, generally, smaller than those available today. The computing hardware was also expensive and less powerful, as were the software applications used to interrogate the databases.

Hardware and software developments, along with data storage devices, have increased in processing speed (e.g., multiple processors), sophistication, and capacity. Moreover, the cost of purchasing and running data-mining systems has dropped considerably from its early days to the point that contract analysts can now afford these systems. Databases comprising many terabytes of information (known as data warehouses) can be accessed for a fee, so analysts do not have to be involved in the collection aspects of the process (which can be considerable).[19] The datasets themselves can now also consist of structured and unstructured data, which was not always the case.

Data mining was originally used by the business sector to assist in market research. However, once intelligence agencies understood the value of this type of analysis, they embraced it and several large-scale data mining projects went operational post-9/11. Nevertheless, concerns about citizens' privacy and civil liberties soon became a feature of debate, because along with data about potential terrorist targets were data about law-abiding people who live respectable

---

"Simply stated, data mining refers to *extracting or 'mining' knowledge from large amounts of data*. The term is actually a misnomer. Remember that the mining of gold from rocks or sand is referred to as *gold* mining rather than rock or sand mining. Thus, data mining should have been more appropriately named 'knowledge mining.'"[20]

lives. There were also security concerns about inadvertent access or deliberate hacking of the data-mining systems by third parties as well as potential penetration by opposition intelligence services.

The value of data mining to law enforcement agencies is the ability to take disparate datasets and, with a few well-designed software applications, allow intelligence analysts to develop complex queries, so they can interrogate these databases to see if certain relationships emerge. These patterns are based on association rules grounded in logic and mathematical concepts. In a sense, these queries are likened to hypotheses that are tested against the data to see if they hold true.

Once relationships start to emerge, other software applications are employed to graphically display the results and allow secondary queries to be run. Like finding a pure gold nugget in a ton of rocks, data mining allows terabytes of information to be processed to find relationships that would be impossible if performed manually (if they could be performed manually, which is not likely).

What does data mining hold for terrorist intelligence analysis? Arguably there are two key strategies that are used by law enforcement and national security agencies: pattern mining and subject-based mining. With the former, analysts query relationships among variables in datasets to discover patterns. Because the databases are relational, this means many more variables can be created by defining them in terms of the existing data (known as derived data). For instance, a new variable may be created by defining it as a data item containing specific attributes, but only if these attributes occur in time before another attribute. Data items from many different relational databases can be queried to produce these new variables. These new variables can then be queried regarding other existing variables or other newly derived data items.

With subject-based mining, the query starts with subject-specific information and then mines a data warehouse to create a profile or dossier of information related to the initiating data. Profiles and dossiers are used here to denote a collection of information that may be either narrow or wide-ranging relating to many aspects of the terrorist target's life.

Being unchained from having to conduct individual queries on stand-alone small datasets and predefined search options, this is a very powerful method for security analysts. This methodology is coupled with multiple relational databases containing terabytes of information that can be interrogated using sophisticated software applications that run on computers with several multicore processors (or distributed across several such servers).

By way of example, if an intelligence analyst is looking for a terrorist cell, he or she might query several databases by using existing data items (variables) along with derived data items. These might also be combined with business-related data that is accessible for a fee from the commercial sector. For instances, considering just these common databases, one can appreciate the power this methodology wields when trying to track down a terrorist target, and one can appreciate why some civil libertarians have recoiled about the method's potential misuse. Common databases include address records, aircraft registrations, airline manifests, birth records, boat registrations, civil court records, company and business registrations, credit card purchase data, credit histories, divorce records, driver license information, freight records, genealogical/family history, geospatial data, hotel/motel reservations, immigration records, landownership records, marriage records, money-movement and bank transfer records, motor vehicle registrations, newspaper archives, occupational licensing records, police criminal records, school and college yearbooks, shipping records, social security records, and online social data including blogs.

Another source of intelligence information is metadata. Metadata is information about the data—that is, metadata summarize individual data. This summary helps make using the specific data simpler. As an example, take the case of a book that has been published. A librarian will house the text as part of a larger holding but will need some method to retrieve the book when requested. So metadata in this case could be an index entry in what used to be a card catalog (see Figure 11.1). Since the 1980s, libraries have converted these paper index cards to digital records.

Law enforcement and national security agencies are particularly interested in metadata, especially where they relate to telephonic and email traffic. Analysis of these metadata has helped investigators make breakthroughs in terrorist cases that would otherwise not have been possible. For instance, Khalid Sheikh Mohammed, the planner of the September 11, 2001, attacks, was located by law enforcement officers analyzing cell phone metadata.

When law enforcement's or national security agencies' information-collection plan includes searching large datasets, manual procedures can be discounted. Analytic software must be used to filter, sort, and

Courtesy of Dr. Marcus Gossler.

Figure 11.1   Metadata held in a library's paper card catalog.

collate the raw data, and then to present the results of the search queries. There are many analytic software packages on the market and most are very sophisticated, delivering elaborate visuals for intelligence briefings and reports.

Covert Sources

The prevalence and accessibility of open-source information have by no means resulted in the wholesale replacement of covert and clandestine data collection, nor of data obtained from confidential sources, even though the unobtrusiveness of open-source methods has always been useful. In the years since the 9/11 terrorist attacks, the problems and limitations of intelligence gathering caused by having agents on the ground have been pointed out many times.[21] Because of the intrinsically safe nature of open-sources information, a high level of consideration and planning is not required to obtain these data compared to organizing data collection by clandestine and covert means.

Clandestine data collection, although akin to covert collection, is different in that clandestine operations operate in the open—aspects of the operation are visible to the terrorist target, but are disguised so that they do not appear to be what they seem. Covert operations, in contrast, are carried out in secret—they are hidden and not visible to the target even in a disguised form. This method is to some degree intrusive, but because the operations are invisible, the target has no knowledge that a counterterrorism campaign is being conducted.

Law enforcement and national security agencies use these methods because attempts to obtain information via open methods might have failed. For instance, secretive methods are used when the target is concealing information. The only way to obtain such data might be to penetrate the terrorist cell's security measures via a surreptitious method.

Undercover Operatives

Undercover operatives attempt to get close to individuals and inside organizations to make firsthand observations. The use of operatives is therefore risky for the operatives and the intelligence service employing them. These risks are both physical and psychological. The operative risks physical harm in the form of bodily injury and death, as well as a range of psychological injuries spanning from mild anxiety to severe psychiatric disorders. The physical risks are more apparent, as one can easily visualize the ramifications of having to penetrate a terrorist organization. The psychological injuries arise from the stresses associated with working in isolation, working in a dangerous environment, and perhaps engaging in activity that is illegal.

The data that can be obtained from an undercover operative can be very valuable because they offer a glimpse of the terrorist's intentions, thereby providing an insight into the target's thinking, rationale, and behaviors that could not be obtained by other means. However, given the risks and the monetary costs of running a field operation, this method is not often the first used. It is usually reserved as a

The objective of the undercover operative is to infiltrate "as deep as possible and [gather information] on the opposition or enemy."[22]

means of final resort, or for targets that pose an imminent danger to the community or national security.

Because the operative will be in direct contact with terrorists, there are a few issues that their commanders keep in mind. Foremost is that the operative's identity must be guarded with utmost secrecy. If knowledge of the operative leaks to the target, not only will the operative's cover be blown, but also the operative is likely to suffer injury or death.

Part of the operative's brief is to obtain evidence of wrongdoing, in a law enforcement context. Evidence may be in the form of admissions, but intelligence data may be in the form of indicators of intent. To capture these data, the operative can either commit the details to memory and then record them later for transmission back to the agency, or use some electronic device that transmits the data live for recording and transcription. The latter is the most reliable and the best solution, as it doesn't rely on the operative's ability to remember the details, which, from an intelligence point of view, can be critical.

Study Questions

1. Explain what is meant by the term *intelligence*.
2. Explain what *intelligence analysis* means.
3. List six sources of information that intelligence analysts use in making their assessments and explain how each source might provide information to aid a terrorism investigation.

Learning Activity

For this exercise, consider yourself a counterterrorist intelligence analyst. Using at least three Internet search engines, search for information about one of these groups: the Kurdistan Workers' Party, the Palestinian Islamic Jihad, or the Muslim Brotherhood. Compile a list of open-source information on your target group. Collate this list into categories: Internet sources available only

continues

> **Learning Activity** (continued)
>
> on the Internet, print publications that are also available online, and references to other sources (e.g., transcribed interviews, recordings, videos). As an analyst, assign a level of quality to each open source of information. This is important because Internet-based information is not regulated for accuracy, given that anyone can publish whatever they like online. Categorize the sources as accurate, doubtful, or indeterminate. Is there any pattern in the quality of information for each category? If not, is the data source skewed one way or another? Do your results suggest that some sources are better than others? What other conclusions can you draw from your brief survey?

Notes

1. Hank Prunckun, *Scientific Methods of Inquiry for Intelligence Analysis,* 2nd ed. (Lanham: Rowman and Littlefield, 2015), 6.

2. Sometimes referred to as open-source intelligence (OSINT).

3. Although for some agencies, particularly military and national security agencies, there may be restrictions imposed by regulations or directives that prohibit the collection, retention, or dissemination of information regarding US citizens. See for instance Army Regulation 381-10, *U.S. Army Intelligence Activities,* and Executive Order 12333, *U.S. Intelligence Activities.*

4. Harry Howe Ransom, *The Intelligence Establishment* (Cambridge: Harvard University Press, 1971), 19. Ransom was quoting Ellis M. Zacharias, a World War II deputy director of the Office of Naval Intelligence. According to Zacharias, only 4 percent of intelligence came from semi-open sources, and a mere 1 percent from secret agents.

5. Ransom, *The Intelligence Establishment,* 20.

6. Richard Helms with William Hood, *A Look over My Shoulder: A Life in the Central Intelligence Agency* (New York: Random, 2003), 73.

7. John J. McGonagle Jr. and Carolyn M. Vella, *Outsmarting the Competition: Practical Approaches to Finding and Using Competitive Information* (Naperville, IL: Sourcebooks, 1990), 4.

8. Pawel Monat with John Dille, *Spy in the U.S.* (London: Frederick Muller, 1962), 120.

9. Frederick P. Hitz, *The Great Game: The Myth and Reality of Espionage* (New York: Knopf, 2004), 86.

10. Prunckun, *Scientific Methods of Inquiry for Intelligence Analysis.*

11. David Shenk, *Data Smog: Surviving the Information Glut,* rev. and updated ed. (New York: HarperCollins, 1997), 25–26.

12. Richard Best and Alfred Cummings, *Open Source Intelligence Issues for Congress* (Washington, DC: Congressional Research Service, 2007).

13. In the counterintelligence context, access to social media data is a reason why intelligence officers should avoid, or at least restrict, the personal information they post online. However, there is a twist to this if the officer is an undercover operative. That is, their undercover persona may need to have a social media presence to "backstop" their cover story or "legend."

14. George Orwell was the pseudonym for Eric Arthur Blair who wrote the fictional novel *Nineteen Eighty-Four.* In this book, Orwell portrayed a totalitarian society where government surveillance is omnipresent. Although he described a system of surveillance that consisted of agents, informants, and two-way "telescreens," the computer monitor and social media could, by analogy, be considered a manifestation of these methods. George Orwell, *Nineteen Eighty-Four: A Novel* (New York: Harcourt, Brace, 1949).

15. Joby Warrick, *The Triple Agent: The al-Qaeda Mole Who Infiltrated the CIA* (New York: Doubleday, 2011).

16. See also accounts about how marketers have exploited online journalism to successfully manipulate public opinion, such as Ryan Holiday, *Trust Me, I'm Lying: Confessions of a Media Manipulator* (New York: Portfolio/Penguin, 2012).

17. Holiday, *Trust Me I'm Lying.*

18. Bruce Hoffman and Christian Ostermann, *Moles, Defectors, and Deceptions: James Angleton and His Influence on U.S. Counterintelligence* (Washington, DC: Wilson Center and Georgetown University, 2014).

19. These would, of course, be unclassified data warehouses, not those of law enforcement, the military, or national security agencies. Nevertheless, these agencies would no doubt find some commercial databases very attractive to the types of issues they are probing and hence may have commercial agreements in place to access business-related datasets, as can any private contractor.

20. Jiawei Han and Micheline Kamber, *Data Mining: Concepts and Techniques,* 2nd ed. (Burlington, MA: Morgan Kaufmann, 2006), 5, original emphasis.

21. Robert Baer, *See No Evil: The True Story of a Ground Soldier in the CIA's War on Terrorism* (New York: Crown, 2002); Melissa Boyle Mahle, *Denial and Deception: An Insider's View of the CIA from Iran-Contra to 9/11* (New York: Nation, 2004).

22. J. Kirk Barefoot, *Undercover Investigation* (Springfield, IL: Charles C. Thomas, 1975), 4.

12

Protection of
Critical Infrastructure

Protection of critical infrastructure concerns itself with safe-guarding key pieces of plant and equipment that provide essential public services. Electricity, water, waste, telecommunications, Internet data centers, transportation, financial services, as well as law enforcement, fire departments, hospitals, ambulances, and other emergency services fall into this category.

Protection of critical infrastructure goes beyond the traditional notion of security to embrace a coordinated approach to protect assets that are essential for a civil society to exist. This coordination draws in prevention, response, and, if required, recovery from a terrorist event. Picture the ramifications of a city without electric power and lights; with hospitals operating on only a few hours of backup generators; with no traffic lights; with cell phone towers unable to pass telecommunications traffic.

Protection of critical infrastructure is a defensive program that is being used worldwide but arguably has its roots in the United States via Presidential Decision Directive 63, issued in May 1998. Protection of critical infrastructure has several goals that may be expressed differently in various countries, but generally center around three objectives: a system for protection, a system for providing warning, and a system for responding to a terrorist attack.

This chapter examines the latter two systems only, because to consider the defensive strategies[1] for each type of plant and equipment associated with the myriad aspects of what can be categorized as critical infrastructure would require an encyclopedic volume. Nevertheless, once a threat assessment and vulnerability assessment are conducted by law enforcement or a security agency, appropriate defense measures can be designed to meet the need for protection, as well as fitting in with the organization's budget and other priorities.

Even though this chapter addresses protection of critical infrastructure from a counterterrorism point of view, it should be borne in mind that such plans also address what are termed *all hazards*. For instance, law enforcement agencies considering the impact of a terrorist event also consider an event occurring because of nature—wildfire, flood, earthquake, tornado, severe storm, and so on.

Threat Assessment

Threat analysis is the first of three integrated phases that law enforcement and security agencies use to develop a counterterrorism plan. The two subsequent phases are vulnerability analysis and risk analysis. The results of these three pieces of analytic work lay the groundwork for crafting programs that address prevention, preparation, response, and recovery (PPRR). In other words, all the techniques discussed in this chapter are intrinsically linked and act as building blocks to form a comprehensive methodology for counterterrorism analysis.

In summary, these steps are (1) identify the threat, (2) explore vulnerabilities to this threat, (3) gauge the likelihood of the threat, (4) assess the consequence of threat, and (5) construct a PPRR plan. Consider the following example of how these steps are applied in practice:

1. Threat: cyber attack via an email-borne virus.
2. Vulnerability: the organization's servers and workstations via the Internet.
3. Likelihood: greater than 85 percent probability.
4. Consequence: moderate to severe loss of computer resources.
5. PPRR plan: attempt to prevent such an attack (prevention); prepare the agency for such an attack if prevention measures fail (preparation); guide the agency in the actions it needs to take to respond to an attack that is under way or has occurred (response); and suggest what needs to be done to aid the agency in recovery once an attack has passed (recovery).

Although discussed here as a coordinated approach to counter terrorism, law enforcement agencies can use any of these analyses on their own, or apply them individually to problems other than terrorism. For instance, a threat analysis could be carried out in relation to gangs,[2] or a risk assessment could be conducted in relation to a person or group acting criminally.

The purpose of carrying out a threat analysis is to identify problems that personnel and physical assets may face.[3] In a law enforcement context, a threat constitutes a person's resolve to inflict harm on another. It is important to note that a threat cannot be posed by a force of nature or natural event—these are hazards. Only people can pose a threat, as they need *intent* and *capability* (or organizations, associations, businesses, and the like, because they are staffed by people).

Threats can be made against most entities—people, organizations, and nations—and this is done by a *threat agent*. The potential harm can come in many forms and can be suffered either physically or emotionally/psychologically. Threat agents do not have to openly declare their resolve to cause harm to constitute a threat, though explicit words or actions make it easier for field operatives to identify the threat agent and for intelligence analysts to assess the threat.

Threat analysis acknowledges two necessary key factors—a threat agent, and an object of the threat (i.e., the target, which does not have to be physical, such as a shopping mall or an individual; it can be intangible, such as the threat to national security or a community feeling insecure about going out in public or attending public events). Stated another way, a threat agent who has intent and capability must be able to harm something. A *terrorist* threat agent could be someone who is intent and capable of making, say, an explosive device.

When law enforcement security analysts assess a threat agent, they are gauging whether the agent has intent and capability to produce harm to a target (this is why naturally occurring events cannot be threats). In deciding whether the agent has intent and capability, analysts need to establish two elements for each of these factors: desire and expectation (or ability) for intent, and knowledge and resources for capability. These considerations are shown in Figure 12.1. As an equation, threat is expressed as:

$$(desire + expectation) +$$
$$(knowledge + resources) = threat$$

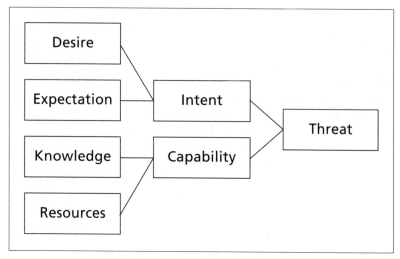

Figure 12.1 Threat Analysis

Desire is described as the threat agent's enthusiasm to cause harm in pursuit of their goal. Expectation is the confidence that the threat agent has that they will achieve their goal if their plan is carried out. Knowledge is having information that will allow the threat agent to use or construct devices or carry out processes that are necessary for achieving their goal. Resources include skills (or experience) and materials needed to act on their plan.

Security analysts consider the context of the threat, their agency's mission, and the list of potential targets when adopting a model to aid them in determining the threat environment. A generic model for calculating threats might look something like the example of a threat summary depicted in Table 12.1. This model can be modified to suit the specific requirements of individual law enforcement agencies.

Although modeling does not eliminate subjectivity, it does provide security agencies the ability to be transparent as to how they calculate threat. In addition, models are not able to eliminate miscalculations because of inadvertent skewing. In Table 12.1, intent is calculated by adding desire with expectation, and in turn this sum is added to the sum of knowledge and resources (and will range from a low of 4 to a maximum of 20). The process of adding limits the spread of values, whereas the process of multiplying any of these

Law enforcement planners use two additional concepts:

*threat intent = the optimism a threat agent
has about successfully attacking a target*

and

*threat capability = the force a threat
agent can bring to bear on a target*

**Table 12.1   Threat Posed to the Metropolis of Orrenville by the
Martyrs of the Righteous**

Scale	Scores	Tally
	Desire	
Negligible	1	
Minimum	2	
Medium	3	3
High	4	
Acute	5	
	Expectation	
Negligible	1	
Minimum	2	
Medium	3	3
High	4	
Acute	5	
Total intent		6
	Knowledge	
Negligible	1	
Minimum	2	
Medium	3	3
High	4	
Acute	5	
	Resources	
Negligible	1	
Minimum	2	
Medium	3	3
High	4	
Acute	5	
Total capability		6
Threat coefficient		12

scores would increase the values. For instance, if all scores were multiplied—that is, substituting multiplication for addition—per the equation, the range would be spread from 1 to 625.

The precision of this wide range of values diminishes law enforcement's ability to accurately determine either intent or capability. Therefore, it is suggested that adding all values, rather than multiplying them, will reduce the spread and therefore maintain the threat coefficient as an *indicator* rather than promote it as a reflection of its absolute condition. Even if desire and expectation, and knowledge and resources, are multiplied, but the resulting sums are added, this would still yield a very wide spread—from 2 to 50—as would the opposite—that is, multiplying the sums that constitute intent and capability, from 4 to 100.

Two additional issues arise when law enforcement agencies use quantitative methods. First, there is still a need to provide conditioning statements so that the reader of the intelligence report understands what is meant by a medium threat intent and capability. And second, unknowns are not accommodated in this model. These unknowns are informally termed *black swans*[4]—unexpected and unforeseeable events or, in this context, threat agents.

The threat coefficient obtained from this analysis is then compared against a reference table to gauge where it sits on the continuum of danger of attack. The scale suggested in Table 12.2 can be varied with additional qualifiers, or it can be collapsed if the number is deemed too many. Likewise, how the incremental breakdown of coefficients is determined will depend on whether the law enforcement or security agency is willing to accept the risk that a threat agent may slip under its gaze by raising the categories of negligible and minimum. In the end, the number and their descriptors need to make sense in the context of the asset being protected. That is, each of the descriptors needs to have a conditioning statement attached to it to define what is meant by negligible, minimum, medium, high, and acute.

Threats are context-dependent, and what forms a threat in a critical-infrastructure setting (e.g., a business setting) does not necessarily form a threat in a military setting or national security setting (though the opposite may be true). One way that law enforcement agencies contextualize threats is to view them as *threat communities*. Some examples of threat communities pertaining to malicious human threats include common thefts, local gangs, organized criminal groups, international or transnational terrorists, state sponsors of terrorism, domestic terrorists

Table 12.2   Example of a Threat-Coefficient Scale

Threat Level	Coefficient
Negligible	4–6
Minimum	7–10
Medium	11–15
High	16–18
Acute	19–20

(including offshoots), insurgents and guerrillas, anarchists, domestic anarchists, cyber-criminals and cyber-vandals, organized national or international criminal gangs, radical political groups, radical rights campaigners, militant single-issue lobbyists, and foreign government intelligence services.

These threat communities can be subdivided into more distinct groups if there is a need—for instance, extremist rights campaigners could be classified into the following extremist subgroups: political extremists, religious extremists, single-issue extremists. Nevertheless, membership in one threat community (or subcommunity) does not exclude a person being a member of another, or several other, threat communities.

To better understand the "who" that compose a threat community, intelligence analysts compile a threat profile. The profile needs to be adequate (perfection is rarely, if ever, obtainable) to understand the threat environment, which aids the next phase in counterterrorism analysis: vulnerability analysis. In the meantime, consider the threat profile shown in Table 12.3 as an example that demonstrates the important aspects of a fictitious threat agent.

Vulnerability Assessment

Vulnerability can be described as a weakness in an asset that can be exploited by a threat agent. In this regard the term *asset* is being used in this chapter to denote plant or equipment associated with critical infrastructure.[5] Viewed another way, vulnerability is an asset's capability to withstand harm inflicted by a threat. Harm can be anything from experiencing a minor nuisance to a situation that is catastrophic.

Table 12.3   Threat Profile for the Fictitious Martyrs of the Righteous

Summary	Observations
Desire	
Targets	Objects that represent Western values, or people who do not ascribe to their interpretation of their faith (including other believers)
Affiliation	Totally autonomous
Recruitment	Educated local ethnic population
Target characteristics	Symbolic and iconic objects that afford high visibility and hence high media coverage
Tactics	Targets mass gatherings, critical infrastructure, communications, mass transport, and distribution chains
Expectation	
Motivation	Radical religious ideology
Intent	Extensive destruction
Tolerance to risk	High
Self-sacrifice	Very accepting
Willingness to inflict collateral harm	Extreme
Knowledge	
Planning	Based on target acquisition intelligence through fixed and mobile surveillance, informants
Information	Open-source data collection as well as access to declassified military manuals
Training	Low-grade, informal facilities. Though training standards are crude, knowledge transfer is effective.
International connections	Training and ideological support
Resources	
Financing	Extortion and kidnapping of the wealthy
Weapons	Improvised explosives and small arms
Skills	Attack vector–dependent: • Computer-based—very low • Electronic/communications—moderate • Small arms—high • Explosives—very high

Vulnerability is a function of several factors: attractiveness of the target, feasibility of carrying out an attack, and potential impact (i.e., potential harm as discussed earlier). This model is shown in Figure 12.2. Usually, these factors entail such considerations as status of the target, potential for the attack to succeed, potential for the threat agent to get away with the attack, and potential to inflict loss. These factors can be weighed against measures to mitigate loss and to deter or prevent attack on an asset.

Formula-based analyses are popular with law enforcement and security agencies engaged in counterterrorism because they allow for transparency. Transparency is important because the assessment can be replicated if necessary. Transparency and replication form the basis of the scientific method of inquiry. Although the procedures vary from agency to agency, they usually follow a basic stepwise formula. The following procedure shows the common approach:

1. Define what constitutes an asset (critical infrastructure, transport network, food chain, distribution hub, or any essential service—e.g., electric power, gas, potable water, sewerage).
2. Sort these assets into categories.
3. Assign a grade or level of importance to each asset.
4. Identify potential impact on the asset if it suffers harm.

There is no single criterion for calculating vulnerability. This is because each class of asset may require special factors to be considered. One general approach is to use a model such as

$$target\ attractiveness + ease\ of\ attack + impact = vulnerability$$

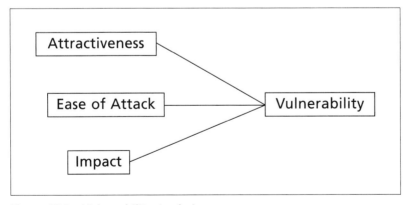

Figure 12.2 Vulnerability Analysis

To operationalize attractiveness, the analyst could ask questions along the following lines and tabulate the results to insert into the model:

- Is the target readily recognizable?
- Is the target the subject of media attention/coverage?
- Does the target have a symbolic status in terms of historical, cultural, religious, or other importance?

Attractiveness is placed in context with the threat agent. For instance, some Islamic extremist groups see assets that represent Western culture or symbolize Western values as attractive.[6] To operationalize the concept of ease of attack, law enforcement analysts ask questions like the following:

- How difficult would it be for the threat agent to predict the peak attendance times at the target?
- Are there security measures in place?

Questions that probe the existence and extent of controls (or lack thereof) are also asked to gauge ease of attack. On the one hand, if there is a high degree of control effectiveness, this will usually reduce ease. On the other hand, if there is a low level of control effectiveness, it will increase ease. But with some targets, even a small reduction in control effectiveness can result in a disproportionate increase in ease of attack. The concept of impact is operationalized by questions like:

- What are the numbers of people frequenting the target?
- In dollar terms (or operation hours, units of production, etc.), what would the financial impact of an attack be if the asset is disrupted, incapacitated, or destroyed?

Impact is predicated on an assumption that terrorists want their attacks to result in large numbers of deaths. This may have been true in the al-Qaeda-focused climate that existed in the early 2000s, but such an assumption may not always be valid. For instance, a nationalist-focused group may someday emerge that seeks to destroy critical infrastructure rather than kill people. In such a case, these terrorists may view heavy public traffic as an inhibitor to ease of attack. The first paradigm is described by counterterrorism scholars as comprising effect-based attacks, whereas the latter are considered event-based attacks, which is the focus of protecting critical infrastructure.[7]

A template used by security agencies for calculating vulnerability might look something like the example shown in Table 12.4. The vulnerability coefficient derived from this analysis is then compared against a reference table to gauge where it sits on the continuum of susceptibility to attack. Law enforcement agencies can increase the scale with additional qualifiers (i.e., conditioning statements), or they can be collapsed if the number is deemed too many. In the end, the number and the descriptors created are crafted to make sense in the context of the asset being protected (the left and center columns of Table 12.5). Qualitative descriptors (i.e., conditioning statements) are, if needed, added for each category (as shown in the right column of Table 12.5).

Note that *consequence* is not a factor that is considered in a threat assessment. It is, however, considered in a risk assessment.

Table 12.4 Vulnerability of the Metropolis of Orrenville's Main Bridge over the Orren River

Scale	Scores	Tally
	Attractiveness	
Negligible	1	
Minimum	2	
Medium	3	3
High	4	
Acute	5	
	Ease of Attack	
Negligible	1	
Minimum	2	
Medium	3	3
High	4	
Acute	5	
	Impact	
Negligible	1	
Minimum	2	
Medium	3	3
High	4	
Acute	5	
Vulnerability coefficient		9

Table 12.5 Example of Vulnerability Coefficients with Qualifiers

Vulnerability	Coefficient	Qualifier (Conditioning Statements)
Negligible	1–3	• Can be successfully attacked only if the threat-agent has an acute-threat coefficient; or • Has little or no importance; or • The range of security measures makes attack very difficult; or • If attacked, the information has little utility to cause harm.
Minimum	4–6	• Can be successfully attacked only if the threat-agent has a high-threat coefficient (or greater); or • Has limited importance; or • The range of security measures makes attack difficult; or • If attacked, the information has only some utility to cause harm.
Medium	7–9	• Can be successfully penetrated only if the threat-agent has a medium-threat coefficient (or greater); or • Has reasonable amount of importance; or • The range of security measures makes penetration moderately difficult; or • If attacked, the information has a moderate level of utility to cause harm.
High	10–12	• Can be successfully attacked only if the threat-agent has a minimum-threat coefficient (or greater); or • Has a sizable amount of importance; or • The range of security measures makes penetration undemanding; or • If attacked, the information has a high degree of utility to cause harm.
Acute	13–15	• Can be successfully attacked only if the threat-agent has a low-threat coefficient (or greater); or • Has a very high level of importance; or • The range of security measures is nonexistent; or • If attacked, the information will cause immediate or extreme harm.

Risk Assessment

Law enforcement and security agencies are no different than businesses that assess risk. In a business context, managers might assess risk to employees in relation to occupational hazards associated with the workplace. The same analytic methods are employed in counterterrorism.

A risk assessment is carried out in relation to almost any situation; it is not just for issues of grave concern. Risk analysis techniques can be applied to situations that may be the target of criminals or criminal organizations (e.g., gangs) not associated with terrorism. Nevertheless, analyzing risk allows law enforcement agencies to recommend measures that will provide owners and operators of critical infrastructure with the ability to either accept the risk as-is or treat the risk (which includes such decisions as to avoid the risk altogether, mitigate the risk, or defer the risk to another person or organization).

Risk analysis is the subject of an international standard. The Swiss-based International Organization for Standardization (ISO) has published a document that puts forward a common approach for dealing with the implementation of risk management that is consistent and effective.[8]

Law enforcement agencies use the analytic process depicted in the following equation for assessing risk:

$$risk = likelihood + consequence$$

The concept of likelihood refers to the probability of "a specific event or outcome, measured by a ratio of specific events or outcomes to the total number of possible events or outcomes." The consequence is defined as "the outcome of an event affecting objects."[9]

Likelihood and consequence are evaluated by law enforcement agencies in the analysis phase of the risk management cycle. This analytic cycle comprises several phases as shown in Figure 12.3.[10] Law enforcement agencies do this using a three-step process:

1. Two scales are used to evaluate a risk rating for the target (i.e., the asset under consideration). These two scales consist of a likelihood scale (see Table 12.6) and a consequence scale (see Table 12.7).
2. The results of these two assessments are then entered into a risk rating matrix (see Table 12.8) that returns a risk rating coefficient.
3. Finally, the risk rating coefficient on the risk evaluation scale (see Table 12.9) is read to determine what actions (if any) are required.

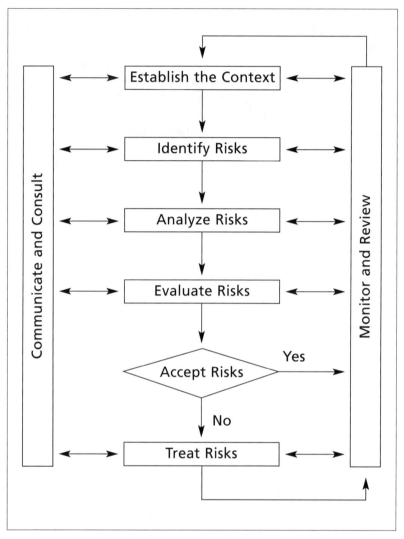

Figure 12.3   Typical Risk Management Cycle

In conducting some assessments, agencies may find that in addition to the descriptors listed in Tables 12.6–12.9,[11] a set of conditioning statements are also necessary, along the lines of those contained in Table 12.5. This also applies to the descriptors contained in Table 12.7. To demonstrate this, examples of low-risk events might include

- An event that would occur rarely and would result in insignificant consequences (reflected in Table 12.8 as E1).
- An event that is unlikely to occur and would result in minor consequences (reflected in Table 12.8 as D2).

Examples of high-risk situations include

- An event that would occur rarely but would result in catastrophic consequences (reflected in Table 12.8 as E5).
- An event that is likely to occur and have minor consequences (reflected in Table 12.8 as B2).

Treating Risk

Once each risk is assessed by a security agency in this way, the risks can be positioned on the rating matrix (see Table 12.8) so they can be compared with each other to prioritize treatment options. Take for instance the following events considered by a state police force:

Table 12.6 Example of a Likelihood Scale

Rank	Likelihood	Descriptor
A	Almost certain	Situation is expected to happen.
B	Likely	Situation will probably occur.
C	Possible	Situation should occur at some time.
D	Unlikely	Situation could occur at some time.
E	Rare	Situation would only occur under exceptional circumstances.

Table 12.7 Example of a Consequence Scale

Rank	Consequence	Descriptor
1	Insignificant	Small impact.
2	Minor	Minor impact.
3	Moderate	Considerable impact.
4	Major	Noticeable impact.
5	Catastrophic	Will cause systems and operations to fail with high impact.

Table 12.8   Example of a Risk Rating Matrix

			Consequences		
Likelihood	1 Insignificant	2 Minor	3 Moderate	4 Major	5 Catastrophic
A Almost certain	Moderate	High	Extreme	Extreme	Extreme
B Likely	Moderate	High	High	Extreme	Extreme
C Possible	Low	Moderate	High	Extreme	Extreme
D Unlikely	Low	Low	Moderate	High	Extreme
E Rare	Low	Low	Moderate	High	High

- The risk posed by a person-borne suicide bomb to a public meeting place could be located at C5 (possibly with catastrophic consequences—therefore, it is an extreme risk).
- Violence because of a street demonstration could be located at B3 (likely with moderate consequences—so the risk is high).

The scale provided in the risk rating (see Table 12.9) is useful for judging whether the policing agency recommends accepting the risk or treating the risk (and, if so, to what extent). Without the risk assessment process, the recommendations of the agency could be called into question as an overreaction or, equally, deemed an underestimate of the seriousness of the situation.

Although the risk rating shows what is a generally accepted distribution of risk levels,[12] law enforcement agencies will make their own judgments as to where these transition points take place. Many

Table 12.9   Example of a Risk Evaluation Scale

Risk Level	Suggested Actions
Low	Manage using standard operating procedures.
Moderate	Outline specific management actions that need to be taken.
High	Create a business continuity plan and a response plan (test annually).
Extreme	Urgent actions are necessary (in addition to those per high-risk threat level).

Some treatment options for critical infrastructure include awareness and vigilance, communication and consultation, engineering
options, monitoring and review, resource management, security
and surveillance, and community capability and self-reliance.[13]

times, this will be a topic for discussion with the political leaders as
a matter of policy. But by using a systematic approach to risk management, security agencies can reduce the likelihood and lessen
consequences through the application of technology, science, or
personal or collective effort.

Response Planning

There are four elements to a terrorism response plan—prevention,
preparation, response, and recovery. Prevention considers the risk
and tries to implement ways that could stop it from happening. Preparedness acknowledges that despite preventative measures, the
event may still occur, so owners and operators of critical infrastructure need to prepare for it. If an attack does occur, response is that
part of the plan that deals with how organizations will mobilize and
act (and what type of action, etc.).

The final element provides guidance for recovery operations.
This aspect of the plan anticipates the worst-case scenario—that is,
preventative measures have failed, and preparation measures may
have mitigated the impact to some degree, but a terrorist attack still
occurred; response has contained and brought the event to an end,
but it is now time to recover from the event's effects.

When compiling a PPRR plan, security agencies plan in such a
way that the four elements have no delineation between them, though
they may be expressed individually in their written plans. Further, the
PPRR elements may be put into action at the same time; for instance,
response and recovery can, and in most cases will, start at the same
time, because they are inextricably linked (as shown in Figure 12.4).
As it is arguable that until recovery starts, the target of attack cannot
function, recovery is considered at the earliest opportunity.

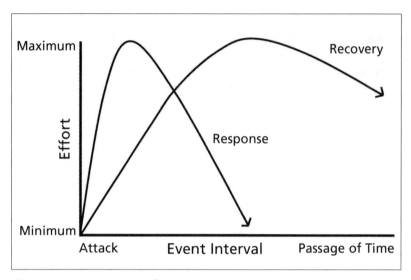

Figure 12.4 Response and Recovery

Finally, though the language used by law enforcers appears in action-oriented terms, the treatments they employ are not always physically based options. Options involving social dimensions are also used, because people are the ultimate targets of an event-based terrorist attack—recall the first pillar of terrorism: "Kill one, frighten ten thousand."

Study Questions

1. List the elements that constitute a threat analysis. Describe each and explain why it is important to understanding a threat.
2. List the elements that constitute a vulnerability analysis. Describe each and explain why it is important to understanding the concept of vulnerability.
3. List the elements that constitute a risk analysis. Describe each and explain why it is important to the understanding of risk.
4. List the elements that constitute a PPRR plan. Describe each and explain why it is important to counterterrorism.

Learning Activity

Suppose the law enforcement agency in your jurisdiction that is responsible for monitoring threats of subversion and terrorism has assessed that the water pipeline that connects the city's drinking supply (say a reservoir of some description) to your city's population is vulnerable to attack by the fictional Martyrs of the Righteous. Using PPRR, devise a plan that considers each of the elements.

Notes

1. This chapter is based on Hank Prunckun, "Threat, Vulnerability, and Risk Assessments," in Hank Prunckun, *Scientific Methods of Inquiry for Intelligence Analysis,* 2nd ed. (Lanham: Rowman and Littlefield, 2015), reproduced here, in an edited version, with permission of the publisher.
2. These methods can also be adapted for dealing with violent gangs. See Hank Prunckun, "Anti-Terrorist and Anti-Gang Intelligence," in Hank Prunckun (ed.), *Intelligence and Private Investigation: Developing Sophisticated Methods for Conducting Inquiries* (Springfield, IL: Charles C. Thomas, 2013).
3. James F. Broder and Gene Tucker, *Risk and the Security Survey,* 4th ed. (Waltham, MA: Butterworth-Heinemann, 2013), 316.
4. See for example a discussion of such unknowns in a number of contexts: Nassim Nicholas Taleb, *The Black Swan: The Impact of the Highly Improbable* (New York: Random, 2007).
5. See for instance Mary Lynn Garcia, *Vulnerability Assessment of Physical Protection Systems* (Burlington, MA: Elsevier Butterworth-Heinemann, 2006).
6. Carl Hammer, *Tide of Terror: America, Islamic Extremism, and the War on Terror* (Boulder: Paladin, 2003).
7. Victoria Herrington, Australian Graduate School of Policing and Security, Sydney, personal communication, May 3, 2009.
8. International Organization for Standardization (ISO), *ISO 31000: Risk Management—Guidelines on Principles and Implementation of Risk Management* (Geneva, 2009).
9. ISO, *ISO 31000,* 5.
10. ISO, *ISO 31000,* 14.
11. Queensland Government and Local Government Association, *Local Government Counter-Terrorism Risk Management Kit* (Brisbane, 2004), 16.

12. Queensland Government and Local Government Association, *Local Government Counter-Terrorism Risk Management Kit,* 16.

13. Emergency Management Australia, *Critical Infrastructure Emergency Risk Management and Assurance,* 2nd ed. (Canberra: Attorney General's Department, 2004), 43.

13

Deradicalization

Deradicalization refers to a process of deprogramming people who have developed radicalized views that have in turn led to violence. This chapter highlights some of the measures adopted by different regions to deradicalize terrorists as well as those attracted to extremist ideology. While this chapter is an introduction to deradicalization, it is important to recognize many of the programs used to deradicalize people are akin to the strategies used to resocialize criminals but without the ideological underpinnings found in deradicalization.

Evident in the processes are similarities such as emphasis on education, psychological counseling, vocational training, and social services. These socioeconomic measures replace efforts to challenge the ideology of individuals and groups. In some cases extremist ideology is tolerated, provided that it does not lead to violence, or help fund violence, so that people's attention can be refocused to more acceptable activities.

Deradicalization is different from counterradicalization or anti-radicalization, which are preventive measures. Deradicalization comes after an individual or group has committed a terrorist act and is aimed at stopping further violence.[1] Given that deradicalization comes after an attack, the perpetrator is often in custody, so the process of deradicalization is institutionally based—often in prisons.

Counterradicalization, or antiradicalization, programs tend to be (but are not exclusively) community or religion based. This chapter examines the three aspects of deradicalization, counterradicalization, and antiradicalization in their various guises and approaches via geographical areas. Moreover, the chapter surveys some of the contrasts between how different global regions approach reversing and countering radicalization. Because of the wide range of cultural, religious, and ethnic backgrounds of terrorists and their supporters, it cannot be expected that any single universal approach to deradicalization exists. However, there are many commonalities in the grievances of individuals and groups. Radicalized individuals are often reacting to an experienced social marginalization or suffer economic disadvantage that leads them to seek out radical groups. These groups will provide politically naive explanations for the wrongs they perceive to have taken place or distorted theological interpretations for people's suffering.

Disengagement, Antiradicalization, Counterradicalization, Deradicalization

Agreeing on definitions about what disengagement, antiradicalization, counterradicalization, and deradicalization may appear on the surface an academic exercise, but failing to understand what is meant by these concepts can cause conflicting expectations and misunderstandings of objectives. Consequently, it is worth providing some sense of the definitions to clarify the uniqueness of each approach.

Disengagement

Disengagement accepts there are always going to be people with radical ideas who will support terrorist ideology. Therefore, the challenge for disengagement is not changing views and ideologies of individuals or groups but ensuring that those views and ideologies are not manifested into terrorist activities or violence. Disengagement is the acceptance of radical ideologies but with the refocusing of those ideologies away from terrorism. The acceptance of extremist ideologies is what separates disengagement from deradicalization, antiradicalization, and counterradicalization—all of which may tend to challenge extremist ideology.

Antiradicalization

According to Lindsay Clutterbuck,[2] antiradicalization is the process used where there is risk of radicalization or extremism. Antiradicalization programs emerge in pre–extremist violence societies and are designed to mitigate the possibility of violence and stop radicalization. Antiradicalization programs may include the types of programs run in schools. In Australia and the United Kingdom, the governments have devoted funding for the development of education packages designed to address radical views. The United Kingdom offers the Prevent Program, which had been legislated as a requirement for teachers to understand. The program teaches how to identify possible radicalization of students. Similarly, the Australian government offers schools its Radicalization Awareness Kit. In an approach similar to that of the UK program, it uses case studies and scenarios to explain the key indicators of radicalization.

Counterradicalization

Counterradicalization is different from antiradicalization through its emphasis on community engagement. Whereas antiradicalization focuses on identifying extremism and early radicalization, counterradicalization aims at reversing the perception that the wider community is marginalizing groups or individuals as extremist groups would suggest. Through sports programs or community outreach activities, counterradicalization programs focus on fostering an inclusive society.

Deradicalization

Particularly in mainstream media, deradicalization has become an umbrella concept for counterterrorism, anti-terrorism, and disengagement. Subsequently, the distinctions and variety of objectives attached to each are lost. Deradicalization occurs when there is a need to target insurgents or terrorists in an environment of high or low violence.[3] Counterradicalization and antiradicalization can be interpreted as processes that may be used prior to getting to a point where deradicalization is required. Deradicalization would occur as an effort to change the ideology of active terrorists, not simply of those likely to be susceptible to committing terrorist acts.

Prison-Based Programs

Many prisons have established deradicalization programs as well as antiradicalization programs through measures such as ensuring that religious teachings are provided by qualified religious instructors. Although there is debate about whether prisons radicalize individuals, some scholars have asserted that a prison, by its structure and environment, provides opportunities for radicalization. Others have suggested that it is not the prison experience that creates the environment for radicalization but rather the immediate post-prison experience. Regardless of the academic debate surrounding this issue, programs to combat radicalization are an important part of prison-based social rehabilitation.

As an example, Thailand has developed a process for deradicalization that is strong on classification of terrorists and uses that classification to determine the most suitable kind of deradicalization program. Inmates are identified as three possible types: (1) supporters with no strong ideological position; (2) those working for groups at an operational level; and (3) group leaders who have strong ideological positions and are highly motivated.[4] This categorization indicates the type of deradicalization rehabilitation that is applied.

In the case of supporters with no real ideological motivation, the deradicalization program is focused on providing vocational education. Those who are classified as supporters tend to be involved with terrorist groups because it provides an income. Consequently, if those prisoners are provided with a means to earn an income after release, they may be less likely to reoffend. This is based on the theory that people are accepted into mainstream society through productive work, social connections, a sense of personal meaning, and community.

Those prisoners who have been classified as part of the operational aspect of a terrorist group are also provided with vocational training, with some group and individual counseling. Those identified as leaders of a group receive less emphasis on vocational training but a greater focus on counseling and group therapy.[5] Central to the counseling process is allowing prisoners to express the difficulties they have experienced in life. The ability for prison staff to show compassion and understanding is described as an important aspect of the deradicalization program.[6]

Community-Based Programs

Community-based deradicalization programs are more akin to counterradicalization and often are organized via government grants to community groups. These programs focus on funding Muslim-based community organizations. To date, deradicalization programs do not examine all ideological or religious expressions of radicalization; rather, contemporary programs tend to target Muslim radicalization. However, many European countries will also target youth at risk of joining white extremist groups.

In the United States and Australia, funding for community-based programs is provided by the government on the theory that the best people able to provide deradicalization of Muslims are other (nonradical) Muslims. The approach taken by these governments is to fund early intervention programs that bring individuals back into the community.

Australia offers a Living Safe Together Grants Programme that funds approximately forty community-based organizations nationwide. Programs include Muslim Youth Leadership and the Mentorship Program. In 2011, the United States offered its Countering Violent Extremism program. Like the Australian approach, the US program was aimed at countering radicalization through addressing community needs, instilling a counterradicalization message, and addressing factors that lead to radicalization.[7]

The Netherlands developed a model for de-racialization that incorporates aspects of security and social work. The model was also adopted by the United Kingdom and aimed to address the spread of radical and extremist ideologies as well as extremist groups. The program starts with police identifying groups or individuals who are considered at-risk and are either placed under surveillance or, if they have yet to commit any criminal acts, directed to social services that assist with housing, training, or education issues.[8]

The underlying theme of community-based deradicalization is disengaging people from radical ideology and providing support and inclusiveness to stem the flow of future terrorists. The sense of marginalization and tendency to blame society for feelings of alienation is viewed to be the catalyst for people to adopt violent extremist ideology.

Collective and Individual Programs

There is a difference in approaching the deradicalization of a group (collective) and of an individual. Collective deradicalization programs often appear more like government negotiation (with groups), while individual programs are centered on integrating the individual back into society.

Collective deradicalization programs require a conducive environment to operate effectively. It may seem surprising, but part of this is that the group possessed a strong leadership. Strong leadership and organizational structure may reduce the impact of the group splintering and provide collective agreement on ceasing violence.

In addition to working with a strong leadership, goals and agreements between the government and group are also required. So too required are the risk of losing public support for the group's activities and the existence of alternative groups.[9] A notable example of successful collective deradicalization is the Irish Republican Army. With a strong leadership and disciplined organizational structure, it was able to disengage from terror with minimal splinter organizations emerging. An additional environmental factor influencing the IRA was the change in global public opinion regarding terrorism as a means for political change. The organization also had a political wing that provided the alternative to violence in reaction to this change in public opinion.

While both collective and individual programs target grievances, the grievances of the collective will often be more political while those of the individual are more likely centered on social services. For individuals, their sense of disenfranchisement leads them to find the explanation for their problems in politics. Consequently, individual programs focus on addressing social issues while collective programs attempt to address political goals.

Geographic Programs

Deradicalization programs are influenced by geography. The location of terror groups reflects the politics of a region and hence the programs reflect the cultural, religious, and social aspects that need to be addressed. Each region is unique, with its own grievances and perceptions of social problems. To address grievances and deradicalize people, an understanding of the unique circumstances of their geographic area is important.

US Programs

In 2017, deradicalization programs were relatively new in the United States, with most still in development. Only since late 2016 has the US judicial system commenced examining certain alternatives to prison sentences. Much of the US approach to radicalized individuals, specifically those supporting terror groups like ISIS, has involved imposing long prison sentences, up to fifteen years in some cases. It appeared early on that the United States was more concerned with punishment as a deterrence rather than rehabilitation—some may say this is a common problem society also has with wider criminal and deviant behaviors.

While in 2018 punishment remains the dominant approach, some deradicalization programs have been tried. Some of the emerging programs have been influenced by European research and experience, such as the encouraging of radicals to view their problems not as a result of religious or cultural victimization but as problems that can be solved through further education and work that leads to a meaningful life. According to those involved in deradicalization programs, individuals will view the solution to their problems through armed struggled and a reorganization of society[10] rather than exploring political and social alternatives, especially those offered in democracies.

As in some European programs, the deradicalization programs being introduced in the United States do not attempt to enter moral or religious discussions with radicals but rather pose questions and highlight logical problems with terrorist plans. This means that rather than attempting to change ideology, a deradicalization program points out problems with a radical course of action by providing peaceful substitute actions. However, advocates of US deradicalization programs have accepted there are limits to this type of program's success. Such programs will not work with all individuals, and it is not always possible to change entrenched views. Therefore, some programs tend to favor disengagement over deradicalization.

European Programs

The Muslim diaspora from the Middle East and Africa in Europe has seen the continent at the forefront of counterradicalization and deradicalization, with European programs pioneering new methods. The Netherlands adopted what can be called both prevention and reduction methods. Using law enforcement to disrupt networks and target radicals, it is also aimed at identifying those at risk of radicalization and offers an outreach service.[11]

The Netherlands concentrates its deradicalization and counterradicalization programs at a local level. Its programs target specific areas rather than adopting a national approach. As an example, the Netherlands developed a program to counter right-wing extremism targeting youth in the city of Winschoten. The city was known for right-wing extremist groups that were attracting young people through concerts and festivals. The counterradicalization program targeted youths on the fringe of the extremist group rather than so-called hardcore members by offering assistance to return to school, find employment, or find housing. The program did not attempt to change their right-wing views; rather it discouraged violent and antisocial behavior. Again, this is type of program is more in the vein of an attempt to disengage rather than deradicalize individuals.

France has taken a similar approach to counterradicalization by targeting specific locations and offering opportunities for disadvantaged people who may be attracted to extremist groups. However, France also teaches political and social values as part of its school education curriculum. The French Ministry of Education mandated that all schools teach civics to students until they reach the age of sixteen. The aim of the program is to instill political and social values that shine a light on simplistic radical views that ignore the wider political context. It expresses what acceptable behavior is and why such values are important to a civil society.

In Germany, several antiracism centers have been established that offer a range of programs aimed at stopping racism. It has also established a radicalization help center as an outreach service to parents or friends of violent extremists.[12] In 2011, an innovative campaign involved the German government sponsoring a "Trojan" t-shirt campaign. Campaign staff attended a neo-Nazi concert and distributed free "white power" t-shirts to those at the concert.[13] The t-shirt logo read, "Hardcore Rebels. National and Free." But when the shirts were washed, the message changed to read, "If your t-shirt can do it, so can you." The t-shirt also had a contact number for those wanting to leave extremist right-wing groups.

In the United Kingdom, deradicalization programs shifted in 2011 from having an emphasis on security to an approach that addressed social disadvantage. It was specifically aimed at those from Muslim migrant communities. Like some European nations, its aim was to address social concerns. At the forefront of addressing extremism in the United Kingdom is a nongovernmental organization by the name of Active Change Foundation. It uses funds to develop resources and training to address extremist politics.

Saudi Arabian Program

Saudi Arabia commenced its deradicalization program in 2004. At first it did not expand to those involved in terrorist activities but soon included those incarcerated in Guantanamo Bay and returning from fighting in places like Iraq. The Saudi program is managed by religious clerics, psychologists, and security personnel. The program offers classes and counseling on sharia law, psychology, vocational training, sociology, history, Islamic culture, art therapy, and athletics.[14] Similar to other programs, it does not attempt to change a person's beliefs but rather attempts to remove the propensity to use violence. The program also emphasizes incorporating the person's family in therapy. Following their release from the program, radicals are monitored by security specialists.[15] Saudi Arabian authorities initially claimed a 100 percent success rate. But in more recent years it acknowledged that there may be approximately 20 percent of program graduates who return to terrorist activities.[16]

North African Programs

Within the North African region, the Kingdom of Morocco has made important efforts to stem radicalization and has extended this program to its expatriates living in Europe. In Morocco the king is the senior authority on religious instruction, having the title Commander of Faith, which provides an opportunity to address religious-based extremism.

Morocco has also established an official register of imams and has created a directorate of religious education that includes training for Muslim leaders to deal with extremist views. In addition to localized efforts, Morocco has established a religious council in Europe to provide instruction for Moroccans living overseas. It is also active in reviewing religious textbooks and school syllabi to ensure there are no radical teachings or calls to violence.[17]

Southeast Asian Programs

Earlier in this chapter we mentioned the Thai approach to deradicalization to highlight the socioeconomic approaches to reeducating members of terrorist organizations. However, it is Malaysia that claims to have had the most successful deradicalization rates in Southeast Asia. In 2016, the Malaysian government stated it had a 97 percent success rate with its deradicalization program. On the surface, the program does not seem significantly different from other programs throughout the world, so this success rate may be questionable. It removes radicalized prisoners from the general population and provides religious and psychological counseling. It also teaches vocational training and provides instruction for prisoners to produce and market products sold on their behalf. The inmates receive the funds from product sales upon leaving the prison.[18]

Study Questions

1. Explain the difference between deradicalization, counterradicalization, and antiradicalization. Discuss why it is important to have definitions.
2. List some of the central ideas behind deradicalization programs.
3. Discuss some of the potential shortcomings of deradicalization programs.
4. Can any of the regions highlighted in this chapter lay claim to having the most effective deradicalization program? Explain your response.

Learning Activity

Find information about a counterradicalization or antiradicalization program in your country or region. Describe the program, highlighting its features, how it operates, and who administers it. Has the program published any data on success rates? Evaluate the program's strengths and weaknesses, and present your findings in briefing-paper format.

Notes

1. Lindsay Clutterbuck, *Deradicalization Programs and Counterterrorism: A Perspective on the Challenges and Benefits* (Washington, DC: Middle East Institute, 2015), 5.

2. Clutterbuck, *Deradicalization Programs and Counterterrorism.*

3. Clutterbuck, *Deradicalization Programs and Counterterrorism.*

4. Nathee Chitsawang, "Deradicalization Programs in Prison," 2017, http://thaicriminology.com/deradicalization-programs-in-prison.html.

5. Chitsawang, "Deradicalization Programs in Prison."

6. Chitsawang, "Deradicalization Programs in Prison."

7. Stefanie Mitchell, "Deradicalization: Using Triggers for the Development of a U.S. Program," *Journal for Deradicalization* no. 9 (Winter 2016–2017), 107.

8. Anne Speckhard, "Prison and Community Based Disengagement and Deradicalization Programs for Extremists Involved in Militant Jihadi Terrorism Ideologies and Activities," in Laurie Fenstermacher and Anne Speckhard (eds.), *Social Sciences Support to Military Personnel Engaged in Counter-Insurgency and Counter-Terrorism Operations: Report of the NATO Research and Technology Group 172*, NATO Science Series (Brussels: NATO, 2011), 3.

9. Samuel J. Mullins, "Rehabilitation of Islamist Terrorists: Lessons from Criminology," *University of Wollongong Research Online* (Faculty of Law) (2011), 7, https://ro.uow.edu.au/lawpapers/225.

10. Brendan I. Koerner, "A Controversial New Program Aims to Reform Homegrown Isis Recruits Back into Normal Young Americans," *Wired*, January 24, 2017, https://www.wired.com/2017/01/can-you-turn-terrorist-back-into-citizen.

11. Riazat Butt and Henry Tuck, *European Counter-Radicalisation and De-Radicalisation: A Comparative Evaluation of Approaches in the Netherlands, Sweden, Denmark, and Germany* (Oslo: Institute for Strategic Dialogue, 2014).

12. Maria Lozano, *Inventory of the Best Practices on Deradicalization from the Different Member States of the EU* (Amsterdam: Impact Knowledge and Advice Centre, 2014), 30.

13. Lozano, *Inventory of the Best Practices on Deradicalization,* 31.

14. Marisa L. Porges, *The Saudi Deradicalization Experiment* (New York: Council on Foreign Relations, January 22, 2010), https://www.cfr.org/expert-brief/saudi-deradicalization-experiment.

15. Porges, *The Saudi Deradicalization Experiment.*

16. Porges, *The Saudi Deradicalization Experiment.*

17. Kingdom of Morocco, *Morocco's Approach to Countering Violent Extremism* (Washington, DC: Moroccan American Center, September 8, 2016).

18. "Zahid Hamidi: Malaysia's Deradicalization Programme Best in the World," *The Star Online,* February 20, 2016, https://www.thestar.com.my/news/nation/2016/02/20/zahid-hamidi-malaysia-deradicalization-programme-best-in-the-world/#Bzglq6qBHup1kwYJ.99.

14

Global Approaches to Counterterrorism

The concept of a global approach to terrorism suggests that all nations are willing and able to assist in addressing the threat posed by terrorists. It also assumes that there is multilateral agreement on what constitutes terrorism. Consequently, it could be assumed that there are terrorists on one side and a united network of nations on the other who are committed to bringing these outlaws to heel.

However, there are complexities that need to be dealt with if such a crucial mass of anti-terrorism opposition is to be achieved. While acts of terrorism are criminal, the political motives of the crime make it difficult to galvanize the support for a global approach. Despite the difficulties and perhaps the impossibility of creating a global approach, there is merit in maintaining it as an aspiration.

A global approach to terrorism is required in the twenty-first century because never has the world been so interconnected and interdependent. It is not a cliché to say that technology has made the world smaller by enabling economies, communication, and transportation to traverse borders. So it is not surprising that terrorism has also become interconnected.

Terrorism's appeal is as vast as the economies, communication, and transportation it uses. While a terrorist cause may be parochial, its ideology and tactics can be broad. Naturally, a well-resourced terrorist group will have far-reaching capabilities that require a global counterterrorism approach.

While accepting these complexities, it is evident that there are mechanisms at play (internationally) that are attempting to build a global approach, even if it is at times working only through narrow international alliances or a collective interest of states. These mechanisms include diplomacy, law enforcement and military cooperation, and humanitarian and community approaches. They take a multipronged approach and, when used concurrently, can create a global approach through use of international resources. These approaches use hard- and soft-power politics and social welfare. Soft power is used in international relations to gain support from other states by economic persuasion or national prestige. Hard power is aggressive and usually involves use of a state's military or security intelligence apparatus to pressure another state into submission.

Contrasting Perceptions

Bodies like the United Nations as well as nations brought together under security pacts such as NATO and the Australia, New Zealand, United States Security Treaty (ANZUS) provide policing and military cooperation and share intelligence to address terrorism. Nevertheless, international governing bodies and international alliances are fraught with divergent geopolitical outlooks that make it difficult to agree on what constitutes terrorism.

Some terrorists enjoy the support of nation-states for a variety of reasons. Whether ideological, political, religious, or economic, terrorists enjoy state-sponsored assistance. In practice, this means it is difficult to have a fully global bipartisan approach. The difficulty in obtaining unpartisan cooperation lies in the disagreement over what constitutes terrorism. This failure to agree on who is, and who is not, a terrorist is a significant issue because labeling who is a terrorist is a matter of political interpretation. Take the following definitions of terrorism as example. In 1937, the League of Nations defined terrorism as "All criminal acts directed against a State and intended or calculated to create a state of terror in the minds of particular persons or a group of persons or the general public."[1] In 1998 the League of Arab States proposed the following definition: "Any act or threat of violence, whatever its motives or purposes, that occurs in the advancement of an individual or collective criminal agenda and seeking to sow panic among people, causing fear or harming them, or placing their lives, liberty or security in danger, or seeking to cause damage to the environment or to public or private installations or property or to occupying or seizing them, or seeking to jeopardize national resources."[2] In 2005 the United Nations defined terrorism as actions "intended to cause death or serious bodily harm to civilians or non-combatants with the purpose of intimidating a population or compelling a government or an international organization to do or abstain from doing any act."[3]

On the surface, the definitions appear somewhat similar, so it would seem possible to have the basis for an international response to terrorism. But behind efforts to define terrorism are larger debates and disagreements on the interpretation of terrorism—all of which are based on political perspectives. To illustrate the point, Iran is known to have supported Hezbollah and Qatar has been linked to lending support to Hamas. Hamas seeks to create a separate Palestine state from an area that it perceives as occupied by Israel. Meanwhile Hezbollah has sought to remove Israel from Lebanon. From a pro-Palestine or pro-Shiite viewpoint, these two groups could be viewed as freedom fighters. But from an Israeli and a broader Western perspective, Hamas and Hezbollah are terrorist organizations.

The United Nations, while it has some definition of terrorism, also recognizes the right for people to fight against tyrannical governments, institutionalized racism, and even colonization. This means that it becomes a matter of interpreting the *cause* from a specific standpoint. The late Yasser Arafat interpreted his cause in an address to the United Nations in 1974:

> The difference between the revolutionary and the terrorist lies in the reason for which each fights. For whoever stands by a just cause and fights for the freedom and liberation of his land from the invaders, the settlers and the colonialists cannot possibly be called terrorist, otherwise the American people in their struggle for liberation from the British colonialists would have been terrorists; the European resistance against the Nazis would be terrorism, the struggle of the Asian, African and Latin American peoples would also be terrorism, and many of you who are in this Assembly hall were considered terrorists.[4]

Assessing his statement with critical attention to the details shows several issues that immediately present themselves for debate—for example, his reference to a *just cause* and liberation from *invaders* is fuel to ignite dispute. Also, his analogy to resistance to the Nazis is contentious because, as history shows, World War II was a fight waged against an immensely militarized nation, not a political resistance that targeted an unarmed civilian population. Additional criticism can be made, but the point is that terrorists will distort facts to suit their cause. Therefore, the problem of a global response to terrorism is in the interpretation of terrorist actions. The political context within terrorism makes it harder to combat globally. It is unlike international crime, which is often driven by simple economic gain, and for which it is therefore easier for nations to agree on a definition.

Given the political dichotomy inherent in terrorism and its relationship to global politics, terrorism can be countered only by groups of states that agree that a specific group is a terrorist organization. Once that agreement is made, it is left to those states to use diplomatic cooperation, military alliances, or joint community and humanitarian approaches to address this issue.

These methods are the three pillars that provide the foundation for a global approach. Without the right blend of each, combating terrorism would be unachievable. Despite the difficulties inherent in the complexities of agreeing on who is a terrorist, these pillars provide a way forward.

Diplomatic Cooperation

Gaining diplomatic cooperation is the first step to forming a counterterrorism strategy. It involves the use of soft international political power. Diplomatic cooperation usually commences with one or more states seeking assistance from other states to deal with a terrorist situation.

Gaining support from other states has several benefits. A coalition of nations can share resources and spread the costs as well as the risks associated with engaging a terrorist group. A coalition, particularly a large coalition, can demonstrate that there is an international mandate for action to address the problem.

Expressions of soft power include influencing states to support counterterrorism activities in return for, say, aid, funding, or other economic inducements. As an example, the United States reportedly provided Pakistan with US$33.4 billion over a fifteen-year period to support US anti-terrorism operations in Afghanistan.[5] Similar to the approaches to counterradicalization discussed in previous chapters, soft power can also be targeted directly at a region or community to address economic or social problems, with the aim of diffusing the influence of terrorist ideology.

Diplomatic cooperation can be expressed in the form of international treaties. The most well-known body for formulating international treaties is the United Nations. In the absence of a definition of terrorism, UN treaties are aimed at addressing terrorism but tend to focus on the criminal aspects of these activities. UN-based treaties focus more on international crime rather than on anti-terrorism specifically.

UN treaties include international anti-hijacking laws, conventions on taking hostages and piracy (see Chapter 10). A focus on international crime is less contentious when compared to trying to forge an agreement on the political interpretations of terrorism, given the number of sovereign states and groups harboring political and religious grievances. Consequently, focusing on criminality instead of politics makes consensus-building more realistic.

Within the realm of diplomatic cooperation there are some cultural and historical circumstances that help shape the type of diplomatic agreements made. For instance, within the Association of Southeast Asian Nations (ASEAN) there is a requirement to maintain sovereignty. ASEAN members assert the value of noninterference in domestic matters of other states. Therefore, addressing transnational crime, and specifically terrorism, becomes problematic, because it is seen as interfering with another state's sovereignty. This sensitivity extends to military cooperation.[6]

Much of the emphasis placed on sovereignty (over cooperation) has its foundations in colonial Southeast Asia. In reaction against colonialism, for many of the postcolonial Asian states this is a delicate issue. Yet the implications of such an attitude mean a lack of coordination of resources including law enforcement, intelligence sharing, and even human rights.

Diplomatic agreements on counterterrorism serve as the basis for more specific cooperation. Once there is consensus on terrorism, diplomatic agreements can pave the way for military cooperation and a range of joint operational and strategic planning. Diplomatic agreements can also provide a path for providing humanitarian and community approaches.

Military Coalitions and Cooperation

Military coalitions and cooperation are extensions of diplomatic agreements about a terrorist threat. The wars in Afghanistan and Iraq are examples of military coalitions: partners working together to combat terrorist organizations or fighting shoulder-to-shoulder. Military cooperation is different in that it provides training, intelligence, weaponry, and the like to another state that is dealing with terrorism.

In 2017, the efforts of Australia and the United States to assist the Philippine government in dealing with the Maute group, Abu Sayyaf, and the Bangsamoro Islamic Freedom Fighters, in the south of the country, constitute an example of such military cooperation. The agreement between Australia and the Philippines included the provision of training to the Philippine military as well as collaborating to improve intelligence analysis, reconnaissance, and surveillance in areas occupied by these terrorist groups. It also included provision of maritime security.[7]

Some forms of military cooperation may have considerable political overtones that lead observers to question the rationale for the response. Military cooperation can also illustrate an important change in geopolitical viewpoints. For instance, in 2017, Iraq and Iran signed a memorandum of understanding that outlined their decision to cooperate in fighting terrorism and political extremism. It focused on border security as well as educational, logistical, technical, and military support.[8] This kind of military cooperation prior to 2003 would have been unthinkable. But with the fall of Saddam Hussein's regime and the rise of a Shiite Iraqi government, the two nations were able to agree on a common terror threat because they shared a common political and religious position.

Military Coalitions

An emerging military coalition is the Islamic Military Counter Terrorism Coalition. The coalition aims to share military and intelligence resources. Headquartered in Saudi Arabia, in 2016 the coalition comprised forty-one members. Covering most regions of the world, it had members in Asia, Africa, and the Middle East. Not all its members enlisted to have a military role, but it had wide support from the Muslim community around the world.

As of early 2018, there had not been any notable operations undertaken by the coalition, nor had there been details about the coalition's strategic interests. However, it is an important development in the global approach to addressing terrorism because it serves to distinguish Islam from the brand of psychotic theology practiced by Muslim terrorists. It is also an appropriate military coalition considering most terrorist attacks take place in Muslim countries. It marks a shift in the way Islamic nations approach terrorism.

Since the 9/11 attacks, the United States has organized several military coalitions. The so-called Coalition of the Willing was assembled in 2003 to remove Saddam Hussein from his dictatorial rule in Iraq because it was a state sponsor of terrorism and wrongly identified as manufacturing weapons of mass destruction. In that instance the coalition was made up of approximately thirty nations, mostly smaller Eastern European nations. The Coalition of the Willing was a contentious alliance because it lacked support from more influential nations and Arab nations. It also failed to secure a mandate from the United Nations. The Coalition of the Willing was an attempt to demonstrate that there was a broad consensus among nations that Iraq posed a threat to global security. However, not all nations viewed Iraq as such, and the subsequent investigation by the Commission on the Intelligence Capabilities of the United States Regarding Weapons of Mass Destruction found that "the Intelligence Community's performance in assessing Iraq's pre-war weapons of mass destruction programs was a major intelligence failure. The failure was not merely that the Intelligence Community's assessments were wrong. There were also serious shortcomings in the way these assessments were made and communicated to policymakers."[9]

Nevertheless, the Coalition of the Willing illustrates the subjectivity involving what constitutes state-sponsored terrorism as well as terrorism in general. Moreover, it is equally difficult to gain consensus on what acts are considered terrorism when the attack is aimed at a military target (see Chapter 4). The experience of the Coalition of the Willing also suggests that military coalitions need to have recognition by the international community to be legitimate.

Legitimacy requires comprehensive diplomatic engagement. Of course, full consensus by the international community is never likely to be achieved, for reasons already discussed, but nevertheless it is not unreasonable for this to be the diplomatic objective. To be successful, a global approach to terrorism requires a strong diplomatic mandate, not just a military coalition alone.

Intelligence Cooperation

For the most part there is an apprehensiveness to share intelligence, not only domestically between different agencies, but also internationally between nations. This issue was highlighted as a significant problem by the 9/11 Commission in its report and remains an ongoing concern.

Interagency rivalry, lack of trust, and failure to communicate were cited as partial contributing factors for the intelligence failure that led to the 9/11 attacks. Perhaps the most important lesson learned from 9/11 is the need to share intelligence.[10] International intelligence cooperation is essential to achieve a global response to terrorism, but cooperation requires considerable trust between nations.

An important development in intelligence cooperation was the creation of fusion centers. Fusion centers can access data from a range of agencies, both national and international. The fusion concept allows for a single access point for critical decisionmaking information. These data may come from law enforcement, the military, as well as myriad other sources relating to terrorist targets.

In a fusion center, data are analyzed and intelligence reports are produced for dissemination to members of the fusion center. The concept is gaining interest in several nations and within political and military alliances. An example of sharing intelligence resources among nations is the North Atlantic Treaty Organization's Intelligence Unit. In 2002, NATO established a Terrorist Threat Intelligence Unit, comprising civilian and military intelligence officers. It provided risk assessments and monitored terrorist threats for NATO's member states. In 2010, this unit was replaced with a new unit, simply known as the Intelligence Unit. With a similar organizational makeup, the new unit widened its intelligence mandate to include transnational threats.[11]

One of the more successful intelligence cooperation arrangements is known as the Five Eyes. This is a group of intelligence agencies from Australia, Canada, New Zealand, the United Kingdom, and the United States. It is one of the longest-standing international intelligence alliances. Emerging from World War II, the Five Eyes today share intelligence on a range of topics, including terrorist threats, and undertake joint intelligence operations. It is recognized as one of the most closely bonded international intelligence-sharing groups. Its success comes from its long-standing history of trust and cooperation, but also from the cultural and political similarities between the participating states. The commonalities of these nations' shared history in conflict have brought about a truly unified approach.

Humanitarian and Community Approaches

Humanitarian and community approaches to terrorism are illustrations of soft power (see Figure 14.1). The types of strategies used in humanitarian and community approaches are similar in various countries. These approaches may include education, creating employment opportunities, providing social welfare services, and implementing programs that alleviate poverty and provide relief from natural disasters.

The aim of humanitarian and community approaches to address terrorism is to remove the "push factors" that lead people to adopt radical ideology, and then go on to commit acts of terrorism. Push factors can be a lack of education and little opportunity to study to gain a skill, high unemployment, insufficient housing, poor health, inadequate food and water, as well as the other trappings of poverty, whether these are brought about by natural disasters or human (political) causes.

Education and Training

The role that education and training play in combating terrorism has many facets. On a base level, they provide individuals and communities with the knowledge and skills that can assist them in gaining employment. On a higher level, they provide literacy and numeracy skills that can empower people by developing their critical thinking, which they can use not only in their daily lives but also to question terrorist ideology. For instance, a problem in some states is that education and training are provided (particularly to the poor) by religious organizations. In some instances, these organizations may harbor religious extremist views that are passed on through the curriculum.

Employment Opportunities

Low-level supporters of terrorism are often involved for financial reasons. In addition to providing education and training, the economic

Courtesy of the US government.

Figure 14.1 Emergency aid supplies arrive in Tacloban, Philippines, November 16, 2013. The Philippine Department of Social Welfare and Development, which was the lead local agency for aid distribution, ensured that these essential supplies reached the municipalities affected by Typhoon Haiyan.

development of communities can provide additional employment opportunities. Capital works programs not only assist in developing community infrastructure but also help create secondary sources of employment.

Another program is a micro-loans scheme aimed at establishing small or cottage-based businesses. Micro-loans are low-cost but high-impact fund advances that can strengthen a poor community's economy by empowering its people. The rationale for providing employment opportunities it to remove economic hardship because experience shows that poverty leads some disenfranchised people to adopt radical political solutions to their problems. In some cases, that radical solution may by the adoption of terrorist ideology.

Social Welfare Services

Even in a robust economic climate there will always be segments of society that fail to benefit from a community's prosperity. This sense of exclusion can build resentment. Those who experience this exclusion tend to be more inclined to be attracted to extremist ideology, which often provides a naive political explanation and a simplistic solution for their economic or social problems.

Human welfare services play an influential role in addressing social disadvantage. If targeted correctly, these services have the potential to help relieve social problems, thereby countering the opportunities militants exploit to recruit new members and garner sympathy in the larger community.

Delivering Humanitarian and Community Approaches

In most instances, governments are the major funders of humanitarian and community approaches. But they are not always at the forefront of service and program delivery. Governments encourage community groups and nongovernmental organizations (NGOs) to provide humanitarian programs.

Aside from the cost-effectiveness of contracting humanitarian programs to NGOs, there are sound political and social reasons to do so. Key motives include creating the perception of distance from the social issue. Distance is particularly useful when a government is being viewed as a cause of the problem. Another reason is a government's ability to influence communities in other nations experiencing similar issues. Working through NGOs, a government can sponsor a humanitarian program to address terrorism in a foreign state without showing a direct hand.

Finally, governments recognize that nongovernmental organizations have a better understanding of the affected individuals. This allows NGOs to run programs that can play a significant part in counterradicalization measures. The establishment of outreach programs within communities at risk of radicalization has become a standard approach to overcoming terrorism.

Scenario Bringing Together the Three Pillars

This hypothetical scenario demonstrates how the diplomatic, military, and humanitarian pillars can work.

Background

Country X is located on the border of Countries A and B. Country X has suffered severe economic recession and high unemployment because of a succession of natural disasters. An organization known as the People's Salvation Front has been conducting a series of terrorist attacks in Country X with the goal of destabilizing the government to take power. The People's Salvation Front has made claims that it is only through a revolutionary act that Country X can enjoy prosperity again. As the terrorist attacks intensify, Country A launches an intelligence operation that determines that the People's Salvation Front is funded by Country Z because of the long-standing grievances between the two countries. Meanwhile Country B has discovered that the People's Salvation Front has plans to expand their attacks into neighboring countries to spread their ideology, with the hope of producing a transnational empire.

Diplomatic Cooperation

Country B has concerns for its national security. It meets with Country A's leaders and the two agree that the People's Salvation Front is a terrorist organization because of the tactics it uses. They both seek security talks with Country X, expressing their concerns. It is agreed that the three countries should jointly approach the United Nations with their fears about the People's Salvation Front. They also agree to propose a motion that the People's Salvation Front be declared a terrorist organization.

The three countries meet with other countries to gain support for their motion. However, Country Z is lobbying at the United Nations too. It is arguing that the People's Salvation Front is a group committed to combating the tyrannical regime in Country X. Country Z also enjoys a great deal of soft power within the United Nations, so it can successfully block any moves to have the People's Salvation Front declared a terrorist organization. Countries X, A, and B are therefore left without a United Nations mandate, but agree action still needs to be taken.

Military Cooperation and Coalition

Countries A and B offer Country X anti-terrorism and intelligence training as well as logistical support for Country X's forces engaged to dealing with the terrorists. The three countries agree to establish a joint intelligence center to share information about the People's Salvation Front.

Through military cooperation, intelligence finds that the People's Salvation Front has established a training base not far from villages in the country's north along the border with Country Z. Countries X, A, and B decide to send a coalition force comprising armed specialists from each country to remove the training base. The coalition force engages the People's Salvation Front at the training base, destroying it. In the engagement, many members of the People's Salvation Front disband and blend into surrounding villages.

Humanitarian and Community Approach

Villages in the north in Country X have suffered some of the worst effects from the nation's economic recession. There is higher than average unemployment and the resulting poverty has made the region susceptible to propaganda espoused by the People's Salvation Front, propaganda that is now spreading throughout the area.

Young unemployed men are particularly attracted to the People's Salvation Front. Country X's government is not trusted in the area because of a clash of ethnic differences but knows there are a couple of NGOs working in the area. Using financial assistance from Countries A and B, Country X offers the NGOs funds to conduct employment and training programs for the local unemployed men. It also seeks to develop several counterradicalization programs. In addition, Country X commences a number of capital works programs using expertise from engineers in Countries A and B. The introduction of capital works and training programs eases many of the economic problems in the area, and there is a decrease in support for the People's Salvation Front to the point that it becomes no more than a political ideology shared by a few hardcore radicals.

Study Questions

1. Explain what are soft and hard power. Describe where soft- and hard-power strategies fit within the three-pillar global approach to terrorism.
2. Discuss how diplomatic cooperation can lead to military cooperation.
3. Explain why humanitarian and community approaches are important aspects of dealing with terrorism.
4. Explain why the United Nations has had difficulty in defining terrorism.
5. Describe some of the problems associated with establishing military cooperation to address terrorism.

Learning Activity

Reread the scenario bringing the three pillars together. Using this case, explain what other options may have been available to Countries X, A, and B, and suggest an alternative outcome based on the options you provide.

Notes

1. League of Nations, *Convention for the Prevention and Punishment of Terrorism* (Geneva, November 1937), 6.
2. League of Arab States, *The Arab Convention for the Suppression of Terrorism* (Cairo, April 1998), 2.
3. United Nations, "With Call for Action, Not More Words: Annan Outlines Plan for Radical UN Reform," March 21, 2005, https://news.un.org/en/story/2005/03/132432-call-action-not-more-words-annan-outlines-plan-radical-un-reform.
4. Yasser Arafat, "General Assembly Speech," New York, United Nations, November 13, 1974.
5. Shahbaz Rana, "War on Terror Aid: Pakistan," *Express Tribune,* September 6, 2017.
6. Chester Cabalza, "Can ASEAN Work Together to Fight Regional Terrorism?" *The Diplomat,* August 9, 2017.

7. Andrew Green, "ADF Counter-Terrorism Team to Head-Up Urban Warfare Training with Philippine Troops in Marawi" (Canberra: Australian Broadcasting Commission, October 24, 2017).

8. "Iran and Iraq Sign Accord to Boost Military Cooperation," *Reuters,* July 23, 2017, https://www.reuters.com/article/us-iran-iraq-military/iran-and-iraq-sign-accord-to-boost-military-cooperation-idUSKBN1A80HJ.

9. Commission on the Intelligence Capabilities of the United States Regarding Weapons of Mass Destruction, *Report to the President of the United States* (Washington, DC: WMD Commission, 2005), 46.

10. National Commission on Terrorist Attacks upon the United States, *The 9/11 Commission Report* (Washington, DC, 2004), Executive Summary.

11. North Atlantic Treaty Organization (NATO), "Intelligence Sharing in Combating Terrorism," http://natolibguides.info/intelligence.

Part 3
Conclusion

15

Can the War on Terror Be Won?

It could be argued that utopian visions are what advance humanity. The thought of ridding the world of cancer, infectious disease, poverty, crime, and illiteracy, and building a permanent peace, is a noble dream toward which nations work every day. Institutions have been established to pursue these ideals, such as the World Health Organization, the United Nations, and hundreds of private think tanks and philanthropic foundations—the Bill and Melinda Gates Foundation, Open Society Foundations, Ford Foundation, Rockefeller Foundation, and the list goes on.

Have the billions of dollars and inestimable hours spent striving toward these goals eliminated the problems? The answer is clear. But has this stopped the world from forging ahead regardless? That answer is also obvious. Nevertheless, the question that could be asked is why humanity pursues goals that are obviously utopian in vision, knowing full well that these goals are never likely to be reached. This short answer is *hope*. It is what makes our species unique.

Societies have many other goals that are less ambitious than eliminating disease or illiteracy, or saving the environment. Take for instance curbing the road death toll. If one were to count the number of local, state, and national road safety campaigns that have been conducted over a century of driving worldwide, as well as the treasury of funds spent on safety research, these would likely be figures of staggering proportions. Yet every year, in every country that has roads and cars, people are injured and killed. Regardless, we know that the issue of road safety has improved since traffic accidents gave rise to the phenomenon. This is due to better road design, safety features built into cars, laws that mandate safer driving practice, and driver education that has led to an improvement in driving skills.

Injury and death still occur because of cancer, infectious disease, poverty, crime, illiteracy, and conflict and war. Can these issues be eliminated? Perhaps not. But asking the question in such simplistic terms isn't the best way to help resolve these problems. And terrorism is just a small aspect of the problem category of crime.

So, what can be done to address terrorism? Although it constitutes only a fraction of what has been defined as crime, by its nature it draws a significant amount of the world's attention. "Kill one, frighten ten thousand." When the September 2001 attacks killed thousands, they frightened the world.

Debating the War on Terror

Writing in 2003, Alan Dershowitz argued that the greatest danger to the world order was from religiously inspired, state-sponsored terrorists.[1] Unlike the assassins of ancient times, who would use a dagger to kill an individual, terrorists have moved to using weapons that kill indiscriminately as well as showing an interest in acquiring weapons of mass destruction. If the analogy with road safety is used, society has not given up on the goal of reducing motor vehicle injuries and deaths. It has taken steps to implement better policies and practices. If the problem of global terrorism is a phenomenon likened to traffic losses, governments can take similar steps to reduce the frequency and severity of terrorist attacks.[2]

Scholars are at odds about whether this can be done and what is preventing it from occurring. Some argue that if we understand the underlying conditions that spawn terrorist grievances, we can address the root causes. Others argue that a tougher stance must be taken, because soft options only cater to the terrorists' demands. There is weight to each argument because the positions posited by the two sides of the debate are supported with various forms of evidence.

Nonetheless, as with any form of debate, much of the debate around terrorism has to do with the persons making the argument, their charisma (or lack thereof), and how they craft their arguments.

From critics of these types of dichotomous positions, we know that many ignore or fail to recognize logical fallacies, limitations of the data on which they rely (or ignore), and restrictions of the analytic methods they employ to draw their conclusions. They sometimes slip into using inductive logic—which on the surface appears reasonable but isn't because the premises are merely cogent, not true like the premises that form a deductive argument. Other times they may be susceptible to confirmation bias when selecting evidence to support their arguments, ignoring evidence that shows the contrary. Moreover, some have obfuscated the spuriousness of their arguments by calling into question peripheral issues of their opponents' positions, often using emotive language and thus diverting the main argument to issues that are tangential to the central debate. There are many other logical traps, as well as evidentiary and analytical pitfalls, that have befallen terrorism scholars trying to answer the question of whether we can win a war on terror.

Coping with Terrorism

There are certainly strategies that governments can take to reduce the frequency and severity of terrorist attacks. The goal with this approach is not to eliminate terrorism but rather to cope with and manage terrorism. This does not mean that society must abandon the aspirational dream of having a terrorism-free world; it means that we need to accept that when we create communities, build cities, and engage in trade and commerce, we introduce the phenomenon of conflict, which needs to be managed. Disagreement, opposing views, and, as human nature attests, violent conflict manifest from hatred, intolerance, and acts of aggression in the pursuit of political advantage and power.

Dealing with terrorism therefore means that we should define what is meant by "manage." If we take the utopian view of a total absence of the phenomenon, then it is likely that this may mean measures that are so oppressive that social values and other community goals will be consequently eliminated in the process. If we return to the analogy of human losses caused by traffic accidents as a way of visualizing the issue, an injury- and death-free road transport system would look much different from what exists today; its operation would likely be so restrictive that the advantages the current system offers would disappear. Transposing these similarities to a terrorism-free world is likely to see a comparable change. The question then is what level of terrorism society can cope with given that it is a utopian view to think the world can become free of all conflict. If we accept this premise, how do we manage terrorism?

Managing Terrorism

Before we can discuss how terrorism can be managed, we must determine what we mean by terrorism. In Chapter 1 we looked at the different forms this crime can take. We noted the taxonomy of terrorism and its typology. This showed that there are four classifications: domestic, transnational, international, and state. Understanding these categories helps us conceptualize terrorism within a framework that can allow us to address the issue. For instance, it is axiomatic that a strategy devised to address domestic terrorism would not be suited for international terrorism. Each category of terrorism needs a tailored approach, even those within the same classification. This is because a domestic terrorism issue in the United States is likely to be different from a domestic group that is operating in Canada, Australia, New Zealand, or the United Kingdom. The situation applies across the taxonomy.

When we look at the typology that applies to each category of terrorism, we realize that the problem of designing countermeasures becomes more complex. Take for example domestic terrorism again; it is not an unvarying form. In Chapter 1 we discussed that terrorism comprises six types: political, religious, limited political, lone-actor, state-sponsored, and criminal. It is also axiomatic that each type within each classification needs a different strategy, and each strategy depends on the geographic context in which it will be applied, as well as the political, social, and cultural norms of that area. In addition to these confounding variables, there is the issue of financial resources—how much tax revenue each community is willing to give to their political leaders to pay for countermeasures; and what personal and collective freedoms they are willing to sacrifice for a given level of management. Some communities might be in more need than others, and hence more willing to do more—take Israel, for instance. Other communities less so, and so the permutations unfold. It is obvious that there is no one-size-fits-all approach.

Strategies and Countermeasures

If these variables affect how communities approach the issue of terrorism, then is it understandable why the debate in the literature has been fraught with disagreement—hard-liners versus humanitarians, in simple terms. Much of what is being advocated one way or another has not been grounded in a theoretical frame that considers the issues just discussed—logic traps, the taxonomy of terrorism, and its typology. It does not account for the geographic setting, or the political, social, and cultural norms of the community. However, if the science of crime management discussed in this book is applied to terrorism, solutions tailored for each issue can be determined. Does this mean there is *a* solution to terrorism? No. There is no single solution because of the dynamic nature of terrorism and the various manifestations of terrorists' targets. Yet it does mean that a custom strategy can be crafted for each type of terrorism.

How would a community do this? Let's take a major US city as a hypothetical example, Boston. As discussed in Chapter 12, Boston would need to conduct a terrorism threat assessment. This analytical report would provide an objective basis for determining whether there is a threat, who the threat is, and, importantly, if the threat has the four factors that are necessary to be a credible threat—that is, desire and expectation, and knowledge resources.

Once a picture of who constitutes a threat has been developed, several methodological approaches to crime control can be applied: traditional, zero-tolerance, community policing, problem-oriented policing, and intelligence-led policing. The last three approaches could be considered offensive strategies because they actively seek to address the problem. The first two are more concerned with taking a defensive (reactive) stance.

In Chapter 10 we discussed the complementary approach of defensive measures. These approaches to crime management are called crime prevention strategies and include the widely used principles of crime prevention through environmental design (CPTED). The other defensive crime prevention measure is that of situational crime prevention, whereby specific forms of crime are managed by designing or manipulating the environment in such a way as to reduce criminal opportunity.[3]

If the terrorism issue is found to be in the international sphere, military options and intelligence operations can be employed. These too were discussed in Chapter 10. Under the legal doctrine of *jus in bello,* small-scale force operations can be initiated, as well as large-scale deployments developed. An example of the former is the 1986 air raid on the former dictator of Libya—the late Colonel Muammar Qaddafi. An example of the latter is the military operation that targeted al-Qaeda and Taliban forces in Afghanistan between 2001 and 2014.

In terms of intelligence operations, these could involve covert preemptive neutralization: killing terrorists in acts of preemptive self-defense. Of course, these options are not the only possibilities for the application of either military or intelligence resources; they merely suggest the types of deployments that are possible when the problem is located overseas.

Conclusion

Although scholars will disagree about the solution to win the global war on terror, it is clear from our brief examination that we must understand the underlying conditions that give rise to terrorist grievances, so we can address the causes. Simultaneously, we must also take a tougher stance. Both approaches are necessary.

The thought that terrorism can be defeated by the routing of a corrupt foreign political regime or the elimination of leaders of a couple of key terrorist cells is precarious. Likewise, providing diversionary programs and creating counternarratives to redirect disaffected people from terrorism-inspired ideology is not as compelling as are focused strategies. Strategies need to be aimed at understanding the threat and then tactically targeting the underlying causes that give rise to extremism. As an overarching doctrinal approach, if the crime triangle theory (comprising an object or victim, criminal desire or the ability to commit a crime, and opportunity) were applied to terrorism, it becomes clear that the 9/11 attacks, as well as the subsequent bombings in Bali (2002) and Madrid (2004), along with the subsequent attacks that took place more than a decade later—Denmark (2015), France (2015, 2016, and 2017), Turkey (2015 and 2017), Germany (2016), Belgium (2016), Britain (2017), Spain (2017), Russia (2017), and Sweden (2017)—were not just well-*organized* attacks; they were also well-*supported* attacks.

In guerrilla warfare, fighters are organized into small units—like terrorist cells—but must rely on the support of the local population.

It is on the support of terrorist organizations and the encouragement given to individuals that law enforcement and military forces would benefit from focusing their intelligence resources. Until the financial and human bases that support these extreme views is diminished, civilized societies can expect high-severity attacks. This strategy aims to break two of the three sides of the crime triangle—criminal desire or the ability to commit a crime, and opportunity.

Take the case of al-Qaeda. It was an autonomous terrorist organization established by bin Laden to recruit fighters and raise money to conduct jihad. Its goal was a paradise on Earth. In Afghanistan, under the Taliban, this paradise was realized. It became a nation where there was no division between "church" and state: religious doctrine was the rule of law. It was a place where politics were based on a puritanical interpretation of the Quran (known as Wahhabism or Salafism). This view of religion rejected all notions of secular or pluralistic values, and adherence to these doctrines was enforced, if necessary, by bloodshed.

The Taliban benefited from al-Qaeda's efforts during and after the Soviet invasion. With this victory fresh in its memory, al-Qaeda set about extending its vision by bringing jihad to the doorstep of other so-called infidel countries: the West in general, and specifically in the United States, which it saw as the "Great Satan."

Bin Laden and other Islamic extremists believed that US troops resident in Saudi Arabia—the holy land of Islam—and America's "aggression" against the Iraqi people (such as the 1991 Gulf War and subsequent economic sanctions), and Israel's territorial occupation, were insults to Islam. These Islamic extremists were driven by a psychotic vision of using guns and bombs, and in the name of Allah they would rid the world of the infidel and in the process create a paradise on Earth.[4] What resulted seemed nothing of the sort (see Figure 15.1).

The United States assessed how this could best be countered. The conclusion was to tackle funding and recruitment/membership. However, this required a large-scale military operation—Operation Enduring Freedom (2001–2014). The operation was aimed at destroying al-Qaeda's safe-haven operational base in Afghanistan. To do this, the Taliban needed to be removed from power by force.

On a tactical scale, it could be argued that through systematic attacks on terrorists' financial bases (e.g., seizing their assets and, where applicable, cutting them off from state sponsors of terrorism)[5], liberal democracies can strip extremists of their ability to purchase

Courtesy of the US Air Force.

Figure 15.1 Nineteen US airmen died, and more than 350 service members and civilians were injured, in the terrorist attack at Khobar Towers, Dhahran, Saudi Arabia, on June 25, 1996.

arms and explosives (and the means to deploy both), thus reducing them to mere "radicals" spouting fanatical dogma. These members can then be subjected to the normal law enforcement methods for dealing with subversives.

As for recruitment, dealing with the underlying factors that give rise to disaffected, dispossessed, and marginalized men and women who are drawn to radical teachings can prevent new recruits from joining movements like al-Qaeda, Hamas, Islamic Jihad, and Jemaah Islamiah—movements that provide meaning for the disgruntled.

An example of this in practice can be seen in aid programs run by both the Australian and US governments in Indonesia.[6] Millions of dollars in foreign aid were provided by these countries on the condition that radical boarding schools (known as *pesantren*) had to demonstrate a far more moderate education curriculum that was not based on anti-Western teachings.

"In view of its dismal record, one wonders why terrorism persists, and what its attraction can be. The answer plainly lies in the deepest, darkest reaches of human nature. And so far, it is inaccessible to us."[7] Terrorism is a multifaceted problem that has no solution. Nevertheless, threat, vulnerability, and risk assessments will help us devise policies and programs that address two sides of the crime triangle— internationally as well as domestically. If we place this approach in the context of the question about what level of terrorism society can cope with, we won't be able to eliminate it, but we can bring it under control. If the two critical pillars of funding and recruitment/ membership can be addressed, then liberal democracies can expect to achieve a confident level of management over the problem.

Study Questions

1. Name the three sides of the crime triangle and explain how each is necessary for a crime to take place.
2. With the advantage of hindsight, discuss how the crime triangle theory could be applied to the terrorist attack of January 7, 2015, on the offices of the French satirical magazine *Charlie Hebdo*.

Learning Activity

In this chapter it has been argued that the so-called war on terror is not winnable because such a goal is only aspirational. Nevertheless, it is posited that, using a logical approach, the threats can be identified, the vulnerabilities recognized, and the risks assessed, so that interventions can be implemented. Knowing that this is not a one-size-fits-all approach, because these assessments must be conducted in the context of numerous confounding variables—domestic versus international threat; political, social, and cultural norms of a geographical area; and so on—give your thoughts about scholars who advocate using a statistical framework to predict future terrorist attacks based on recognizing past patterns of attacks. Research this statistical approach and argue either for or against this position as a viable option for managing terrorism.

Notes

1. Alan M. Dershowitz, *Why Terrorism Works: Understanding the Threat, Responding to the Challenge* (New Haven: Yale University Press, 2003).

2. Henry Prunckun and Philip B. Mohr, "Military Deterrence of International Terrorism: An Evaluation of Operation El Dorado Canyon," *Studies in Conflict and Terrorism* 20, no. 3 (1997).

3. Based on the crime triangle theory, which comprises an object or victim, criminal desire or the ability to commit a crime, and opportunity. The theory postulates that if any one of these elements is missing, a crime cannot be committed.

4. The promise of paradise comes "in the form of the perfect Islamic society here and now or, this failing, in the after-life." Carl Hammer, *Tide of Terror: America, Islamic Extremism, and the War on Terror* (Boulder: Paladin, 2003), 323.

5. As one example, Iran is known to have provided arms and training to Shiite militias, including Hamas in Gaza, Hezbollah in Lebanon, and the Houthis in Yemen, and it supported the regime of Bashar al-Assad in Syria.

6. John Kerin, "U.S. Aims at Terror Schools," *Weekend Australian*, October 4–5, 2003.

7. Thomas P. Raynor, *Terrorism: Past, Present, Future* (New York: Franklin Watts, 1982), 146.

Bibliography

Adorjan, Michael, Tony Christensen, Benjamin Kelly, and Dorothy Pawluch. "Stockholm Syndrome as Vernacular Resource." *Sociological Quarterly* 53, no. 3 (2012).

Alfred, Charlotte. "20 Years Ago, a Shadowy Cult Poisoned the Tokyo Subway." *World Post,* March 20, 2015. https://www.huffingtonpost.com/2015/03/20 /tokyo-subway-sarin-attack_n_6896754.html.

Anonymous. "Just Terror Tactics." *Ramiyah,* May 4, 2017.

Anti-Defamation League. "Anti-Abortion Violence: America's Forgotten Terrorism." September 4, 2012. https://www.adl.org/news/article/anti-abortion -violence-americas-forgotten-terrorism.

Arafat, Yasser. "General Assembly Speech." New York, United Nations, November 13, 1974.

Austrac. *Regional Risk Assessment on Terrorism Financing 2016 South-East Asia & Australia.* Canberra: Commonwealth of Australia, 2016.

Australian Broadcasting Corporation. "Sovereign Citizens: Terrorism Assessment Warns of Rising Threat from Anti-Government Extremists." *7.30 Report,* December 1, 2015. http://www.abc.net.au/news/2015-11-30/australias -sovereign-citizen-terrorism-threat/6981114.

Australian Charities and Not-for-Profits Commission. "Protecting Your Charity Against the Risk of Terrorism Financing." https://www.acnc.gov.au/ACNC /Edu/ProtectTF.aspx?TemplateType=P.

Baer, Robert. *See No Evil: The True Story of a Ground Soldier in the CIA's War on Terrorism.* New York: Crown, 2002.

Baldwin, Clare, and Andrew Marshall. "Between Duterte and a Death Squad: A Philippine Mayor Fights Drug-War Violence." March 17, 2017. https://www.reuters.com/article/us-philippines-drugs-mayor/between -duterte-and-a-death-squad-a-philippine-mayor-fights-drug-war-violence -idUSKBN16N33I.

Barefoot, J. Kirk. *Undercover Investigation.* Springfield, IL: Charles C. Thomas, 1975.

251

Bartholomees, J. Boone, Jr. "A Survey of Strategic Thought." In J. Boone Bartholomees Jr. (ed.), *Guide to National Security Policy and Strategy.* Carlisle, PA: US Army War College, 2004.

Begley, Patrick. "Sydney Siege Over: Lindt Café Gunman Forces Hostages to Appear in Videos." *Sydney Morning Herald,* December 16, 2014.

Best, Richard, and Alfred Cummings. *Open Source Intelligence Issues for Congress.* Washington, DC: Congressional Research Service, 2007.

Boehmer, Elleke. "Postcolonial Terrorist: The Example of Nelson Mandela." *Parallax* 11, no. 4 (2006).

Boggs, Carl, and Tom Pollard. "Hollywood and the Spectacle of Terrorism." *New Political Science* 28, no. 3 (2006).

Bolt, Andrew. "The Dark Side of Nelson Mandela." *Herald Sun,* December 8, 2013.

Bolton, David. *The Making of Tania Hearst.* London: New English Library, 1975.

Bonanno, George A., and John T. Jost. "Conservative Shift Among High-Exposure Survivors of the September 11th Terrorist Attacks." *Basic and Applied Social Psychology* no. 4 (2006).

Bowyer Bell, John. *Terror out of Zion: Irgun Zvai Leumi, LEHI, and the Palestine Underground, 1929–1949.* New York: St. Martin's, 1977.

Brandt, Patrick T., and Todd Sandler. "What Do Transnational Terrorists Target? Has It Changed? Are We Safer?" *Journal of Conflict Resolution* 54, no. 2 (2010).

Broder, James F., and Gene Tucker. *Risk and the Security Survey.* 4th ed. Waltham, MA: Butterworth-Heinemann, 2013.

Bunyan, Nigel. "Senior Muslim Lawyer Says British Teenagers See ISIS As 'Pop Idols.'" *The Guardian,* April 5, 2015.

Butt, Riazat, and Henry Tuck. *European Counter-Radicalisation and De-Radicalisation: A Comparative Evaluation of Approaches in the Netherlands, Sweden, Denmark, and Germany.* Oslo: Institute for Strategic Dialogue, 2014.

Cabalza, Chester. "Can ASEAN Work Together to Fight Regional Terrorism?" *The Diplomat,* August 9, 2017.

Cassella, Stefan D. "Reverse Money Laundering." *Journal of Money Laundering Control* 7, no. 1 (Summer 2003).

Chairman of the Joint Chiefs of Staff. *Antiterrorism.* Joint Publication 3-07.2. Washington, DC: US Department of Defense, 2010.

Chitsawang, Nathee. "Deradicalization Programs in Prison." 2017. http://thaicriminology.com/deradicalization-programs-in-prison.html.

Clutterbuck, Lindsay. *Deradicalization Programs and Counterterrorism: A Perspective on the Challenges and Benefits.* Washington, DC: Middle East Institute, 2015.

Commission on the Intelligence Capabilities of the United States Regarding Weapons of Mass Destruction. *Report to the President of the United States.* Washington, DC: WMD Commission, 2005.

Council of Europe. *Convention on the Prevention of Terrorism.* Treaty Series no. 196. Warsaw, 2005.

Crenshaw, Martha. *Explaining Terrorism: Causes, Processes, and Consequences.* New York: Routledge, 2011.

Cronin, Audrey Kurth. "Sources of Contemporary Terrorism." In Audrey Kurth Cronin and James M. Ludes (eds.), *Attacking Terrorism: Elements of a Grand Strategy.* Washington, DC: Georgetown University Press, 2004.

D'Alfonso, Steven. "Why Organized Crime and Terror Groups Are Converging." 2014. https://securityintelligence.com/why-organized-crime-and-terror-groups-are-converging.

Davis, Brian L. *Qaddafi, Terrorism, and the Origins of the U.S. Attack on Libya.* New York: Praeger.

Dean, Geoff, Peter Bell, and Jack Newman. "Dark Side of Social Media: Review of Online Terrorism." *Pakistan Journal of Criminology* 3, no. 3 (January 2012).

Dershowitz, Alan M. *Why Terrorism Works: Understanding the Threat, Responding to the Challenge.* New Haven: Yale University Press, 2003.

Dixon, Lloyd. "Compensation Policies for Victims of Terrorism." *RAND Review* (Summer 2002).

Ehrenfeld, Rachel. *Narco-Terrorism.* New York: Basic, 1990.

Elliott, Paul. *Assassin: The Bloody History of Political Murder.* London: Blandford, 1999.

Emergency Management Australia. *Critical Infrastructure Emergency Risk Management and Assurance,* 2nd ed. Canberra: Attorney General's Department, 2004.

European Union. *Terrorism Situation and Trend Report.* The Hague: European Union Agency for Law Enforcement Cooperation, 2017.

Federal Emergency Management Agency (FEMA). *Managing the Consequences of Terrorist Incidents: Interim Planning Guide.* Washington, DC, July 2002.

Federation of American Societies for Experimental Biology. "Report on Animal Rights Extremism." March 24, 2014. http://www.animalrightsextremism.info/news/media-conferences-and-press/faseb-report-on-animal-rights-extremism.

Financial Action Task Force. *The Role of Hawala and Other Similar Service Providers in Money Laundering and Terrorist Financing.* Paris: Organization for Economic Cooperation and Development, October 2013.

Ganor, Boaz. "Terrorism: No Prohibition Without Definition." October 7, 2001. https://www.ict.org.il/Article.aspx?ID=1588#gsc.tab=0.

Garcia, Mary Lynn. *Vulnerability Assessment of Physical Protection Systems.* Burlington, MA: Elsevier Butterworth-Heinemann, 2006.

Garrison, Arthur. "Defining Terrorism: Philosophy of the Bomb, Propaganda by Deed, and Change Through Fear and Violence." *Criminal Justice Studies* 17, no. 1 (September 2004).

Glasse, Cyrill. *The New Encyclopedia of Islam.* New York: Altamira, 2003.

Green, Andrew. "ADF Counter-Terrorism Team to Head-Up Urban Warfare Training with Philippine Troops in Marawi." Canberra: Australian Broadcasting Commission, October 24, 2017.

Gregg, Heather S. "Defining and Distinguishing Secular and Religious Terrorism." *Perspectives on Terrorism* 8, no. 2 (2014).

Gregg, Richard B. *The Power of Non-Violence.* Philadelphia: Lippincott, 1934.

Grierson, Jamie. "Litvinenko Inquiry: Russia Involved in Spy's Death, Scotland Yard Says." *The Guardian,* July 31, 2015. https://www.theguardian.com/world/2015/jul/30/litvinenko-inquiry-russia-involved-spy-death-scotland-yard.

Gross, M. L., and D. R. Vashdi. "The Psychological Effects of Cyber Terrorism." *Bulletin of the Atomic Scientists* 72, no. 5 (2016).

Grothaus, Nick. *Right-Wing Terrorism.* 2011. http://handofreason.com/2011/featured/right-wing-terrorism.

Guevara, Che. *Che Guevara on Guerrilla Warfare.* With an introduction by
    Major Harris-Clichy Peterson. New York: Praeger, 1961.
Hammer, Carl. *Tide of Terror: America, Islamic Extremism, and the War on Ter-
    ror.* Boulder: Paladin, 2003.
Han, Jiawei, and Micheline Kamber. *Data Mining: Concepts and Techniques.*
    2nd ed. Burlington, MA: Morgan Kaufmann, 2006.
Havocscope. "Human Trafficking Victims Prices, 2017." http://www.havocscope
    .com/black-market-prices/human-trafficking-prices.
Heitland, Jon. *The Man From U.N.C.L.E. Book: The Behind-the-Scenes Story of
    a Television Classic.* New York: St. Martin's, 1987.
Helms, Richard, with William Hood. *A Look over My Shoulder: A Life in the
    Central Intelligence Agency.* New York: Random, 2003.
Hersh, E. D. "Long-Term Effect of September 11 on the Political Behavior of
    Victims' Families and Neighbors." *Proceedings of the National Academy of
    Sciences of the United States of America* 110, no. 52 (2013).
Hillier, Bill. "Democratic Popular Front: We Are Marxist-Leninists." In John
    Gerassi (ed.), *Towards Revolution,* vol. 1. London: Weidenfeld and Nicolson,
    1971.
Hitz, Frederick P. *The Great Game: The Myth and Reality of Espionage.* New
    York: Knopf, 2004.
Hoffman, Abbie. *Steal This Book.* Cambridge, MA: Da Capo, 1996.
Hoffman, Bruce. *Inside Terrorism.* Rev. and expanded ed. New York: Columbia
    University Press, 2006.
Hoffman, Bruce, and Christian Ostermann. *Moles, Defectors, and Deceptions:
    James Angleton and His Influence on U.S. Counterintelligence.* Washington,
    DC: Wilson Center and Georgetown University, 2014.
Holiday, Ryan. *Trust Me I'm Lying: Confessions of a Media Manipulator.* New
    York: Portfolio/Penguin, 2012.
Howard, Michael. "What's In a Name? How to Fight Terrorism." *Foreign Affairs*
    8 (January–February 2002).
Ilardi, Gaetano Joe. "Prison Radicalization: The Devil Is in the Detail." Confer-
    ence paper presented at the Global Terrorism Research Centre, Melbourne,
    Monash University, December 31, 2010.
Institute for Economics and Peace. *Global Terrorism Index 2016.* New York,
    2016.
International Organization for Standardization (ISO), *ISO 31000: Risk Manage-
    ment—Guidelines on Principles and Implementation of Risk Management.*
    Geneva, 2009.
"Iran and Iraq Sign Accord to Boost Military Cooperation." *Reuters,* July 23,
    2017. https://www.reuters.com/article/us-iran-iraq-military/iran-and-iraq-sign
    -accord-to-boost-military-cooperation-idUSKBN1A80HJ.
Jackson, Richard. *Writing the War on Terrorism: Language, Politics, and
    Counter-Terrorism.* Manchester: Manchester University Press, 2005.
Jacobsen, David, with Gerald Astor. *Hostage: My Nightmare in Beirut.* New
    York: Donald I. Fine, 1991.
Jenkins, Brian Michael. "International Terrorism: A Balance Sheet." *Survival* 17,
    no. 4 (July–August 1975).
———. "The New Age of Terrorism." In David G. Kamien, *The McGraw-Hill
    Homeland Security Handbook.* New York: McGraw-Hill, 2006.
———. *The Study of Terrorism: Definitional Problems.* Santa Monica: RAND,
    1980.

John, Tara. "Boko Haram Has Kidnapped Dozens of Schoolgirls, Again: Here's What to Know." *Time,* February 26, 2018. http://time.com/5175464/boko -haram-kidnap-dapchi-schoolgirls.

Kahn, David. *The Codebreakers: The Story of Secret Writing.* New York: Macmillan, 1967.

Kamal, Muhammad. *The Meaning of Terrorism: A Philosophical Inquiry.* NCEIS Research Paper 1, no. 1. Melbourne: University of Melbourne, 2008.

Kamienski, Lukasz. "Defining Terrorism: Issues and Problems." In Frank Shanty (ed.), *Counterterrorism: From the Cold War to the War on Terror,* vol. 1. Santa Barbara: Praeger Security International, 2012.

Kaplan, Eben. "Targets for Terrorists: Chemical Facilities." December 11, 2006. https://www.cfr.org/backgrounder/targets-terrorists-chemical-facilities.

———. "Tracking Down Terrorist Financing." Council on Foreign Relations, April 4, 2006. https://www.cfr.org/backgrounder/tracking-down-terrorist -financing.

Kearns, Erin, Allison Betus, and Anthony Lemieux. "Why Do Some Terrorist Attacks Receive More Media Attention Than Others?" March 5, 2017. https://ssrn.com/abstract=2928138.

Kerin, John. "U.S. Aims at Terror Schools." *Weekend Australian,* October 4–5, 2003.

Kingdom of Morocco. *Morocco's Approach to Countering Violent Extremism.* Washington, DC: Moroccan American Center, September 8, 2016.

Kirchner, Lauren. "Whatever Happened to 'Eco-Terrorism'?" January 27, 2015. https://psmag.com/environment/whatever-happened-to-eco-terrorism.

Kirkpatrick, David D. "Qatar's Support of Extremists Alienates Allies Near and Far." *New York Times,* September 8, 2014.

Klausen, Jytte. "Tweeting the Jihad: Social Media Networks of Western Foreign Fighters in Syria and Iraq." *Studies in Conflict and Terrorism* 38 (2015).

Koerner, Brendan I. "A Controversial New Program Aims to Reform Homegrown Isis Recruits Back into Normal Young Americans." *Wired,* January 24, 2017. https://www.wired.com/2017/01/can-you-turn-terrorist-back-into-citizen.

Laqueur, Walter. *The New Terrorism: Fanaticism and the Arms of Mass Destruction.* New York: Oxford University Press, 1999.

League of Arab States. *The Arab Convention for the Suppression of Terrorism.* Cairo, April 1998.

League of Nations. *Convention for the Prevention and Punishment of Terrorism.* Geneva, November 1937.

Lesce, Tony. *The Shotgun in Combat.* Cornville, AZ: Desert, 1979.

Lewis, Bernard. *The Assassins: A Radical Sect in Islam.* London: Weidenfeld and Nicolson, 1969.

———. "The Isma'ilites and the Assassins." In Marshall W. Baldwin (ed.), *The First Hundred Years: A History of the Crusades,* 2nd ed., vol. 1. Madison: University of Wisconsin Press, 1969.

Lewis, John E. "Testimony Before the Senate Judiciary Committee." Washington DC, May 18, 2004. https://archives.fbi.gov/archives/news/testimony/animal -rights-extremism-and-ecoterrorism.

Lichtblau, Eric, and Eric Schmitt. "Cash Flow to Terrorist Evades U.S. Efforts." *New York Times,* December 6, 2010.

Lozano, Maria. *Inventory of the Best Practices on Deradicalization from the Different Member States of the EU.* Amsterdam: Impact Knowledge and Advice Centre, 2014.

Mahle, Melissa Boyle. *Denial and Deception: An Insider's View of the CIA from Iran-Contra to 9/11*. New York: Nation, 2004.

Makdisi, Ussama. "'Anti-Americanism' in the Arab World: An Interpretation of a Brief History." *Journal of American History* (September 2002).

Manheim, David, Patrick B. Johnston, Joshua Baron, and Cynthia Dion-Schwarz. *Are Terrorists Using Cryptocurrencies?* Santa Monica: RAND, 2017.

Maremont, Mark, and Christopher S. Stewart. "FBI Says ISIS Used eBay to Send Terror Cash to U.S." *Wall Street Journal*, August 10, 2017. https://www.wsj.com/articles/fbi-says-isis-used-ebay-to-send-terror-cash-to-u-s-1502410868.

Marighella, Carlos. *Minimanual of the Urban Guerrilla*. Boulder: Paladin, 1985.

Marts, Jon. "Radicalization in Danish Prisons." In *Danish Institute for International Studies Brief* (2008).

McCauley, Clark, and Sophia Moskalenko. "Mechanisms of Political Radicalization: Pathways Toward Terrorism." *Terrorism and Political Violence* 20, no. 3 (2008).

McCusker, Rob. "Organised Crime and Terrorism: Convergence or Separation?" *Standing Group Organised Crime eNewsletter* (European Consortium for Political Research) 5, no. 2 (May 12, 2006).

McDermott, Jeremy. "The FARC and the Drug Trade: Siamese Twins?" September 4, 2014. http://www.insightcrime.org/investigations/farc-and-drug-trade-siamese-twins.

McGonagle, John J., Jr., and Carolyn M. Vella. *Outsmarting the Competition: Practical Approaches to Finding and Using Competitive Information*. Naperville, IL: Sourcebooks, 1990.

Meyers, Jeffrey. *Joseph Conrad: A Biography*. New York: Scribner's, 1991.

Mitchell, Stefanie. "Deradicalization: Using Triggers for the Development of a U.S. Program." *Journal for Deradicalization* no. 9 (Winter 2016–2017).

Monat, Pawel, with John Dille. *Spy in the U.S.* London: Frederick Muller, 1962.

Moore, Jack. "Hawala: The Ancient Banking Practice Used to Finance Terror Groups." *Newsweek*, February 24, 2015. http://www.newsweek.com/underground-european-hawala-network-financing-middle-eastern-terror-groups-307984.

Moran, C., K. Brohi, M. Smith, and K. Willet. "Lessons in Planning from a Mass Casualty Event in U.K." *British Medical Journal* 359 (2017).

Mullins, Samuel J. "Rehabilitation of Islamist Terrorists: Lessons from Criminology." *University of Wollongong Research Online* (Faculty of Law) (2011). https://ro.uow.edu.au/lawpapers/225/.

Nacos, Brigitte. *Terrorism and Counterterrorism*. 5th ed. New York: Routledge, 2016.

———. *Terrorism and the Media*. New York: Columbia University Press, 1994.

National Abortion Federation. "Violence Statistics and History, 2017." https://prochoice.org/education-and-advocacy/violence/violence-statistics-and-history.

National Commission on Terrorist Attacks upon the United States. *The 9/11 Commission Report*. Washington, DC, 2004.

North Atlantic Treaty Organization (NATO). "Intelligence Sharing in Combating Terrorism." http://natolibguides.info/intelligence.

Oliver, Willard M. "The Fourth Ear of Policing: Homeland Security." *International Review of Law, Computers, and Technology* 20, nos. 1–2 (2006).

Olson, Dean T. "Financing Terrorism." *Law Enforcement Bulletin* 76, no. 2 (February 2007).

O'Neill, William G. "Terrorism and International Law: Why Conventions Matter." *Daily Star,* October 28, 2004.

Orwell, George. *Nineteen Eighty-Four: A Novel.* New York: Harcourt, Brace, 1949.

Owen, Mark, with Kevin Maurer. *No Easy Day: The Autobiography of a Navy SEAL.* New York: Dutton, 2012.

Parry, Jonathan. "Just War Theory, Legitimate Authority, and Irregular Belligerency." *Philosophia* 43 (2015).

Patrikarakos, David. "Social Media Networks Are the Handmaiden to Dangerous Propaganda." *Time Magazine,* November 2, 2017. http://time.com/5008076/nyc-terror-attack-isis-facebook-russia.

Pierce, William Luther, writing as Andrew Macdonald. *The Turner Diaries.* Charlottesville, VA, National Vanguard, 1978.

Porges, Marisa L. *The Saudi Deradicalization Experiment.* New York: Council on Foreign Relations, January 22, 2010. https://www.cfr.org/expert-brief/saudi-deradicalization-experiment.

Powell, William R. *The Anarchist Cookbook.* New York: Lyle Stuart, 1971.

Prunckun, Hank. *Counterintelligence Theory and Practice.* 2nd ed. Lanham: Rowman and Littlefield, 2019.

———, ed. *Intelligence and Private Investigation: Developing Sophisticated Methods for Conducting Inquiries.* Springfield, IL: Charles C. Thomas, 2013.

———. *Scientific Methods of Inquiry for Intelligence Analysis.* 2nd ed. Lanham: Rowman and Littlefield, 2015.

Prunckun, Henry (ed.). *Cyber Weaponry: Issues and Implications of Digital Arms.* New York: Springer, 2018.

———. "The First Pillar of Terror—Kill One, Frighten Ten Thousand: A Critical Discussion of the Doctrinal Shift Associated with the 'New Terrorism.'" *The Police Journal: Theory, Practice, and Principles* 87, no. 3 (2014).

———. *How to Undertake Surveillance and Reconnaissance: From a Civilian and Military Perspective.* South Yorkshire, UK: Pen and Sword Military, 2015.

Prunckun, Henry, and Philip B. Mohr. "Military Deterrence of International Terrorism: An Evaluation of Operation El Dorado Canyon." *Studies in Conflict and Terrorism* 20, no. 3 (1997).

Qaddafi, Muammar. *The Green Book.* Tripoli: Green Book World Center for Research and Study, 1980.

Queensland Government and Local Government Association. *Local Government Counter-Terrorism Risk Management Kit.* Brisbane, 2004.

The Quran. Translated by Abdullah Yusuf Ali. 1934.

Rana, Shahbaz. "War on Terror Aid: Pakistan." *Express Tribune,* September 6, 2017.

Ransom, Harry Howe. *The Intelligence Establishment.* Cambridge: Harvard University Press, 1971.

Rapoport, David C. "The Four Waves of Modern Terrorism." In Audrey Kurth Cronin and James M. Ludes (eds.), *Attacking Terrorism: Elements of a Grand Strategy.* Washington, DC: Georgetown University Press, 2004.

Ratcliffe, Jerry H. *Intelligence-Led Policing.* 2nd ed. New York: Routledge, 2016.

Raynor, Thomas P. *Terrorism: Past, Present, Future*. New York: Franklin Watts, 1982.
Regal, S., and S. Joseph. *Post-Traumatic Stress*. Oxford: Oxford University Press, 2010.
Regens, James L., Amy Schultheiss, and Nick Mould. "Regional Variation in Causes of Injuries Among Terrorism Victims for Mass Casualty Events." *Front Public Health* 3 (2015).
Reuter, Christopher. *My Life Is a Weapon: A Modern History of Suicide Bombing*. Princeton: Princeton University Press, 2004.
Roberts, Adam. "Counter-Terrorism, Armed Force, and the Laws of War." *Survival* 44, no. 1 (Spring 2002).
Robinson, B. A. "The 'Concerned Christians' Cult—Originally of Denver CO." 2002. http://www.religioustolerance.org/dc_conc.htm.
Sabir, M., and N. Aslam. "Impact of Suicide Bombing on the Cognitions of Victims." *Journal of Behavioural Sciences* 21, no. 1 (2011).
Samuel, Henry. "French Minister Agrees That Lack of Mosques Encourages Radicalisation." *The Telegraph*, April 7, 2015. http://www.telegraph.co.uk/news/worldnews/europe/france/11519452/French-minister-agrees-that-lack-of-mosques-encourages-radicalization.html.
Sarre, Rick. "Gun Control in Australia." *Salus Journal* 3, no. 3 (2015).
Schmid, Alex. "Strengthening the Role of Victims and Incorporating Victims in Efforts to Counter Violent Extremism and Terrorism." The Hague: International Centre for Counter-Terrorism, August 2012.
Scott, John. "Rational Choice Theory." In Gary Browning, Abigail Halcli, and Frank Webster (eds.), *Understanding Contemporary Society: Theories of the Present*. London: Sage, 2000.
Seib, Philip. "Mainstream Media Outlets Are Dropping the Ball with Terrorism Coverage." *The Conversation,* June 1, 2017. https://theconversation.com/mainstream-media-outlets-are-dropping-the-ball-with-terrorism-coverage-78442.
Seib, Philip, Dana M. Janbek, and Andrew Hoskins. *Global Terrorism and New Media: The Post–Al Qaeda Generation*. London: Routledge, 2010.
Shankar, Abha. "Social Media Emerges As a Valuable Terrorist Fundraising Tool." April 20, 2016. https://www.investigativeproject.org/5314/social-media-emerges-as-a-valuable-terrorist.
Sheehan, James. "Violent Jihadism in Real Time: Al-Shabaab's Use of Twitter." January 2013. https://www.start.umd.edu/sites/default/files/files/publications/research_briefs/STARTResearchBrief_AlShabaabsTwitterUse.pdf.
Shenk, David. *Data Smog: Surviving the Information Glut*. Rev. and updated ed. New York: HarperCollins, 1997.
Silverman, H., and D. Ruggles. *Cultural Heritage and Human Rights*. Singapore: Springer Singapore, 2008.
Simon, Jeffrey D. *The Terrorist Trap: America's Experience with Terrorism*. Bloomington: Indiana University Press, 1994.
Simon, Jeremy M. "The Credit Card–Terrorism Connection: How Terrorists Use Cards for Everyday Needs and to Fund Operations." May 15, 2008. https://www.creditcards.com/credit-card-news/credit-cards-terrorism-1282.php.
Smith, Laurence Dwight. *Cryptography: The Science of Secret Writing*. New York: Dover, 1943.

Southern Poverty Law Center. "Active Antigovernment Groups in the United States, 2015." https://www.splcenter.org/active-antigovernment-groups-united-states.

Speckhard, Anne. "Prison and Community Based Disengagement and Deradicalization Programs for Extremists Involved in Militant Jihadi Terrorism Ideologies and Activities." In Laurie Fenstermacher and Anne Speckhard (eds.), *Social Sciences Support to Military Personnel Engaged in Counter-Insurgency and Counter-Terrorism Operations: Report of the NATO Research and Technology Group 172,* NATO Science Series. Brussels: NATO, 2011.

Statista. "Global Terrorism Index 2017." https://www.statista.com/statistics/271514/global-terrorism-index.

Stitt, Nathan. "Terrorism Media Coverage Playing into Extremists' Hands, Academic Warns." March 24, 2017. http://www.abc.net.au/news/2017-03-24/terrorism-media-coverage-is-helping-terrorists-academic-warns/8381780.

Sunga, Lyal S. *The Emerging System of International Criminal Law: Developments in Codification and Implementation.* The Hague: Kluwer Law International, 1997.

Tagliabue, John. "Bombings Laid to Mafia War on Italy and Church." *New York Times,* July 15, 1994. http://www.nytimes.com/1994/07/15/world/bombings-laid-to-mafia-war-on-italy-and-church.html.

Taleb, Nassim Nicholas. *The Black Swan: The Impact of the Highly Improbable.* New York: Random, 2007.

Tamek, Mohamed. "Morocco's Approach to Countering Violent Extremism." Presentation at the Washington Institute for Near East Policy, Washington, DC, May 16, 2014.

Thony, Jean-François. *Money Laundering and Terrorism Financing: An Overview, 2002.* Versailles: French Court of Appeals, 2000.

United Nations. *The Criminal Justice Response to Support Victims of Acts of Terrorism.* Rev. ed. New York, 2012.

———. *Report of the Secretary-General's High-Level Panel on Threats, Challenges, and Change: A More Secure World—Our Shared Responsibility.* New York, 2004.

———. "With Call for Action, Not More Words: Annan Outlines Plan for Radical UN Reform." March 21, 2005. https://news.un.org/en/story/2005/03/132432-call-action-not-more-words-annan-outlines-plan-radical-un-reform.

United Nations Educational, Scientific, and Cultural Organization (UNESCO). *Terrorism and the Media: A Handbook for Journalists.* Paris, 2017.

United Nations High Commission for Human Rights, Human Rights Terrorism, and Counter-Terrorism, *Fact Sheet* no. 32 (2008).

United Nations Secretary-General. *First Global Symposium on Supporting Victims of Terrorism.* New York, September 9, 2008.

University of Chicago. "Attacks by Year." http://cpostdata.uchicago.edu/search_results_new.php.

US Department of the Army. *Field Manual* no. FM-5-31: *Boobytraps.* Washington, DC: US Department of Defense, 1965.

———. *Improved Munitions Handbook* no. TM 31-210. Washington, DC, 1969.

———. *A Military Guide to Terrorism in the Twenty-First Century.* Washington, DC: US Department of Defense, 2007.

US Department of Defense. *Department of Defense Dictionary of Military and Associated Terms.* Joint Publication no. 1-02. Washington, DC, October 18, 2008.

———. *Dictionary of Military and Associated Terms*. Washington, DC, 2017.

US Department of Justice, Federal Bureau of Investigation. *Terrorism 2002–2005*. Washington, DC, 2017.

US Department of State. *Patterns of Global Terrorism*. Report of the Office of the Coordinator for Counterterrorism. Washington, DC, April 29, 2004.

US Senate, Select Committee to Study Governmental Operations with Respect to Intelligence Activities. *Alleged Assassination Plots Involving Foreign Leaders*. Washington, DC: US Government Printing Office, 1975.

"Vice President Tells West Point Cadets 'Bush Doctrine' Is Serious." *Department of Defense News*, June 2, 2003.

Wahdatyar, Hashim. "How Opium Fuels the Taliban's War Machine in Afghanistan." *The Diplomat*, October 28, 2016.

Walsh, Declan. "WikiLeaks Cables Portray Saudi Arabia As a Cash Machine for Terrorists." *The Guardian*, December 6, 2010. https://www.theguardian.com/world/2010/dec/05/wikileaks-cables-saudi-terrorist-funding.

Walzer, Michael. "Five Questions About Terrorism." *Dissent* 49, no. 1 (2002).

Wang, Peng. "The Crime-Terror Nexus: Transformation, Alliance, Convergence." *Asian Social Science* no. 6 (June 2010).

Warrick, Joby. *The Triple Agent: The al-Qaeda Mole Who Infiltrated the CIA*. New York: Doubleday, 2011.

Weikart, Richard. "The Origins of Social Darwinism in Germany, 1859–1895." *Journal of the History of Ideas* 54, no. 3 (July 1993).

Weinstein, Adam. "The Real Largest State Sponsor of Terrorism." *Huffington Post*, March 16, 2017. https://www.huffingtonpost.com/entry/the-real-largest-state-sponsor-of-terrorism_us_58cafc26e4b00705db4da8aa.

West, John. "Hamas Fighters Are Gaza's Idols". *Reuters*, December 26, 2000. https://www.paldf.net/forum/showthread.php?t=5586.

White House. "Address to a Joint Session of Congress and the American People." September 20, 2001. https://georgewbush-whitehouse.archives.gov/news/releases/2001/09/20010920-8.html.

———. "Combatting Terrorism." *National Security Decision Directive 138*. Washington, DC: April 3, 1984.

Wilkinson, Paul. *Terrorism and the Liberal State*. London: Macmillan, 1977.

Yerak, Becky. "'Suspicious' Crowdfunding Activity on the Rise, U.S. Watchdog Says." *Chicago Tribune*, October 15, 2015. http://www.chicagotribune.com/business/ct-crowdfunding-fincen-sars-1015-biz-20151015-story.html.

Index

Australia, 15, 35, 43, 47, 85, 108, 114,
115–116, 140, 153, 155–156, 171,
213, 215, 224, 228, 244; Five Eyes
intelligence alliance, 153, 230;
government, 248
Australian Security Intelligence
Organization, 35
Austro-Hungarian Empire, 33
aviation security, 148–149, 163–164,
178

Bangsamoro Islamic Freedom Fighters,
52, 228
Bashar al-Assad, 250n5. *See also* ISIL;
ISIS; Syria
Basque Armed Revolutionary Workers'
Organization, 38
Basque Homeland and Liberty, 12, 52
Bastille Day, 22, 164
Bill and Melinda Gates Foundation, 241
bin Laden, Osama, 61, 113, 170, 247
Black Hand, 17
Black Panthers, 32, 35
Blair, Eric Arthur, 190n13
body scanners, 164. *See also* aviation
security
Boko Haram, 21–22, 52, 110, 134
border security, 162–163, 228
Borough Market attack, 73–74, 165

C³I. *See* command, control,
communication, and intelligence
Caribbean, 35
Castro, Fidel, 35, 103
CBRNE. *See* chemical, biological,
radiological, nuclear, and explosive
weapons
Central Intelligence Agency, 103, 178;
covert operations, 172; political
action group, 173; psychological
operations, 173; special activities
division, 173
Chechen Republic, 47
chemical, biological, radiological,
nuclear, and explosive weapons,
102–103
chemical: attacks, 36–37, 135; warfare,
166; weapons, 36, 102–103, 156
Cheney, Dick, 157
chlorine, 135

CIA. *See* Central Intelligence Agency
civil rights, 35; movement, 40
COINTELPRO, 40
Colombia, 13, 109
Columbine High School, 13
command, control, communication, and
intelligence, 6
command-and-control, 174
Conrad, Joseph, 17, 25fn25. *See also*
The Secret Agent
conventional warfare, 5, 6, 19, 32, 37
counter-battery fire, 78
counter-propaganda, 128
counterradicalization, 211, 212, 213,
215, 218, 227, 233, 235
counter-revolution, 31
counter-strategy thinking, 78
counterterrorism, 22, 134, 187, 192,
193, 200–201, 213; analysis, 192,
197, 199, 202; Australia, 155–156;
Center for Strategic
Counterterrorism Communications,
127; defensive strategies, 78;
defined, 161–162; human rights,
158–159; international conventions,
148–152; Italy, 153–155; military
law, 156–158; plan, 192; policy, 4,
152, 223–235; rule of law, 147–159;
United States, 152–153; versus anti-
terrorism, 161–162
CPTED. *See* crime prevention
crime prevention, 22, 245
crime triangle theory, 246–247,
249–250n3
criminal terrorism, 45–46; defined, 13
critical infrastructure, 71, 101, 141,
153; protection, 191–208
crowd-funding, 108, 114
crypto-currency, 117–119
Cuba, 103, 112
cyber attack, 102, 141, 192
cyber bomb, 100
cyber weapons, 100–102, 105n19
cyber-crime, 76, 153
cyber-criminal, 197
cyber-terrorism, 76, 141
cyber-vandal, 197
cyphers, 166–167

Damascus, 113

About the Book

What is terrorism? How do terrorists operate—what are their means, targets, and motivations? How can governments prevent terrorist attacks from happening? Henry Prunckun and Troy Whitford address these questions in their systematic, comprehensive exploration of terrorism and counterterrorism.

Notably, this authoritative text:

- Explains complex issues in an objective, accessible way.
- Traces the phenomenon of terrorism through history.
- Examines law enforcement as well as intelligence and military operations.
- Features case studies from around the world.
- Includes learning aids for students.

Designed to appeal to both students and instructors, the text enables readers to deepen their understanding of terrorism today and learn what is being done to combat it.

Henry Prunckun is a research criminologist at the Australian Graduate School of Policing and Security (AGSPS), Charles Sturt University. He previously served as a senior counterterrorism policy analyst and has held a number of operational postings in investigation and security. **Troy Whitford** is lecturer in intelligence and security studies at AGSPS.